War and Peace in Jalémó

War and Peace in Jalémó

The Management of Conflict in
Highland New Guinea

Klaus-Friedrich Koch

Harvard University Press   Cambridge, Massachusetts   1974

© Copyright 1974 by the President and Fellows of Harvard College
All rights reserved
Publication of this book
has been aided by a grant
from the Andrew A. Mellon Foundation
Library of Congress Catalog Card Number 73-92579
ISBN 0-674-94590-5
Printed in the United States of America

Acknowledgments

I received my training in anthropology at the University of California, Berkeley. With great respect and admiration I remember the late Professor T. D. McCown, whose scholarship, humanism, and magnanimity remain for me a lasting source of inspiration and reflection. Professors Laura Nader, Eugene A. Hammel, and Herma Hill Kay guided the original analysis of the field data in my thesis. Laura Nader has encouraged my work in the anthropology of law and conflict since my first year of graduate study. This book represents one of several case studies in her comparative law project (see Nader, Kay, et al. 1966).

Many people helped me in Irian Jaya (West New Guinea). Professor Soegarda Purbakawatja, then Rector of Universitas Tjenderawasih, and his staff led me through an overwhelming maze of government offices and mediated my requests for numerous permits from the immigration, customs, and police authorities. The late Reverend F. J. S. Rumainum, Chairman of the Synod of Geredja Kristen Indjili (G.K.I.), and the Reverend M. Koibur assisted me in many ways. They let me stay in their guest house in Jayapura, vouched for me as a foreign resident in an area not yet under government control, and supported my application for flight services of the Missionary Aviation Fellowship. Mr. H. Worthington, manager and chief pilot of the M.A.F., and his staff provided transportation between the coast and the interior and accommodation in Sentani. The Roman Catholic Mission (O.F.M.) in Sentani also offered me its generous hospitality.

In the field I received help from the staff of the G.K.I. mission station in Angkuruk, the Reverend S. Zöllner of the Rheinische

Missions-Gesellschaft, Dr. W. H. Vriend of the Nederlands
Hervormde Kerk, and Mr. K.-D. Peters, an agricultural engineer
temporarily associated with the R.M.G., and their families.
Throughout my stay in the field, I depended on their sympathy
with my work. They invited me to stay in their houses for
several weeks in the beginning and during sporadic visits to
Angkuruk, and took care of my mail and the supplies that I
stored at the station. I obtained valuable linguistic data from
the Reverend S. Zöllner and useful cartographic material from
Dr. Vriend. Mr. Peters enhanced my knowledge of local ecology.

The people of Pasikni tolerated my intrusion into their village
with great forbearance. I cannot claim that all of them welcomed my presence though most had begun to accept it when
I left. A few men did more than indulge my curiosity: with
great patience they taught me much of their way of life. On the
pages of this book they appear as anonymous informants; in
the field they were my friends: Avésa and Óaklaxevak of
Kénanghólómó, Wasa, Kepolok, and Sue of Longkopini, Taling
and Pavéon of Nelelum, Saxoóngkól and Jéxék of Jekjekpini,
and Halim of Seraxanpini.

Paul Bohannan, Laura Nader, and Claire Rosenfield read an
earlier draft of this manuscript and their wise comments
obliterated many obscure paragraphs and guided my revisions.

Discussions with my students at Harvard, especially with
Andrew Arno, Donald Brenneis, Wynne Furth, Carol Green-
house, and Letitia Hickson clarified the theoretical implications
of this study. Letitia Hickson constructed Figure 16.

I express my gratitude to all people who have helped me
during the various stages of my work, and record my particular
appreciation of the patient encouragement I received from
Ann Orlov, Editor for the Behavioral Sciences of Harvard
University Press, who shepherded this book on its way
from pen to print.

My field research was supported by fellowships from the
Social Science Research Council and the Wenner-Gren Foundation for Anthropological Research. The Robert H. Lowie

Museum at Berkeley provided funds for the shipment to the United States of a complete collection of Jalé artifacts, which I donated to the University of California. I gave a similar collection to Universitas Tjenderawasih in Irian Jaya.

Klaus-Friedrich Koch
Cambridge, Massachusetts
July 1974

Contents

Illustrations

War and Peace in Jalémó

Note on Terminology, Orthography, and Cases

In the interest of readability I use very few Jalé words. Double quotation marks indicate a fairly literal translation of vernacular terms ("net" pig); single quotation marks appear with interpretative renditions of Jalé expressions ('dowry' pig).

English kin terms for relatives other than members of the nuclear family usually appear in composite expressions that designate a person's exact genealogical position (father's sister's son, son's daughter, and so on). Other terms, like uncle, cousin, and brother-in-law, occur only where the specific kinship link is obvious from the context. Quotation marks ("child") indicate a person's terminological inclusion with a class of primary relatives. The expressions half-brother and half-sister denote a person's agnatic siblings and the adjective uterine signifies a common mother.

The following letters in Jalé words differ in their sound value from their corresponding symbols in the International Phonetic Alphabet (Chao 1968): e = [ɛ] as in pen, é = [I], higher than the [e] in the French été, o = [ɔ] as in rock, ó = [ʊ] as in the German rot; f = [ɸ], a bilabial fricative, softer than the [β] in the Spanish abogado, h = [x] a velar fricative as in the Scottish loch, ng = [ŋ], a velar nasal as in singing (ng before k representing the uvular nasal [ɴ]), w = [ʋ], a dentilabial semivowel as in verse, v = [b] as in big but gliding toward [ɥ] as in the French huit, x = [ʁ], an uvular fricative as in the Dutch vragen. The pronunciation of all other letters follows closely their conventional phonetic values; thus, the initial consonant in Jalé should be pronounced like the English "y" in yard.

I have numbered the dispute cases in the order in which they appear in this book from 1 to 53. Cases 1 to 14 are included in Chapters IV, V, and VI, cases 15 to 53 in Appendix A. An asterisk preceding the case number distinguishes disputes that arose or continued during my stay in the field from those that had ended before my arrival.

Introduction: Fieldwork in Jalémó

In isolated parts in the swamps and mountains of western New Guinea, now the Indonesian province of Irian Jaya, live peoples who have never had direct contact with that cultural agglomerate called "Western civilization."[1] The last places where the steel axe, first vehicle of Western influence par excellence, was not known have probably disappeared since 1960. Yet in many a valley in the eastern Snow Mountains the steel axe is still a thing most people have only heard about from neighbors who have seen it on trading trips into areas nearer to a mission station than their own.

It was only toward the end of the 1950's that expeditions first penetrated the vast quadrangle between the 139th and 141st meridians, eastern longitude, and the 4th and 5th parallels, southern latitude (Brongersma and Venema 1960). This area contains roughly one fourth of the Snow Mountains, a range that traverses the island of New Guinea from the west to the border with eastern New Guinea (under Australian administration). By 1966 half a dozen landing strips for small aircraft existed in this area, which includes the most formidable landscape in the whole central range. The rugged terrain delayed the arrival of missions and governments—both colonial and national—in this part of the island and contributed to the astonishing isolation of its population from contact with places where several churches and the Dutch and later the Indonesian administration had set up stations earlier. Here, as in other parts of New Guinea, habitation by foreigners has been utterly dependent upon support by air.

Because of the virtual absence of foreign influence in most of its valleys, the eastern Snow Mountains offer unexcelled opportunities for the kind of ethnological research that seeks to study the indigenous life of a people before contact with foreign cul-

1 Southwestern Pacific and Irian Jaya

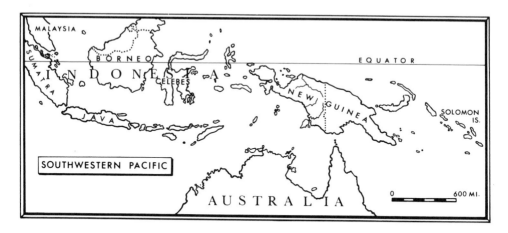

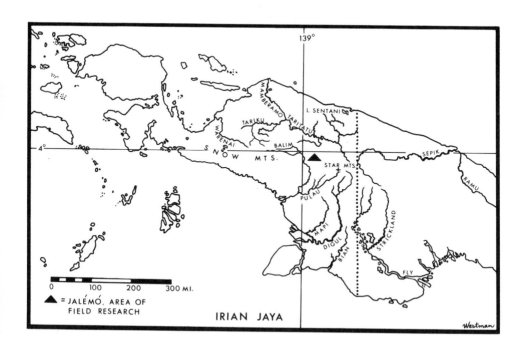

tures caused exogenous change. In New Guinea, the extension of colonial police and military control, or, as its agents prefer to say, the establishment of "law and order," has always first and most decisively altered the way in which a society managed the prevention and resolution of interpersonal and intergroup conflicts. Therefore, albeit not for this reason alone, I selected the eastern Snow Mountains for studying an indigenous system of conflict management among a New Guinea people.

The Jalémó Area

I worked in the valley of the upper Jaxólé, a southern tributary of the Hablifuri, which flows into the Taritatu River. Not until 1961, when a mission station was built at Angkuruk in the Jaxólé Valley, had mission or government patrols made contact with the people in this area. Sixteen years before they had first experienced machine technology in the form of a catastrophe: in 1945 an American military reconnaissance plane crashed into a forested ridge a few miles south of Angkuruk.

The people of the Jaxólé Valley and their neighbors in adjacent valleys with whom they share a common language do not have a name that denotes them collectively. The Dani of the Balim Valley, forty miles to the west, refer to all the country beyond the high mountain range that borders their valley in the east as *jalé-mó*, call the people there *jalé-énap*, and their language *jalé-ane*. In the Jaxólé Valley, in turn, the people speak of the country lying still further east as *jalé-mó* and refer to its inhabitants and their language as *jalé*. By the same process each of these peoples refers to country in the west as *hóvóla-ma*, call the people there *hóvóla-énap* and their language *hóvóla-ane*. This means that the expression *jalé* and its opposite *hóvóla* have geographic or directional referents in some Dani languages. They are predicates rather than names of particular peoples. Nevertheless, I arbitrarily restrict the use of these terms and call Jalé that population which (1) lives east of the Balim, (2) shares a common language which is different from, though related to, the Dani of the Balim Valley, (3) has a cultural tradition which is in many aspects distinct from that of the Dani people, and (4) concentrates its settlements in the Sévé, Jaxólé, and Ovaxak Valleys, north of the central divide, and in the Seng Valley, south of it. I assign the name Jalémó to that area which is inhabited by the Jalé people so defined. On the basis of gross inferential computations, I estimate that about ten thousand Jalé live in this area.

Geographical coordinates place the Jalémó roughly between 139°15′ and 139°30′ eastern longitude and 4° and 4°20′ southern latitude. In the northeastern portion of this quadrangle people have settled who speak a non-Dani language. They belong to a

2 The Central Jalémó

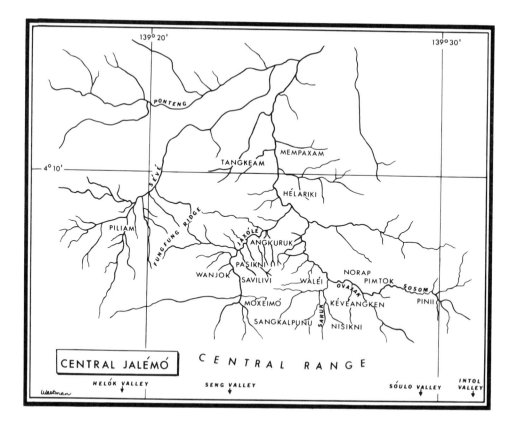

culture area that extends toward the Sobger River in the north
and the Star Mountains in the south of the Central Range. Their
neighbors in the east speak OK languages, the distribution of
which extends across the international boundary into the Territories of Papua and New Guinea (Healey 1964). The main
border between the Jalémó and Dani country is outlined by the
Central Range and a northern spur branching out at 139°15'
eastern longitude. South of the range the Jalé settlements that
I discovered in the Seng Valley separate Dani country from the
Jalé people's eastern neighbors. However, fragmentary ethno-

3 The Jaxólé and Ovaxak Valleys

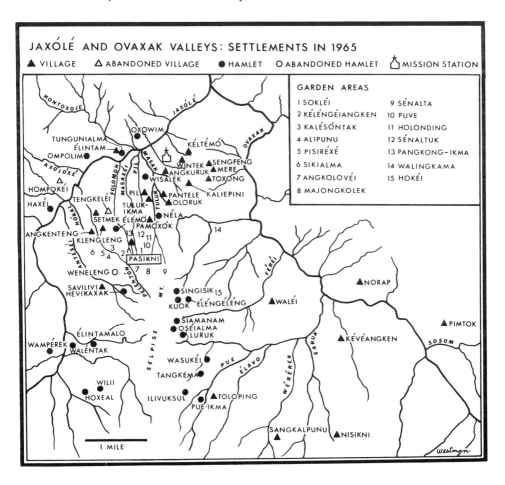

JAXÓLÉ AND OVAXAK VALLEYS: SETTLEMENTS IN 1965

▲ VILLAGE   △ ABANDONED VILLAGE   ● HAMLET   ○ ABANDONED HAMLET   ⌂ MISSION STATION

GARDEN AREAS

1 SOKLÉI	9 SÉNALTA
2 KÉLÉNGÉIANGKEN	10 PUVE
3 KALÉSÓNTAK	11 HOLONDING
4 ALIPUNU	12 SÉNALTUK
5 PISIRÉXÉ	13 PANGKONG–IKMA
6 SIKIALMA	14 WALINGKAMA
7 ANGKOLOVÉI	15 HOKÉI
8 MAJONGKOLEK	

1 MILE

Westman

graphic observations made by early expeditions southwest of the Jalémó (Lorentz 1913, van Nouhuys 1913) and recent comparative linguistic data (Bromley 1967) demand that the suggested boundaries of culture areas be considered hypothetical. A meaningful historical ethnology of the Jalé requires the comparative study of specific cultural and bio-anthropological problems in the three contiguous culture areas—not yet possible from available data.[2]

History of Contact

In 1960 the Protestant Church of Irian Jaya (Geredja Kristen Indjili, G.K.I.) decided to begin mission work in the mountainous interior.[3] An agreement with American missions active in the country designated the Jalémó as G.K.I. territory. In March 1961 an exploration team, consisting of a German theological and a Dutch medical missionary and three coastal men in G.K.I. service, reached the Sévé Valley from the Balim. After a few weeks' stay in the village of Piliam the team moved into the Jaxólé Valley, a day's walk farther east.

On trading trips to eastern Dani villages, people from the Sévé Valley had heard about the establishment of a government post at Wamena (1956) and several mission stations (since 1954) in the Balim Valley; and a few men in Piliam owned steel axes when the mission team arrived. The Jaxólé Valley people did not participate in these contacts, because a long-standing war had cut off virtually all communication with the Sévé Valley.

Between April and September 1961, an air-strip was built in Angkuruk, two miles south of the confluence of the Jaxólé and Ovaxak Rivers. At first, the people reacted to the arrival of strange men and things with bewilderment. Low-flying reconnaissance planes of the Missionary Aviation Fellowship frightened the Jalé. In their anxiety they temporarily stopped garden work, slaughtered many pigs, and initiated underage boys. Yet they approached the strangers with cautious curiosity and very soon recognized the practical value of a steel axe.

In the beginning most people accepted one to two cowrie shells as wages for a day's labor constructing the air-strip. Only

1 Aerial view of the Jaxólé Valley looking south to the Central
Mountain Range (*Courtesy of Archief Topografische Dienst,
Delft, Netherlands, 1962*)

a few workers were willing to save their daily earnings in the form of a small wire piece. The mission exchanged twenty-seven pieces (a number based on the Jalé numeral system) for one axe, and by October 1961 it had redeemed assets, often from joint accounts of several Jalé men, for about thirty axes. The mission exchanged an approximately equal number of axes for land, pigs, and carrier services. During the first two months of construction work, an average of two hundred and fifty people from villages in the Ovaxak and Jaxólé Valleys helped every day with the clearing and leveling of the ground; thereafter, the number dropped to about fifty. The Jalé did very little work on the station between September 1961 and August 1962, presumably because their neglected gardens threatened famine. In the fall of 1962 a large number of people—up to a hundred a day—returned to improve the air-strip. At this time the men demanded steel axes and until March 1963 approximately three hundred and fifty axes were paid. Women and children, however, continued to accept wages in salt and cowrie shells. Then all help was suddenly suspended when a native died in a clinic which had been built in the meantime. In November people began to work again, this time mainly for cymbium shells, which the mission so far had used exclusively as an exchange commodity for pigs and as gifts. The value of one cymbium shell, depending on its size, was fixed at one half to three axes. The wire pieces were now replaced by ten-sen coins, which remained the functional equivalent of the earlier wire currency. From May to July 1964 the number of workers employed for cutting timber, building roads around the station, and clearing mission land temporarily increased to two hundred a day. Between 1964 and 1966 the labor force fluctuated with the size of building projects, seasons for garden work, and changing conditions of peace and war.

By 1965, the permanent staff on the Angkuruk station consisted of three Europeans with their families and half a dozen coastal people, including a schoolteacher and a male nurse. The mission established the first outpost at the old base in Piliam in November 1961, but moved it to the nearby village of Porongkoléi in November 1963. Another air-strip was opened there in August 1964. In February 1962 a second post was built in

Jangkaléi in the Ponteng Valley, a few miles north of Piliam, and abandoned half a year later. The next outpost was established in Wanjok, located four and a half miles south of Angkuruk in the Jaxólé Valley, in March 1963; a fourth, in Hélariki, three miles north of Angkuruk, in August 1963. Work on the last branch station near Waléi in the Ovaxak Valley, four miles east of Angkuruk, began in March 1965. All outposts were staffed by school teachers or catechists from the coast.

In 1966, approximately ten boys between the ages of ten and sixteen attended school fairly regularly at each station. In Angkuruk most boys lived in a dormitory on the station and served as helpers there. A cursory survey showed that, with a few exceptions, the fathers of these boys were dead; some of them also had no elder brother, and others were not born in Angkuruk or nearby villages. On the other hand, most dropouts had been from intact families. The pupils were taught elementary arithmetic, reading and writing, and Christian religion in Indonesian. In 1964 the Angkuruk station started a school for

2   Throughout the Jalémó high cliffs and torrential rivers make traveling slow and hazardous

adult men, who responded much less favorably than the young. By that time several of the schoolboys as well as a few adult men had been taken to the capital, Sukarnapura (formerly Hollandia, now Jayapura), on the coast and to other mission stations in the interior.

The Jalé people believe that "Hollantia" is the home of all foreigners, Europeans and coastal people alike, and they refer to them collectively as *ap tuang* (from the Indonesian *tuan* for "mister," "sir"). I think I failed in my efforts to describe to my friends my home, "Amerika," as a land beyond the great "salt-water lake" that Jalé visitors to the coast had reported to their incredulous relatives.

Proselytizing began soon after the mission's arrival with the discouragement of heavy garden work on Sundays. The people accepted this tabu and simply compared it with their custom of not working when a funeral takes place. In 1963 the pastor began to conduct part of the Sunday service in the Jalé language. In 1965 the schoolboys in Angkuruk attended the Sunday services regularly, and one or two dozen adults from villages located near the station usually participated as well. Beginning in October 1964, services were held at irregular intervals on the air-strip, and prior announcement of these occasions brought together a much larger audience. When I left the field in 1966, the mission had not experienced any overt hostility to church practices. But neither had Christianity gained any influence among the people, with the probable exception of the incipient indoctrination of the schoolboys. Christian beliefs as expounded in the parables and exposed in prayers were accepted and respected as part of the *tuang* way of life and contrasted with "what we do and think."[4]

The mission exerted greater influence through its medical services. By 1964 framboesia, which was fairly common in Jalémó, had been eradicated in most valleys. People came to the hospital with any dermatological ailments and with injuries resulting from accidents, but had hardly begun to seek medical treatment for internal disorders and diseases. The importation, presumably from the Balim, of a contagious dermatosis predominantly affecting the upper thigh, the groin, and the lumbar regions was attributed to the *tuang* people because the disease afflicted the schoolboys first. Since its cure is simple, the malady caused a prolonged suffering only to those unfortunate victims to whom travel to the station was barred by current hostilities between their villages and Angkuruk.

An agricultural engineer associated with the mission who came to Angkuruk in August 1963 also achieved some success with his work. Between 1964 and 1966, a farm complex to house cattle, pigs, sheep, goats, and several kinds of fowl was built at the station. Experimental cultivation of peanuts, cabbage, maize, and other vegetables produced satisfactory results. The farm's studboar was in great demand, and a white strain ran through many a litter in the surrounding villages. In 1965 the mission began to distribute peanuts, maize, and cabbage plants to the local villagers, who generally accepted the new crops. Though soil and parasitological conditions and, as a matter of course, Jalé economy prevented any intensive cultivation of these crops, they nevertheless soon began to have a practical value. While cabbage and maize were grown to be sold back to the mission, the peanut became a highly valued, if scarce, nutriment. During 1966 a few Jalé people acquired chickens and some men built ponds for fish they obtained from the mission's hatchery.

Until 1966 cultural change effected by mission activity was largely limited to and contingent upon the acceptance of a few technical and dietary novelties that had an immediately recognizable value and, as such, could readily be incorporated into the traditional economic system. The importation of cymbium and cowrie shells, both of which were known but very scarce in Jalémó before 1961, increased the wealth of the people in villages around Angkuruk and the outposts, and gave them an advantage in their trade with more distant areas. No perceptible change had occurred in the people's social philosophy with the exception of an incipient acceptance by schoolboys of ideas taught by the mission. In fact, the people already recognized the schoolboys as being different from their age-mates. Clothes, access to new knowledge, and, generally, their membership in a group with a distinct identity had set them apart as the *tuang* children. It was certain that they would become principal agents in the inevitable process of adulteration of traditional Jalé culture.

Police came to Angkuruk for the first time in July 1963, after eleven people from the Jaxólé Valley had been killed and eaten in a massacre at Piliam in the Sévé Valley. They stayed for half an hour, during which a report of the incident was drawn up. Two months later the mission was forced to request police protection when a throng of men threatened to break into a storage room in an attempt to seize cymbium shells and axes as indemnification for the death of relatives slain at Piliam. The mission people were blamed for the massacre because they had encouraged the resumption of traffic between the Jaxólé and Sévé Valley villages.

In May 1964 a police patrol made a preliminary inspection of the wreckage of the U.S. plane that in 1945 had crashed into a mountain ridge south of the populated section of the Jaxólé Valley. Three months later, in August, a joint patrol of Indonesian policemen and American military personnel from the U.S. Embassy in Jakarta came to investigate the wreck and to retrieve the remains of the plane's crew. Informants remembered that when the plane crashed intense terror seized the Jaxólé people. Panic-stricken, they temporarily suspended garden work, slaughtered pigs en masse, and violated premenarcheal, pregnancy, and post-partum sex tabus. Later, a few courageous men visited the wreck. News of their discovery of incomprehensible things spread throughout the region. The people, however, shunned the place, and not until almost twenty years had passed—after the search expeditions had come and gone—did some men venture to exploit the wreck for pieces of aluminum straps that could be hafted to adze handles in place of stone blades. I estimate that only about a dozen of these aluminum adzes had been made by 1966.

In October 1964 the mission radioed for police protection a second time. A "big man" from the village of Angkuruk had singlehandedly wrecked the school dormitory after the boys who took care of one of his pigs had negligently let its leash be burnt in the fireplace. The policemen, the pastor remembered, "upon our request just talked with [the man] but did not take any further action."

The next government patrol was flown into Angkuruk on February 22, 1966, a day after a *tuang* boy had been killed on the station. The party consisted of a civil servant, two policemen, and two soldiers. They stayed four days, during which they recorded the incident and demonstrated the use and effect of a rifle. Two months later, in early May 1966, the mission feared a revenge attack in connection with the recent killing and radioed again for police protection. Two members of that patrol were still in Angkuruk when I left Pasikni in July. In the meantime punitive police actions, following abortive attempts to settle disputes, had given the Jalé people a thorough experience with the power of foreign control backed by the use of firearms.[5]

Problems of Fieldwork

When I arrived at Angkuruk on October 27, 1964, where I spent the following eight weeks as a guest of the mission, I had yet to decide whether to settle in a Jalé village or work among the non–Dani-speaking people further east. Two conditions determined my choice of the Jalémó as a fieldwork area. First of all, a cannibalistic feast which took place on the air-strip less than three months before my arrival (Koch 1970a), along with my own judgment of the contact situation, convinced me that virtually nothing of importance to my study of a traditional New Guinea Highland culture had changed since the mission came into the Jalémó three years before. Second, the high quality of the linguistic material put at my disposal by the pastor enabled me to learn the Jalé language faster than I had anticipated. I made several exploratory trips to villages in the Jaxólé and Ovaxak Valleys and chose the village of Pasikni as my research site. I liked Pasikni on my first view. It is one of the most populous villages in the area, built on relatively dry ground on the east slope of the beautiful Jaxólé Valley, and attractively located high above the valley floor at a comfortable altitude of 5,200 feet.

On December 21, 1964, I set up camp in Pasikni and started

the construction of a simple house at the edge of the village. My lack both of cymbium shells and of the right kind of steel axe for the payment of labor, as well as a war between Pasikni and the neighboring village of Savilivi, delayed its completion until the end of March 1965.

The people of Pasikni received me with suspicion and mistrust. The two men who uttered a few inviting words were, as I later learned, immigrants themselves; and the man who first offered to sell a piece of land where I pitched my tent had no rights to it. Several months later those who had become my friends told me that the old men had been particularly strongly opposed to my decision to stay in their village. And they had expressed their disapproval in the proper idiomatic language of inhospitality: "He is not to defecate and urinate on our ground." When the people gradually discovered that I stubbornly persisted in my plan, they apparently decided to take advantage of the situation and soon distinguished themselves as an extraordinarily mendacious and mendicant lot.

3   Pasikni with the author's house in foreground

My gravest problem in those early days was the necessity of adapting my expectations to a mode of thought that I could not easily appreciate. I also found it difficult to realize that all textbook and field manual anthropology had to wait until I had learned some elementary forms of interaction that would not antagonize my hosts. Moreover, my early unpopularity, as well as my eventual acceptance, provided the Jalé, who love to sing and have an admirable talent for instant composition of new lyrics to go with their old tunes, with events and matter for expression. A stanza that became popular dealt with my solitary efforts to build a house:

> No man comes to bring timber
> Nobody comes to bring timber
> There is no timber to be seen
> But he keeps asking for help.

One song praised the salt I had brought to Pasikni with these lines:

> I walk up to his house, losing my breath
> I walk up for the salt, losing my breath
> I walk down to my house, swiftly move my feet
> With salt in my net, swiftly move my feet.

The poet of another song looked upon the evening market scene at my house, which the women created daily when they came to trade vegetables for salt or cowrie shells:

> They don't see their husbands
> They don't see their children
> With their food they surround
> His house of palmwood.

Many of these husbands, of course, knew that I needed only a small fraction of the food I accepted and would be happy to share it with them when, after a while, they followed their wives and lamented their empty stomachs.

I did not begin any systematic research before April. By then, however, I had acquired sufficient fluency in the language and enough familiarity with local customs so that observation and interviewing ceased to be a haphazard enterprise. I had also begun to realize how reasonable the people's behavior toward me was: the pragmatics of cultural relativity had vindicated its dogma.

In early September I interrupted my stay in Pasikni for nine weeks. When I returned many people welcomed me "back home." An old man who strongly agitated against my intrusion in the beginning had died during my absence. His relatives lost no time in telling me that he had changed his mind and affirmed his approval with the customary blessing: "May he remain well while he lives amongst us." My work became easier now because the people talked more freely and willingly, but I still had to wait for several months before I was granted the privilege of entry, by a contrived formal initiation, into the last of the nine men's houses in the village. Although all Jalé men's houses are sacred, some are more sacred than others; and this one was the most sacred of the Pasikni men's houses.

My second sojourn in Jalémó lasted until July 4, 1966, bring-ing the total number of months spent in the field to seventeen and a half, during which time I made several trips into near and distant regions of the Jalémó, including an extended journey across the Snow Mountains which led to the discovery of Jalé villages in the Seng Valley south of the Central Range. Two years later these friendly people, who had presented me with a pig to show their hospitality, killed and ate two white mis-sionaries traveling through their valley and now figure in Christian annals as "fetish men, sleuth-like, arrogant and crafty —practicing their devilish arts amidst indescribably ghoulish scenes of savagery" (Manning 1969: 113).

In my work I relied on the standard techniques of observation and interviewing. With both approaches I encountered several obstacles that I could never overcome. Since the women and their small children live in separate huts, I was unable to obtain any good information on family life and on routine interaction be-tween husband and wife and between parents and children. For the same reason I was never able to join a group of females in any of their activities, and neither could I conduct any real interviews with women. Consequently, I could not record the most important processes of socialization.

Moreover, I think that I also failed in recording adequately the round of daily life in the men's houses. Although I spent many days and nights in these houses, it was only toward the end of my stay in the field that I felt that the men ignored my presence. I always wished I had lived with them, but, alas, I could not. Imagine a round hut with an open fireplace in the center, with a living space of a hundred and sixty square feet that you share with fifteen or more persons, with a ceiling height of less than five feet, and with the light falling through a small entrance hole barely illuminating the interior. Then you understand why the most committed participant observer will not be able to live there—along with his papers, books, typewriter, camera, medicine box, clothing, and other gear—and still do his work.

Again, I resented having to spend valuable time on the boringly mundane problems of housekeeping. While I never ceased enjoying my life in the bush, routine necessities dulled the experience considerably. I had three boys in succession to help me around the house. The home of the first one was a distant village on the south side of the Central Range, from where he had originally come to live with relatives in the village of Waléi in the Ovaxak Valley. He attached himself to me while I was still in Angkuruk, but he resigned from his job shortly after I had finished my house. The next helper, who was from Pasikni, stayed a few months, until I dismissed him when he began to supplement my generous gifts with thefts from my stores. The third boy, named Hólóap, who had occasionally helped out from the beginning, turned out to be a loyal little friend, and people regarded him as my adopted son. He cleaned the house, chopped wood, washed my clothes, carried my camera, learned to make tea, and took care of my kerosene lantern. His cheerful diligence and versatile abilities greatly mitigated the burden of my own cultural domesticity.

I intensely enjoyed learning the Jalé language. Like all Papuan languages it has a terribly complicated grammar in which infixes and suffixes and six conjugated forms of six basic tenses can modify the stem of a verb several hundred ways. I considered it an attractive challenge to master the transformational rules, but my more sustained intellectual enjoyment came from a gradual comprehension of the metaphorical properties of Jalé speech. The richness of poetic images and the fantastic symbolism of semantic analogies never failed to rouse my admiration.

One of the many mistakes that I made during the first months of interviewing had unfortunate consequences. Whenever I had understood the description of some behavior and wanted to get an explanation, my question began with *"nóngke faxet,"* which literally means "for what?" but like the French "pour quoi?" also means "why?" What I did not know then was that this interrogative expression implies disapproval or even reprimand whenever the behavior referred to is obvious but requires justification of motive. No Jalé thinks that he has to justify routine behavior, much less ritual actions that he should not talk about at all. My questions became less awkward only after I had learned that the semantically appropriate inquiry into the meaning of an act was *"nóngke ólók?"*—"expressing what?"— although I suspect that my informants detected my naiveté before I did. But even in the end I did not understand every talk I heard. Nevertheless I acquired a considerable, if studied, ability to metaphorize my public speech.

The people appreciated my efforts, and I felt rewarded when friends commended me for my incipient oratorical skills. A rather grim situation evoked the first flourish. I had resolved to retaliate for immoderate thefts from my limited supply of knives, salt, and matches by a young boy and so tore out several tobacco plants from his father's yard, which I subsequently burned in the fireplace of my courtyard. In the inevitable confrontation with the irate owner of the plants, I managed to justify my action in the idiom appropriate to the case. I said, "Your son took away my knives, he took away my salt, he took away my 'fire-making things,' he made a fire and the flames spread. They spread afar, and they ate your tobacco. Your own son made cigarettes from your tobacco. Your own son smoked your tobacco."

Fortunately, I had to suffer only a few unpleasant encounters of this kind. Although some of them were more dramatic, all ended auspiciously because I could depend on my friends to defend and support me. I took care to terminate each dispute soon, always an easy task that required nothing more than an apology and a gift. To the unhappy tobacco grower I said a day after our bout, "Because what happened gave me a bad heart, I scolded you. Because I scolded you, I have come to bring you this [a pack of tobacco]." This customary statement of regret and an equally standardized expression of understanding from him dissolved all animosity between us.

As far as I know sporadic and temporary quarrels never put me in danger and I remember my astonishment over a note the mission sent me by special messenger after the *tuang* boy had been killed on the station: "The Tengkeléi people are angry with us. The schoolboys say that they want to eat one of us and, if the flesh tastes good, the others as well. They are furious because Kóxal was killed. They say we haven't guarded him properly."

My knowledge of Jalé ideology is, to an extent, filtered through the minds of the men. These men, of course, were limited in number. Since control of information is a vital aspect of the total system of social control, and since secrecy maintained within an in-group is coupled with a pervasive distrust of strangers, it took a long time to establish the friendships with a few men that were necessary for intensive work. Altogether I had ten main informants with whom I worked regularly. Mutual sympathy created in the course of casual visiting and occasional gift exchanges primarily determined my choice of each. Other considerations that influenced my selection were a man's intelligence, apparent knowledge, and didactic ability, his prospective willingness to cooperate, and my need to have informants of all age groups and from as many men's houses as possible.

Most interview sessions took place in my house or at my fireplace in the courtyard. They were private in the sense that informants often refused to begin or continue a session in the presence of casual visitors or in the presence of other in-

4 Taling, the author's oldest friend and most knowledgeable informant

5   Halim and Pavéon, the author's best friends

formants whose kinsmen were involved in the case under review
and exploration. Some time after I had started regular interviews
my informants began to describe these occasions as "talking
school."[6] The expression reflects their understanding of the
situation as one of formal instruction. The student's use of pen
and paper marked the process and distinguished it from ordinary
teaching.

Younger informants, between twenty and thirty years of age,
were occasionally reprimanded by elders of their residence
groups for "talking school" even toward the end of my stay.
However, the initial general hostility against their cooperation
dwindled after I began to reward them for their services with
gifts of steel axes and shells.

My informants received other benefits through their association with my household. While my tobacco lasted, I shared it
with them, knowing, of course, that for Jalé men smoking and
talking belong together in any discussion. Many meals in my
house turned into parties when I had bartered loads of cooked
vegetables from the women. Informants and any of their kinsmen and neighbors who happened to be visiting could make
their common fare a delicate dish with unrestrained helpings of
my salt, a Jalé's most relished condiment. Hunting marsupials
and birds with me was another attractive diversion, but my
friends' disappointment with my refusal to use the gun against
their enemies never waned.

Usually only one or two informants at a time were inter-
viewed. Often an informant requested a "secluded" session,
either to discuss a matter he did not want anyone else to know
or to entrust me with a secret that he was not supposed to know
or, if he did share it with others, should not tell to an outsider.
For example, many parts of the sacro-ritual complex associated
with the men's house are ideally known only to "men of knowledge," those who have undergone a secondary initiation ceremony. However, young men who knew some aspects of it would
confidentially impart their knowledge provided nobody else
was around. Likewise, an older man who had undergone the

initiation would explain the sacred lore on condition that I did not talk about it with my younger friends.

The study of kinship relations was the most important task for an understanding of Jalé social organization and, especially, for an analysis of conflict behavior. It was also the most difficult problem to pursue. The shallowness of genealogical knowledge frustrated my genealogical inquiries again and again. Worse yet, the construction of pedigrees was especially difficult and time-consuming because every person has at least two names, either one of which may be used by different relatives. Uttering the names of certain kinsmen, such as affines and agnates of ascending generations, is, moreover, tabu. Nevertheless, in the end I had recorded the genealogies of over fifty truncated lineages resident in Pasikni along with detailed data on the marital and residential history of their members.[7]

Much less troublesome was the collection of the dispute cases which form the basis of this study. Unlike all ritual activity, many of them were public affairs to which I had immediate access. I discussed most cases that occured during my stay with several informants on different occasions. Treating what I call "memory" cases in the same way, I noticed a surprising ability of the people to recite in remarkably congruous phrases critical statements made during past disputes. This ability puzzled me until I could follow the incredibly rapid flow of dispute orations and discovered that the Jalé employ rather stereotypical sets of accusatory and defensive speech patterns. I have, therefore, occasionally included literal quotations in the account of a case that I did not witness myself. I could date events in memory cases by parametric correlations with the computed age of a few selected living people, whose ages were calculated in relation to the absolute dates of 1945, the year of the plane crash, and 1961, the year when the mission arrived, and by the mean age difference of four to five years between siblings.

About half of the cases occurred or continued during my stay in the field; the others represent accounts of past conflicts that informants remembered. I have found that these two kinds of cases differ in one significant respect. While most memory cases, regardless of the original grievance, involve violent retaliation, the majority of disputes that took place in the course of my fieldwork did not result in violence. This discrepancy relates to the very nature of Jalé conflict management. In the absence of judicial authorities disputes that the principals settled by private negotiation and grievances that remained without any redress tend to gain little public knowledge and fall into oblivion. On the other hand, conflicts that escalated into warfare are more readily remembered. These impediments to empirical research have an unfortunate consequence. I will not be able to make quantitative estimates concerning any relationship between type and outcome of disputes and the parties involved in a particular kind of conflict. Therefore, I am forced to indicate relative frequencies on the basis of my observations and discussions with informants by expressions like "usually," "often," or "rarely"—a wholly unsatisfactory if unavoidable device.

My field data are deficient also in another important respect. As my discussion of the social organization will show and as many cases will document, the pig has an extremely important place in Jalé society. Virtually all secondary social relationships, those not determined by birth, are validated and solemnified by pig exchanges. Various modes of conflict management incorporate such transactions as well. Since most adult men most of the time have multiple obligations to reciprocate pigs within the context of their exchange relationships, it is customary to keep one's assets secret. People frequently hide their pigs in the house of a neighbor during visits of relatives from other villages if they owe these relatives a pig and do not wish to satisfy claims or unvoiced expectations at that time. Because of this ingrained reluctance of the Jalé to expose to others the quantity and quality of their pigs, I have failed to obtain sufficiently reliable information on socioeconomic relationships that could best be described and analyzed in terms of pig exchanges.

When I left the village, my friends insisted that I come back —with a lot of steel axes and big cymbium shells, of course. Would I return? Wasa, the best medicine man in the village, father of my "adopted" son, able teacher and patient informant, knew the answer. "If the banana tree that I planted in my garden when you had come to live among us bears its fruits toward the source of the Jaxólé River, you will come back. If the fruit stand bends toward where the river flows, we will know that we won't see your face again." I imagine the bananas grew toward the mountains, but old Wasa may not be around to remember his prediction.

I An Anthropological View of Conflict

This book deals with one big question: What are the political prerequisites for the transformation of a dyadic conflict into a triadic relationship between the opponents and a third party who can resolve their dispute? It is this problem which has stunted the institutionalization of peaceful means of settling disputes in New Guinea societies as well as the development of effective international arbitration. As long as the principals must rely upon negotiation in their search for a settlement, resort to force or capitulation remain their sad alternatives.

Every social group must cope with conflicts among its members and between itself and other groups. Rather than being something pathological, enmity and disputes are a normal part of social life. A conflict arises when a person or a group suffers or believes it has suffered an infringement of a right. Whether or not a right constitutes a legal claim or a customary expectation may be an interesting problem in jurisprudence; for the Jalé such a distinction is meaningless.

I view a conflict or a dispute as a confrontation arising from at least partially incompatible interests of opposing parties. Potential consequences of incompatible interests include strife arising from competition for the control of resources or positions of power and ideological disagreement about values or norms.

If we ignore the hypothetical fight of two marooned men for the exclusive control of a small desolate island, the outcome of a conflict as a social process depends not only on the strength of the involved parties but also on the influence and participation of other persons. By outcome I mean a resolution of the conflict that may but need not be an actual settlement by which the problem that led to the confrontation is solved. If no settlement occurs, the resolution merely marks an intermediate phase in the history of a conflict.

Although the opposing parties may have an interest in prolonging a conflict and even exacerbating it over a certain period of time, people involved in the dispute either as principals and their supporters or as agents of political control will ultimately seek to end the conflict. In international relations, for example, a military ideology that desires to resolve a conflict by coercion may find advantages in aggravating it until resort to force becomes an "acceptable" method of confrontation. Similarly the Maoist strategy of revolutionary warfare incorporates the protraction of hostilities as an ingenious tactic aimed at final victory.[1]

A Procedural Model of Conflict Management

I distinguish six processes of conflict management in terms of the procedures that combine the dimensions of intervention by a third party and outcome in different patterns (see Figure 1).

In negotiation both principals seek a mutually acceptable settlement without the intervention of a third party but often with the aid of supporters.

In mediation a third party intervenes in a dispute to help the principals achieve an agreement. Three modes of intervention are possible: either principal may solicit the mediator's aid, or an administrative agency may appoint the mediator, or the mediator may intervene on his own initiative as a party interested in conciliation of the conflict (and he may even enforce his aim by imposing sanctions on both sides). Judicial mediation represents a special mode of this procedure. It occurs when a judge compels the principals to reach an agreement which he subsequently ratifies by formal verdict.[2] Regardless of the particular circumstances that brought the mediator into the conflict, both principals must agree to his intervention. The resolution need not but often does involve a compromise, an agreement that requires a mutually satisfactory adjustment of each principal's initial demands.[3]

Adjudication demands the decision of a third party who has the official authority to render a judgment. Either principal may seek his intervention or he may exercise this role ex officio. The institutionalization of this process tends to formalize the norms of conduct and judicial procedure and requires means that enforce compliance with the decision.

In arbitration both principals consent to the intervention of a third party whose judgment they agree to accept.[4] This procedure includes situations where a contract or charter provides for the appointment of the arbiter by only one of the principals or by a constituted administrative agency. Industrial disputes, for example, are often settled by this method.[5] When both principals agree to perform an ordeal or a divination and accept the outcome as a decision, a special kind of arbitration results, one in which the third party is a nonhuman agent. The Jalé, for example, employ this technique in deciding guilt or innocence in incest cases.[6]

Through coercion one principal imposes the outcome and alone determines his concession, if any, to the opponent. The threat or use of force often aggravates the conflict and impedes a peaceful settlement. This situation, which Boulding has viewed as "one of the great organizational problems of mankind" (1962: 432), often leads the parties into warfare.

1 Processes of conflict management

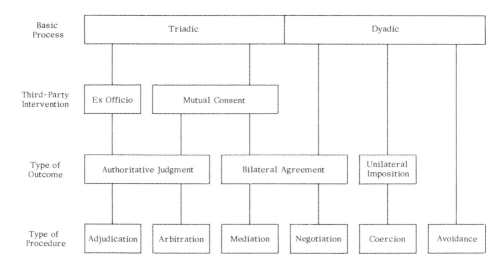

Avoidance represents a procedure of indirect confrontation in which one principal takes no action to obtain redress for a wrong or a curtailment of his interests, although his withdrawal tactics may induce his opponent to make amends.

These definitions of procedures that contrast the significant variables of a dispute process (see Figure 2) denote ideal types in Weber's (1956: 14) sense. The involvement of supporters in the conflict represents a nondistinctive variable since these may participate in every type of procedure, although their roles may range from that of a litigant's attorney in government courts to that of a hired assassin in the world of the Cosa Nostra. Certainly the form and scope of their participation impinges upon the outcome of a dispute, as, for example, in cases of "bargain justice" where collusion between prosecution, defense, and bench often results in an arbitrated decision.[7] Furthermore, any particular conflict may go through several procedures during different phases of its management before reaching a final resolution. An industrial dispute, for example, may go through an initial period of negotiation between labor and management, enter a phase of coercive action with strikes and lockouts, and end with an arbitrated settlement after a court order has terminated the work stoppage.

2 The contrastive variables of procedures

Type of Procedure	Third-Party Intervention		Outcome		
	Ex Officio	Mutual Consent	Authoritative Judgment	Bilateral Agreement	Unilateral Imposition
Adjudication	+	−	+	−	−
Arbitration	−	+	+	−	−
Mediation	−	+	−	+	−
Negotiation	−	−	−	+	−
Coercion	−	−	−	−	+
Avoidance	−	−	−	−	−

Different procedures need not be limited to consecutive phases of a dispute process; the principals may employ several methods concurrently and, as negotiations in industrial conflicts during strikes and the so-called Paris peace talks during the Vietnam War evince, the relative failure or success of the parties in their coercive strategies influences their efforts in negotiation and vice versa. Yet, these concepts of procedures have analytical significance because they do not confuse criteria of office, such as that of an appointed judge or of an agency such as a court, with the performance of a role, that is, with the activity of those engaged in the management of a conflict. My model obviates a distinction between political and legal methods of conflict management. While such a distinction may be important to philosophical discourses on "justice," its analytical value for comparative research is questionable as long as the analysis focuses upon institutions rather than upon function and process. All processes of settling disputes are to some degree political activity, even though in some societies the rhetoric of public policy may obscure the political nature of the courts' activities. In Jalé society a distinction between political and legal processes is as meaningless as a distinction between law and custom.[8]

The model provides a conceptual framework for developing theories that attempt to explain the form and function of empirical relations between types of procedure and other cultural variables.[9] Comparative research may elucidate, for example, the conditions that promote, hinder, or eliminate the possibility of dispute settlement through negotiation or mediation and those which facilitate or require arbitration or adjudication by discovering the structural requisites—political and economic realities of the allocation of power and the control of resources—for the institutionalization and use of these different processes. The exploration of these patterns within a society may focus on differences in the relations between the parties, the type of their dispute, and the normative content and administrative structure of the legal system.[10] Cross-cultural studies may seek to discover correlations between the relative predominance of particular procedures of conflict resolution and the nature of other structural, behavioral, and ideological aspects of societies. Studies of African and Chinese societies have shown, for example, that the choice of mediators usually depends on the relations between the parties and the type of their conflict.[11] Mediation facilitates and relies upon the communication of any beliefs, arguments, and evidence that both principals and the mediator deem important for reaching an agreement. Unlike adjudication—which follows essentially from retrospective evaluation of the dispute in terms of juridically relevant norms—mediation seeks a consensual resolution that favors a relatively amicable continuation of the relationship.[12]

Procedure in Jalé Society

A comprehensive theory of conflict resolution would link together all types of procedure and their correlated sociological variables in one complex model. My aim in this book is much more modest, since it is completely defined by the nature of Jalé conflict management. Jalé society lacks not only forensic institutions like courts and offices whose incumbents exercise a delegated judicial authority, but even more rudimentary institutions such as forums convened to discuss a dispute. Nor do the Jalé have positions of political leadership that empower their incumbents to exercise control over a local community and to adjudicate disputes among its members.

Furthermore, although my own observations of behavior and informants' descriptions of customary modes of conduct could be collated in a catalogue of rules, the Jalé themselves do not formulate any legal norms.[13] Rather, they speak of their behavior either as "what we do," which describes a right and approved course of action, or as "what is not done," which refers to wrong and reprehensible conduct. According to their reasoning, no trouble among people need arise if everybody fulfills his obligations and refrains from violating the rights of others. A pragmatic consequence of this principle subjects any conduct that contravenes these expectations to negotiation or mediation at best and potentially to coercive or retaliatory action—procedures that seek redress for grievances in forceful confrontation with the opponent.

Thus I see the aim of this study as an attempt to explain the absence of a third-party authority in Jalé processes of conflict management, the resultant impediments to a peaceful settlement of disputes, and the correlated tendency of an aggrieved party to resort to violence in his efforts to obtain redress. In other words, I intend to show why in Jalé society the feeble procedures of mediation that do exist have not developed into a viable triadic system of conflict management. An examination of my conclusions in the light of cross-cultural evidence will further elucidate the results in a wider theoretical framework.

Although anthropologists may not agree in their use of terms like law and custom, they commonly accept two methodological premises. The first demands that the ethnographer investigate law and conflict in a society's total cultural context—as influencing and being influenced by the system of social relations that structure the behavior of people. The other insists that the most productive approach analyzes actual dispute cases.[14] This book should reflect the value of these principles for my research among the Jalé. The anthropologist has another important task to fulfill. He has to tell the reader under what conditions he conducted his research. The field, after all, is his "laboratory," and as the physicist needs to describe the set-up of his experiments, so must the anthropologist explain the circumstances under which he made his observations, talked to his informants, and studied the culture of the people.

In the Introduction I have already explained the opportunities and limitations that I encountered in my work among the Jalé. The next chapter will describe the Jalé way of life and their political organization and thus set the stage upon which the social dramas develop that become crystallized in abstract form as cases in the notebook of the ethnographer. My analysis of the cases will show how relations of kinship and residential association between the principals to disputes and the political situation in which disputes arise determine to a decisive degree the procedures of their resolution. The following synopsis describes the dominant patterns.

In disputes within the patrilineage the co-residents of the principals can exert a mediating pressure toward a peaceful settlement as long as the parties live together. Their intervention and formal avoidance tactics between the principals tend to prevent forceful retaliation. The performance of a reconciliation ritual can repair the solidarity of a lineage if the parties have formally severed their relationship. However, when an agnatic descent group has moved apart, the diverging territorial alignments of the principals impédes peaceful procedures, and revenge actions become a likely choice for an injured party seeking redress. The involvement of two residence groups in a conflict appear to weaken lineage solidarity, and acts of violent retaliation and counter-vengeance resemble the patterns of confrontation between villages or different wards, demarcated sections of a village, especially when the residential separation of the parties resulted from a previous dispute. Furthermore, the absence of daily interaction delays or even precludes a final reconciliation of the principals. In this situation a minor grievance may lead to a war between several villages.

Unlike conflicts within the lineage, disputes between husband and wife endanger only their conjugal relations and not the solidarity of a whole group. However, every severe marital conflict also involves the woman's kinsmen because it threatens to disrupt the affinal exchange relationship that the marriage established. They share an interest in the continuation of the exchanges with the husband and his agnates—who may have participated in the reciprocative gift transactions that validated the union—and thus both sides may seek a reconciliation of the spouses. In this situation the transfer of pigs and other gifts within the context of the existing exchange pattern represents a functional equivalent to the reconciliation rite terminating disputes among agnatic kinsmen.

While in conflicts between husband and wife people other than the spouses' closest consanguineal relatives rarely intervene and if they do, usually attempt to reconcile the parties, in direct confrontations between affines each party can rely on the support of his men's house group. If the dissolution of the marriage has severed the principals' affinal relationships, pig seizures become a common method of redress.

Disputes between non-kin members of a ward can be managed peacefully as long as they actually live together in the same place and, especially, if hostilities with other groups demand concerted military action, but—as in conflicts within the lineage —a spatial separation of the parties inhibits negotiations and may promote resort to force, which then tends to precipitate a chain reaction of violent vengeance. However, if a person absconds from his ward to escape punishment after he has committed an offense, this action may mitigate the injured party's wrath and thus alleviate the danger of revenge.

In disputes between unrelated members of neighboring wards two factors may restrain the parties from resorting to forceful retaliation in the pursuit of their interest: the mediating efforts of a principal's co-residents with affinal links to his opponent or members of his men's house group and the recognition that undisturbed garden work and effective defense against an outside enemy requires amity among neighbors. The relatively greater jeopardy experienced by foreign residents in inter-ward conflicts signifies the importance of amicable relationships between autochthonous lineages for maintaining peace within the village community. Unless a person has suffered bodily injury, a dispute between neighbors remains amenable to a compromise settlement through negotiation. Altercations, usually after dusk, bring a grievance to public attention and serve to express hostile sentiments in nonviolent fashion. In this situation "big men" have a chance to intervene and, regardless of their residential association, unfailingly appeal to both parties to exercise restraint. However, bodily injury in a retaliatory action tends to elicit a revenge attack which often initiates a war. Yet the same factors that inhibit the outbreak of violence continue to operate in reducing the virulence of armed combat. If someone has been killed, one revenge death normally ends the fighting, and emigration of the person responsible for the war, like an offender's temporary abscondence in intra-ward conflicts, decreases the chance of further vengeance.

Although parties belonging to different villages may succeed in settling a dispute over, for example, an abduction, mistaken pig seizures, or garden land by peaceful negotiation, an unsuccessful verbal confrontation in these cases often leads to forceful retaliation, which is the usual method of seeking redress for adultery, wanton pig theft, and pillage of crops. Since in inter-village vengeance anyone's pig may be seized from the foraging grounds of the opponent's village, every dispute between strangers jeopardizes not only a party's co-residents but also his neighbors in other wards. Consequently, an unresolved conflict between individuals from different villages affects the political relationship between whole communities and often prevents any negotiation altogether if a new dispute arises between different persons.

Generally, the probability that a confrontation results in armed combat increases with geographical distance and paucity of affinal relationships between the local groups involved in the conflict. The same conditions also impede an early settlement when villages in different regions participate in the war. In this situation alliances are created by default rather than by considerations of affinity and traditional amity, and unsatisfied claims to compensatory pigs among allied wards greatly inhibit the conclusion of a peace treaty that all parties honor.

In summary, my analysis of disputes among the Jalé will conclude that the lack of political integration and the absence of judicial authorities make coercive self-help an institutionalized procedure of conflict management. Unless common interests based upon kinship and co-residence intervene, conflicts in Jalé society have a pronounced tendency to escalate into warfare. The implications of my analysis go far beyond an understanding of conflict management among a small population in the Highlands of New Guinea in that they provide insights into the problems of international war and peace.

II The Jalé Way of Life

The Jalé people live in compact villages built along the middle ranges of the valley slopes, which through centuries of extensive cultivation have lost the original cover of virgin forest around the inhabited areas. Under favorable topographical conditions several villages sometimes occupy a single deforested zone. Major tributaries of the main rivers or low, brushwood-covered, traverse ridges usually separate a cluster of villages from the nearest neighboring settlements. I call these areas districts because the people recognize them as distinct residential localities.

Regions are much larger areas that are separated from each other by a main river or a major forested mountain ridge. Although no synonyms for the generic expressions district and region exist in their language, the people refer to a cluster of neighboring villages and to areas comprising adjacent districts by specific names. Many are named after one of the local villages, others after a prominent geographic feature such as a river or an especially abundant kind of vegetation within the area. Neither region nor district represents a fixed political division, but residential proximity determines alliance politics in inter-village conflicts.

Residence Patterns

The size of Jalé settlements varies considerably. The smallest villages have two dozen or fewer houses and the largest more than a hundred. To each village belong one or more smaller settlements located in distant garden areas which I call hamlets and homesteads. A hamlet is a group of houses which are temporarily occupied during agricultural seasons by people who have their permanent residence in the base village. For Pasikni the distances between garden hamlets and the village vary from a half-hour to a two-hour walk. In addition to the process of gradual expansion of cultivated land, catastrophic events such as defeat in war or an epidemic may result in the permanent occupation of a hamlet by one or several lineages. Over time these hamlets become independent villages, after having passed through a stage of continued association with the natal ward of the founding lineages in ritual activities such as initiation.[1] Homesteads are the homes of one man and his family who, for one reason or another, move away from the village to live permanently in one of his gardens.

Except for the very small ones, most villages comprise two or more wards, residential units consisting of a large men's house and a cluster of smaller family huts built in its immediate vicinity. The big men's house, which is also called "sacred house," is the domicile of all initiated males of a ward, whose autochtonous lineages hold the house as communal property. In some wards only one lineage occupies the men's house, but usually several lineages from different sibs live together. I use the term "sib" to denote an unbounded population segment whose members believe themselves to be descendants of a common ancestor, and "lineage" to denote a group of relatives who can trace their genealogical connnections through a known apical ancestor.

Occasionally a single man or a lineage may build a separate, small men's house adjacent to the ward's main men's house. These adjunct men's houses may become the nucleus of a new ward and, after removal to a different site, may develop into a "sacred house" by gradual enforcement of certain tabus and, finally, by its use for initiations.

A family hut is principally the domicile of a married woman and her uninitiated sons and unmarried daughters, but her own or her husband's widowed or divorced mother may also live with her. In a polygynous marriage co-wives with their children may maintain a joint household, but more frequently each lives in a separate hut. Most family huts are built by the woman's hus-

6 Bird's eye view of the village of Pasikni

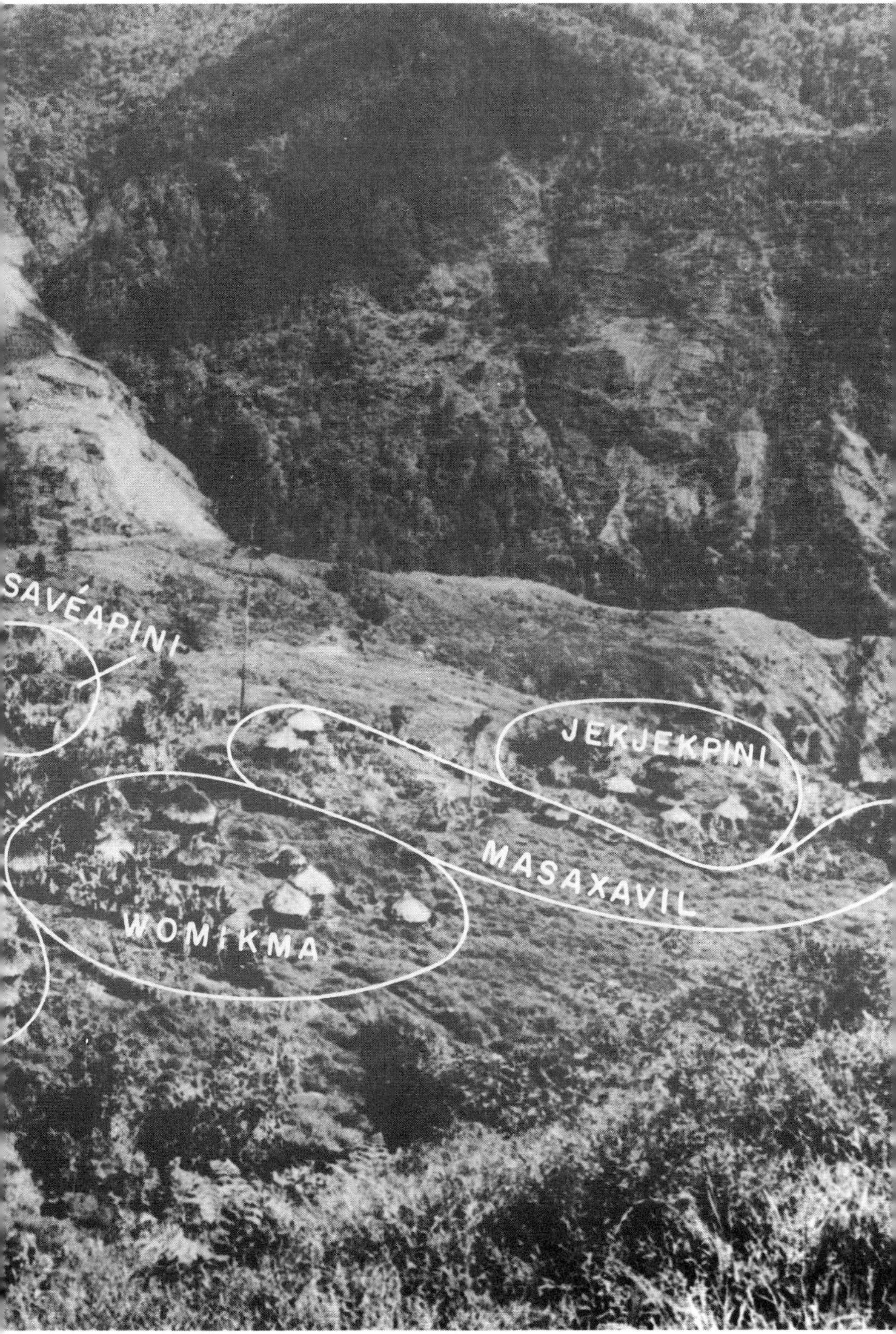

SAVÉAPINI
JEKJEKPINI
MASAXAVIL
WOMIKMA

band, but occasionally an adolescent boy builds one for his mother if his father is dead or senile. When he marries, his wife will live in this hut.[2]

These three types of domicile have the same basic design. A round wall of wooden planks and four central poles carry a conical roof which is made of imbricating layers of pandanus leaves or casuarina bark folded over concentric vine-lashings that connect the rafters. The entrance is a rectangular hole, cut out during the building process, which can be closed with one or two boards. The floor is raised above the ground and a sleeping platform built under the roof is reached by climbing a notched log that leads to an opening on its periphery. On both floors the space between the four central poles accommodates the fireplace. In every family hut, and occasionally in a men's house as well, one or two separate enclosures on the ground floor serve as pig pens, which only in rare instances have a separate doorway.

The entrances of the domiciles face the thoroughfares running through the wards in an irregular layout, and while average distances between any two family huts range from nine to fifteen feet, the sacred men's houses—preferably built on a stretch of elevated ground—usually stand apart by thirty feet or more from the group of family huts. In addition to its size and location, a men's house is differentiated from a family hut by the linear designs painted on the outside walls on both sides of the entrance with red ochre and white clay. Because of its ritual status, females and uninitiated boys must neither enter the men's house nor pass through its courtyard. The area opposite its entrance is particularly sacred. In this sanctum, the men store the sacred nets which belong to the house. These nets—because of their sooted appearance also called "black nets"—hang along the wall and contain various objects of ritual significance that have been kept by succeeding generations of the resident lineages.

Subsistence, Trade, and Cooperation

Climate, soil conditions, and technology base Jalé economy on a subsistence agriculture that requires shifting cultivation by slash-and-burn, drainage, and fencing methods. Although land resources are plentiful, the prolonged fallow periods necessary for a recovery of the ground has resulted in a contingent pattern of shifting residence. Given an average crop season of eight to ten months, the Jalé leave their base villages about twice every year and take up residence in dispersed hamlets. While a hamlet usually belongs to one ward, tenancy rights in a particular locality may bring lineages from different wards together in one settlement. Although it may happen that for short intervals most wards of a village have moved to their hamlets, their autonomous planning makes it impossible for all inhabitants of the larger villages to live in their gardens at the same time.

Residence arrangements are basically the same in the garden hamlet and in the village, but the households of two brothers or a father and his son, usually separate units in the village, are occasionally combined under one roof during a seasonal stay at the hamlet. Unlike the sacred men's house in the village, every men's house in a garden settlement is the property of an individual man who may accommodate other men with their sons who have not built a men's house for themselves.

The Jalé, like other New Guinea Highlands peoples, reserve most of their gardens within and outside the village for the sweet potato. In addition they grow taro, yams, pandanus, pitpit, sugar cane, bananas, and a variety of leafy vegetables. Other cultivated and wild-growing plants provide the materials for the men's penis sheath and ratan dress, the women's apron, netting yarn, and, along with animal bones, for the few tools, utensils, and ornaments used by these people.[3]

Compared with the quantity of vegetables in their diet, the Jalé eat very little animal food. Women, occasionally in small groups, gather insects and their larvae and catch lizards, mice, and frogs. With bow and arrow the men hunt birds, bats, and arboreal or terrestrial mammals found in the forest, especially marsupials, such as the tree kangaroo and phalangers, and giant rats. Although a few men in Pasikni know some trapping devices, they very seldom use this method.

The only domesticated animals found everywhere are the pig and the dog. In every village only a few men own dogs; they seem to be kept mainly as pets, but some have achieved a wide reputation as good hunting dogs. While the Jalé make no attempt to control their dogs' mating habits, they exercise great care in the breeding of pigs. The pig assumes an extremely important place in Jalé culture. Apart from constituting a nutritional resource and a trade object, every pig is a potential vehicle for the validation or reaffirmation of social relationships. All major events in a person's life cycle, the setttlement of serious disputes, and the ratification of a peace agreement require the transfer of pigs.

Tabus restrict the use and consumption of almost any kind of vegetable and animal resource for men and women during particular periods of their life, but the most severe restrictions imposed on edible substances apply to pig's fat. "Men of knowledge" use pig's fat in virtually every supplicative, protective, and curative rite, and initiated males upon reaching full maturity need it for greasing their bodies. This cosmetic use of the fat is a prerogative of men, who claim that women neither know of its application in rituals nor recognize it as the source of the oily appearance of their skin.

While the pig and staple crops are ubiquitous, other valued goods are unevenly distributed in the Jalémó. Some villages or whole regions depend on trade to supplement rare resources and to acquire products that are locally unavailable. Pasikni and the nearby villages of Klengleng and Angkenteng, for example, have access to a salt brine on the bank of the Jaxólé River. Since it is the only known brine in the Jalémó, these three villages exploit their virtual monopoly of production in trading with people who supply them with adze blades, stone scrapers, ratan cuirasses (out of eastern Jalémó), palm bows (from northern Jalémó), and other products for which no resources exist in the upper Jaxólé Valley. Moreover, as most nut-pandanus trees abound only at higher altitudes, many bunches reach the Jaxólé villages in exchange for salt bundles.[4]

A different kind of exchange exists between the Jaxólé Valley and the Seng Valley, located south of the Central Range. Since the men in Pasikni and surrounding villages have to cut the material for their ratan dress in the lower parts of the Seng

Valley and since one expedition there usually requires a journey lasting almost two weeks, they are entirely dependent on the hospitality provided by the local people. The Jaxólé Valley people reciprocate lodging, food, and help with the preparation of the ratan by providing similar accommodation and meals when their hosts come for salt and by helping them with the processing.

Unlike trade in other parts of New Guinea, trade in Jalémó is not a commercial enterprise pursued to gain wealth. While most intra-regional trade follows lines of kinship, trading partnerships connecting two persons of different, especially distant, regions are usually based on friendship ties created by a mutual interest in exchanging goods. Children of the original partners often perpetuate their parents' trade relationships; the use of kinship terms between family members of trading partners indicates the strength of these arrangements.

Cooperation also characterizes Jalé communal work patterns. Just as all members of a men's house and many of their relatives living in neighboring wards collaborate at least once in a genera-

7   People from all valleys of the Jalémó get their salt at a few wells on the bank of the Jaxólé River

tion in the task of rebuilding a men's house, ward neighbors help each other with the construction of family huts. But while all residents participate in getting the material for their men's house, only the agnatic kinsmen of the owner of a family hut and other locally residing consanguineal and affinal kinsmen regularly assist him in cutting lumber and thatch and carrying the material to the village. Women often help transport building supplies for their family huts, but their main job is to prepare an opulent picnic for the workers on building day.

Neighbors and relatives living in other wards also extend reciprocal services at funerals. Nobody receives any reward for helping with the preparation of a pyre for cremating a corpse, although the event requires a particular kind of pig exchange. The surviving relative who is responsible for burning the body— a man's brother, a woman's husband, or a son of the deceased —must give a pig to the kinsman, usually an affine, who has carried the body to the pyre. The recipient of this "corpse" pig must return a "wood" pig. Disputes that I heard involving

8 On visits to relatives and friends in near and distant villages, men trade goods, seek wives, and recount old and new adventures of war

arguments over funeral pigs suggest that both prestations imply a notion of compensation for handling a corpse and for incinerating someone's relative.

Pig breeding necessitates intra-village cooperation, because nobody likes to keep a boar for long. Unlike hogs a boar cannot be let onto the foraging area lest its owner become liable for unwanted pregnancies and injuries inflicted upon other pigs. A boar must, therefore, be penned and fed inside the hut or led to root by a leash. Since an owner receives no payment for letting his boar impregnate other people's sows, only the claim to reciprocal services induces a man to keep one male piglet in a litter for breeding purposes. Consequently, a man brings up a boar only if he and his co-resident relatives happen to raise a reasonable number of pigs at the same time. On the village level the informality and unpredictability of this pattern creates a problem when an unsettled dispute between wards disturbs neighborly relationships.

The construction of bridges and fences involves more limited communal cooperation. A group of men who have a common interest in convenient access to their gardens on the far side of a river will put a bridge across, but anyone who does not participate may subsequently use the crossing. The same idea of public utility applies to the long stone walls and embankments which fence land under cultivation against the pigs' foraging areas. Horticultural work itself, however, is an individual enterprise. Although two brothers, especially if neither has a family, or a young man and his sister's husband may team up to prepare a plot, cooperation in clearing, planting, and harvesting goes little beyond coordinating the cultivation of an area where one or two lineages hold title to particular tracts of land.

Inheritance

A person acquires title to land through inheritance and primary cultivation. A third possibility of assuming ownership of gardens requires payment of a "Cordyline" pig. This name implies a symbolic replication of planting a hedge of Cordyline cuttings by which the owner of a tract of land both marks its

9 Neighbors and relatives help to build a men's house (facing page)

10 —and are treated to a sumptuous picnic from a large earth oven

boundary and prevents the soil from sliding. Most cases involve immigrants who convert cultivation privileges granted to them into ownership rights through such a transaction. Commonly the immigrant pays the pig many seasons after he has first worked on his host's land, and often the "planting of the Cordyline," as the Jalé say, occurs after the death of the original owner when the pig is transferred to his heirs.

Both male and female children inherit their father's gardens and trees, but the shares allotted to girls are considerably smaller than those given to sons. The trees and fields given to a girl represent a dowry payment, since such property is transferred to her in several portions immediately following her marriage. The arrangement applies only if her husband's place of residence allows him to prepare the land for her—which is the case in all intra-village marriages. While a man controls use and exploitation of his wife's land and trees, not he but their children ultimately gain ownership of these resources. If a man's wife dies before their children have grown up, he may continue to work on her land until his remarriage, when the gardens revert to his wife's brothers. They may later return part of the land to his sons provided their affinal exchange relationship with their deceased sister's husband continues. If the couple has a son old enough to make his own gardens, he will be the direct heir of his deceased mother's land regardless of his father's possible remarriage.

Unlike his sister, a son inherits land and trees from his father in a continuous process which starts when he begins to do independent garden work. By the time he marries, a young man already owns a substantial portion of his father's gardens and some of his trees. When a man dies, his sons divide the land and trees that their father had retained for his own use. If he dies without children, his closest agnatic kinsmen share his estate, but all gardens and trees belonging to his wife remain her property. If the children of the deceased are still small, his brother(s) will keep his estate in custody and transfer the property to them when they grow up. Similarly, if a man is survived by several sons only one of whom has reached adulthood, it will be this eldest brother who is responsible for the distribution of their father's estate among his siblings.

As a rule, upon a man's death his closest agnatic male relatives inherit his movable property, while a woman's personal belongings go to her sisters or daughters. Whether siblings or descendants become the main heirs depends on whether or not the deceased was married and on the age of his children, if any. Thus his brother(s) will take a man's weapons, tools, and ornaments if he has no son old enough to use these objects. If a man leaves neither a brother nor a son, his father's brother's son usually inherits these things. His family hut remains in the possession of his widow but as long as she continues to live there, but her son assumes ownership of the hut if it becomes the residence of his own wife. If a widow remarries, the first of her husband's agnatic heirs to need a domicile or the timber takes her hut, as he would the adjunct men's house and garden shed of the deceased.

The clear definition of ownership domains, the paucity of movable property, abundant land resources, and simple patterns of inheritance are probably responsible for the infrequent occurrence of disputes over property among relatives.

Life Cycle

An infant spends his first year in uninterrupted bodily contact with his mother, hanging in a carrying bag on her back throughout the day and cuddled in her arms when she sleeps. During their second and part of their third years, children are still carried in the string bag on most trips to the gardens, but gradually they are trained to ride on the nape of the mother's neck or on the father's shoulder. Toward the end of the fourth year, a child begins to walk about alone. At seven or eight years of age boys begin to spend less time with their mothers. While a girl continues her close association with her mother or elder sisters and other female members of the household, a boy now starts to play with his peers and to practice arrow-shooting with a small

hardwood bow and short reed stalks. He may occasionally accompany his father or elder brother to the gardens and help with
minor chores.

Most boys enter the men's house when they are between
eleven and thirteen years old. An elaborate initiation ceremony
dramatizes their separation from the matrifocal household and
their incorporation into the community of men.[5] For the next
two or three years, they lead a carefree, playful life, spending
much of their time with peers on bird-hunting outings and in
competitive games that encourage agility and marksmanship.
Gradually they begin to participate fully in economic activities:
first, by helping their father and brothers with garden work and
by guarding their pigs; later, by cultivating plots for themselves.

Although a young boy's elders generally encourage rather
than demand his participation in the daily work routine, they
insist that he diligently perform all assigned tasks. Punishment
for negligence and disobedience is quick and painful. A father or
elder brother may severely beat or even burn a young boy for
repeatedly failing to bring firewood, for losing sight of a young
untrained pig, or for indulging in horseplay with potentially
harmful grass spears. They may crop his ear if he should steal
food from his people or violate a dietary tabu.

By the age of fifteen or sixteen a boy has acquired all necessary
skills for independent work in the economic field. Two or three
years later, after his elders have pronounced him ready to anoint
his body with pig's fat, a boy begins to wear the long penis
gourd. These paraphernalia mark his adult status, which means
being both sexually mature and fit for marriage.

Girls do not undergo an initiation ceremony, but at their first
menstrual period they must observe several tabus and cooperate
in the performance of certain ritual acts. Most girls have their
menarche between seventeen and nineteen, a relatively late age
which appears to be common in New Guinea Highlands populations (Malcolm 1966). A girl of this age is capable of pursuing
efficiently all horticultural and housekeeping tasks required of
adult, married women. Besides child-rearing, the typical jobs

of a mother include the preparation of meals for her family, tending the pigs of her husband and sons, and making nets for them. She must also plant, weed, and harvest the plots prepared for her by her husband or son and may have to help her husband plant and weed his own fields.

No girls should have sexual intercourse before menarche, which is believed to open her vagina to make penetration possible. Boys are effectively discouraged from having intercourse until they have reached maturity by the threat that an earlier copulation would damage their vitality and make them decrepit. As a consequence few Jalé have experienced sexual intercourse before marriage, since most girls are married before they have had their menarche, and because copulation with a married woman entails the risk of being punished for adultery by the offended husband.

Severe restrictions on sexual intercourse continue throughout a person's married life. A man sleeps in the men's house at least every other night lest he be ridiculed and accused of sexual greed.

12   Boys learn to use their bows in competitive games

As soon as a woman advises her husband of her pregnancy, he ceases to sleep in his family hut altogether. After birth sexual intercourse should not take place for about four years, until the child is weaned.

While initiation perpetuates the agnatic descent group as a small residential community of males, a marriage establishes alignments between two lineages, who exchange specially named pigs to validate the union.[6] The husband furnishes 'marriage' pigs to his wife's agnates, who provide his wife with 'dowry' pigs.[7] Exchanges of pigs and other gifts occur throughout the marriage, though in later years it is the husband's sons who perpetuate this relationship with their mother's kinsmen.

A boy's initiation into the sacred men's house and a girl's marriage represent complementary acts of incorporation. The entry of the boy into the house of his agnatic kinsmen ritually emphasizes his membership in his father's moiety. The marriage of a girl to a member of her mother's moiety deprives her own moiety of her procreative faculty. Consequently the transfer of

13   —and imitate their elders' dancing in cheerful play

pigs that certifies an initiation and the one that validates a
marriage proceed in opposite directions (see Figure 3).

At one time during his youth or early adulthood, a man participates in a secondary initiation, which confers a new ritual
status upon him. Men who have passed the rite are eligible for
instruction in the "sacred lore," which includes ritually effective,
esoteric formulae. These expressions are so powerful that young
boys who hear them inadvertently are believed to lose their
vitality and become decrepit. Those initiated are respected as
"big men," men with "body" or "substance," or "sacred men,"
but in this context the literal translations are better glossed as
"men of knowledge." As adult males these gnostics perform all
rituals connected with warfare, life crises, and economic pursuits,
which include, for example, a sacramental meal held inside the
men's house at which sweet potatoes are offered to the founding
ancestors when the first crops from a new garden have been
harvested. Through the secondary initiation the "men of knowledge" control the dissemination of their esoteric knowledge and

14   Girls learn to make nets (and all other domestic skills) at an
early age

sustain the male-female dichotomization that pervades Jalé culture.[8]

Both the primary and secondary initiation are rituals that transform the identity of a Jalé male through the mediation of those men whose status the neophyte acquires by his participation in the ceremony (see Figure 4). Seen as a prolonged process of social maturation, the two initiation ceremonies space a Jalé man's acquisition of prestige and power. In a society where an egalitarian access to resources prevents the accumulation of wealth, age and the control of knowledge represent an alternative basis for the exercise of authority.

Social Structure and Political Organization

The Jalé divide their population into named exogamous moieties, each of which comprises a number of named patrilineal sibs, the members of which may live dispersed over several regions of the Jalémó. Mythological data and folk history suggest that the sibs were originally localized clans which became scattered over wider areas as a result of emigration after a defeat in war, an epidemic, or a famine. Furthermore, the Jalé in acknowledging a common affiliation with members of their sib always refer to

3 Initial complementary pig prestations between moieties at marriage and initiation

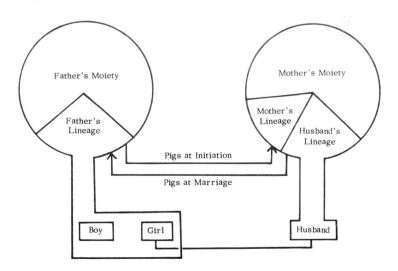

15 Inside a men's house

16 Boy emerging from his men's house the morning after his
        initiation (facing page)

a place of origin rather than to an ancestor. The three main causes of dislocation have effected residential fissions in recent times. The presence of isolated immigrant lineages in a village can often be traced to a war which forced a man to leave his home and establish an exile residence with distant relatives or trading partners. Sometimes a whole new village develops from the simultaneous occupation of an uninhabited locality by several lineages belonging to different sibs.[9]

I use the term sib-fragment to denote a cluster of lineages belonging to the same sib that have residential contiguity in a ward or a village. In the absence of traceable genealogical connections, people belonging to the same sib-fragment acknowledge a closer relationship among their constituent lineages than with other lineages of their sib settled in different villages. The Jalé describe a lineage of their own sib to which they can trace no genealogical link as "a stem by itself." The distribution of the various sibs in the valleys of the Jalémó is very uneven. Some sibs which trace their place of original settlement to localities near Pasikni and are indeed numerously represented in this village have no members, or only very few, in many of the more distantly located villages in the Sévé and Ovaxak Valleys. Several sibs, the original homes of which are in other regions, are not at all represented in Pasikni.

4 Transformations of social identity of Jalé males

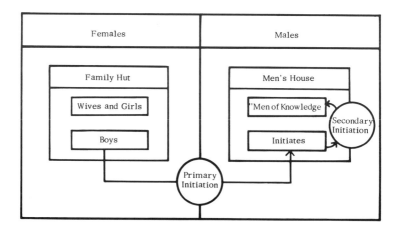

The Jalé term for sib is "head." How many "heads" belong to either moiety is not known. The people say that many more "heads" than those they can list exist in distant regions. In Pasikni about two dozen sib names are familiar, and eight of them refer to sib-fragments which have become autochthonous in the village.[10]

Sib-fragments and lineages are autochthonous if their members believe that their ancestors have founded the men's house of their ward of residence. Descendants of immigrants who settled at an established ward and acquired title to land on village territory become indigenous residents when genealogical links between these immigrants and their living descendants are no longer traceable.

The categorization of a person's relatives outside his natal family derives from an Omaha-type system of classification with patrilineal descent, moiety exogamy, and proscribed marriage with a member of his mother's patrilineage, and produces five distinct reference sets of relatives.[11] One set comprises Ego's own lineal relatives, his agnates. Another set contains Ego's mother's agnates. The children of his female agnates form a third set, but they are terminologically not segregated from his own and his brother's children. Two more reference sets comprise his affines who, except in very rare cases of double affinity between two lineages, include either his wife's agnates or his sister's husband with his agnates (see Figure 5).

What I call a reference set are relatives who share certain rights, responsibilities, and expectations in relation to Ego. Pig exchanges formalize most of these relationships. A man shares with his male agnates a common concern in the initiation of their sons and brothers into the men's house and, later, in their marriages. Anyone in this set may negotiate for a woman and provide part of the required marriage considerations on behalf of a junior agnate. Although an individual lineage member holds unrestricted rights to the produce of his labor and can transfer tenancy privileges to affines and immigrants, agnates regard arable land as their common property and cooperate in the main economic tasks of clearing new garden land and building houses.

Seniority gives a man limited authority or, at least, more influence in deliberations concerning the coordination of his set's economic activities. Politically, a set of agnates forms a power group that always supports and defends a member in a conflict with other groups.[12] If one is killed, his kinsmen seek to revenge his death. The descent group as a whole is also liable for any offense perpetrated by one of its members upon a person from another ward or village. If a man steals a pig, injures or kills someone, he places his kinsmen in unmitigated jeopardy of retaliation. Only in disputes within the men's house community of co-resident lineages do the Jalé appear to make a pragmatic distinction between individual responsibility and corporate liability.

A man's relationship with his maternal kinsmen in a way perpetuates the pattern of gift exchanges that his father established by his marriage and in which he begins to participate quite early in his life. When a child is about five or six years old, he formally enters the exchange network between his own and his mother's agnates. The father or an elder brother gives the child a small pig on a leash with the instruction to present it to his mother's brother or mother's sister. The Jalé believe that a mother's brother who does not receive this special pig will damage the vitality of his "child" by a curse or some other ritual trick. Some time later, the recipient of this gift returns a pig to the child.

5 Reference sets (core ranges)

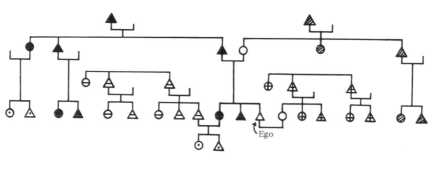

		Agnates			Affines, linked by wife
		Maternal kinsmen			Affines, linked by sister
		"Children"			

Often a boy receives this animal at his initiation. Later in his life a man exchanges pigs, garden produce, and traded goods with his mother's agnates on a reciprocal basis. Upon his mother's death he provides them with a mortuary pig, called "net" pig, and receives a "lung" pig in return.

The reciprocity in formal gift exchanges contrasts with the asymmetrical nature of other relationships in the mother's brother–sister's child dyad. A strictly observed tabu on using their personal names most conspicuously reflects a circumspect and deferential attitude toward one's maternal kinsmen. In the wider kinship realm strong restrictions supported by automatic sanctions of sickness prohibit any participation in butchering and eating the body of a slain enemy who belonged to one's mother's sib, father's mother's sib, or mother's mother's sib. Likewise, a person must not eat from the "head" pig that rewarded the slaying of his own or his parents' maternal sib members.

Generally, a man's relationship with his sister's children reverses his relationship with his mother's agnates. Obligations and rights he has toward the latter convert into rights and obligations toward the former. For example, a man who is to provide a mortuary pig for his mother's agnates will receive a pig of the same category from a sister's son upon her death. Just as his maternal kinsmen have provided a pig at his initiation so will he furnish a pig at the initiation of his sister's son. Throughout his life a man can expect hospitality and protection from his mother's agnates and sister's children if a war forces him to leave his home or if he seeks temporary refuge when a reprehensible action has brought him into conflict with members of his own local group.

With his own marriage, and that of his sister, a man adds new dimensions to the net of his social relationships defined by birth. Again, obligatory pig exchanges are the major aspect of these affinal links. As with mother's brother–sister's child relationships, the degree of mutual help and frequency of interaction depend on residential distance, but the name avoidance in this case is bilateral. Because no Jalé wants to waste the opportunity to increase the scope of his exchange operations by his marriage, it happens only in very rare cases that a man marries the "sister" of his own "sister's" husband or that two brothers or agnatic cousins share the same set of uxori-lateral kinsmen.

Kinship and residence determine virtually all enduring social relationships of the Jalé people. Their society lacks governmental institutions and political offices. Only the biological factors of sex and relative age define ascribed status and, by their ritual implications, determine differential access to certain resources. These conditions leave few opportunities for achieving positions of control and influence beyond the limited realms of family, descent group, and immediate residential community.

For an understanding of Jalé conflict management, the distinction between principles of descent and joint residence is critical.[13] A Jalé descent group consists of co-resident members of an agnatic lineage. As these lineages rarely comprise more than a very few adult men, their political power is minimal compared with that of their whole men's house group. A men's house group, however, comprises several lineages that originated in different localities. Consequently, residence rather than descent not only determines allegiance but also constitutes the basis of concerted political action. Immigration, however, is not the only process that produces a residential accretion of different lineages. Intra-village warfare, unresolved conflict between agnates, and, rarely, a man's decision to build his family hut in his wife's natal ward may induce a single man or a whole lineage to leave the ancestral men's house and take up residence at a neighboring ward.

It appears then that the male members of an agnatic lineage in Jalé society represent a small set of kinsmen who live together and, bound by customary obligations, cooperate in the two critical processes that maintain the traditional organization of the society, marriage arrangements and initiation. The descent group functions mainly as an anchorage for social identification but also supplies the membership and resources that political leadership extending beyond its limited genealogical realm requires. Given the fragmented lineage structure of men's house groups, however, that leadership is extremely limited in scope and power.

Leadership

The Jalé use the term "big man" to refer to those individuals whose opinion they respect more than the view of other men. This term, however, also denotes any adult male, especially every "man of knowledge," so that the behavioral context alone defines its connotation, a man with influence. The Jalé abstract from this context conspicuous qualities that distinguish a particular man from his peers. These distinctive attributes conform entirely to the general Highlands pattern of "big body," "big voice," and "big hand."[14]

My own observations substantiated this trifocal categorization and detected physical fitness, persuasive eloquence and assertiveness, and a superior ability to provide pigs to be the prominent features of Jalé "big men." The expression "big hand" by no means connotes generosity, because virtually every pig prestation must be reciprocated in kind. The real significance of "big hand" is a man's readiness to part with a pig whenever he sees a chance to increase his credit balance. Moreover, he must be prepared to supply pigs on behalf of others who happen to be unable to fulfill a demand.

In Jalé society, then, a man gains renown as "big man" in this restricted sense through his competence in creating debt relationships with consanguineal relatives and non-kin members of his men's house group. The main occasions which call for his intervention are their marriages and initiations and times when they need to satisfy claims for indemnity payments.

Most wards in a Jalé village acknowledge one or two men's house residents as "big men." Their ability to furnish pigs depends to a decisive degree on their position within their descent group. Since by his marriage a man creates a pig-exchange relationship with his wife's kinsmen, the eldest of a group of "brothers," who regularly marries first, can exploit his seniority by helping a junior agnate when he incurs the obligation to pay a pig. For example, a man often provides his younger brother's initial marriage pig, although a boy may sometimes give up his pig for his elder brother as well. Still, the advantage of raising pigs in his own family hut considerably increases a married man's chances of supplying pigs for his juniors. The larger his own kin group or, in a wider realm, the more sib brothers who live in his men's house, the more frequently will a man have an opportunity of showing a "big hand."

While every Jalé always favors his own agnates over non-kin members of his men's house, a customary obligation of mutual help nevertheless applies to all of his co-residents. Therefore, a man can hold and gradually increase his lead over his junior kinsmen and their age mates as a creditor and maintain his position until a member of the succeeding generation establishes himself as a broker, so to speak, for his younger co-residents. Since Jalé economic transactions lack any consideration of usury, a "big man" never acquires wealth through his brokerage. The benefits of the system accrue in the successful management of exchange balances.

A "big man's" ability to obtain pigs from his debtors assumes particular importance when one of his kinsmen initiates a war or when his men's house group decides to revenge an attack upon a ward resident. Since any support rendered by an allied men's house or by individuals from other wards or villages requires gifts of pork, a "big man's" superior solvency usually enables him to supply more pigs than others in his ward. He may provide the pigs either directly to his relatives and friends from other groups or indirectly by giving pigs to his kinsmen for distribution among their affines and friends. These contributions have long-range political consequences, because allies who are dissatisfied with the gifts they receive may withhold their support or even change sides in future hostilities between the parties originally involved in the conflict.

A conspicuous measure of assertiveness is a prerequisite for successful operations in the multiple exchange circles that customary obligations establish for every man. Unless a man masters the idiomatic rhetoric concerning pig transactions and knows the tally of past exchanges for his whole lineage, he cannot achieve recognition as a "big man." Certainly, a man's brokerage activities reinforce any talent for persuasive declamations, because his position as a creditor induces him to speak up more often than his junior kinsmen in matters concerning the whole men's house group.

Ability to argue is indispensable in exerting influence on economic policy and plans for political action in conflict situations; seniority and the size of a "big man's" descent group alone do not suffice in this respect. For example, in two Pasikni wards the acknowledged "big man" has an elder brother, but both these men are quiet and unobtrusive individuals who never engaged actively in any public dispute involving their wards that occurred during the time I lived in the village.

The relative size of his lineage nevertheless conditions the emergence of a "big man." In small wards where no lineage has a clear majority, no "big man" may emerge. For example, there is no "big man" in one small Pasikni ward where the four adult men belong to four different sibs, nor at another ward where seven men belonging to six different lineages of four different sibs share the men's house. Conversely, in the largest ward, where 40 percent of all adult male villagers live, two men belonging to the most numerous sib fragments are recognized as "big men."

In Jalé wards, then, a "big man" is typically an elder, non-senile member of an autochthonous agnatic descent group with a larger membership than co-resident lineages, who possesses managerial finesse and unusual competence in verbal tactics. This combination of genealogical position and personal qualities allows him to maneuver his exchange relationships to the advantage of his kinsmen and non-kin members of his men's house group by providing pigs for them in times of need.

In a way, therefore, the Jalé "big man" is a benefactor rather than a headman who has power to direct the activities of his kinsmen. Furthermore, as kinship and residential links with other men only partially determine his readiness to provide pigs for them, so the recipients base their loyalties to him on tenuous considerations of expediency. Certainly, his status gives a "big man" no adjudicative authority over the people of his ward. As my conflict cases will show, he is neither obliged nor ever asked to settle disputes or mediate in conflicts. During 'shouting matches' and fights within the village his conduct is not different from that of other elders who occasionally interfere in a public dispute or violent brawl by urging restraint. When his own kinsmen are among the contestants, however, his exhortations may meet with a more receptive response.[15]

In Jalémó, a "big man" performs his most conspicuous political role as spokesman for his lineage or sib-fragment in connection with warfare. There are three principal occasions when a "big man" exercises this role: First, in a public evening address to the village he announces his kinsmen's decision to cease hostilities after they have scored a revenge killing or if they wish to avoid an escalation of a battle into a prolonged war. Second, in a laudatory statement he welcomes contingents of allied men's houses who come to his ward to perform a dance, after which they receive pork and pigs. Third, at a peace ceremony he makes a formal declaration denouncing the regrettable effects of warfare and affirming his kinsmen's desire to end the hostilities "forever." On the whole, then, a "big man's" political status derives from the prestige he gains in his role as a pig broker, which gives him limited authority as a spokesman for his kinsmen and his ward in inter-ward and inter-village conflicts.

III Methods and Ideology of Conflict Management

In this chapter I describe the various methods by which the Jalé seek to remedy a wrong and explain their notion of liability as the key concept in their jural ideology. Their language appears to lack concepts that could be translated as mediation or negotiation. Certainly, both methods are used, but the people themselves conceptualize their patterns of conflict management according to five distinct modes of antagonistic interaction: altercation, scuffle, sorcery, avoidance, and warfare.

Altercation or the 'Shouting Match'

The expression 'shouting match' (altercation) denotes a confrontation which is defined by the following features: (a) both parties involved in the conflict actively participate in the event, (b) by making a complaint and accusation or a rebuttal and counter-accusation, (c) in loud and rapid speech that always contains reprimands and/or threats and often includes (d) denigrating insults, shaming affronts, and curses.

The presence of the first feature helps to differentiate an altercation from a simple reprimand, where one party scolds another who either does not respond at all or does so only in a supplicantly defensive manner. But this distinction does not always suffice to identify an event as an altercation. Therefore, several observers may not use the same expression in describing a particular situation. For example, people who watch a man scold his son at a picnic for his failure to collect firewood may report the incident as an altercation, whereas both father and son may talk about a reprimand. Similarly, the two opponents may view their encounter differently. The boy may complain about the altercation with his father; and the latter may speak of having "scolded" his son. In this instance the father may even

want to emphasize his intention to instruct his son in filial duties
and may, therefore, describe his speech as "teaching." Generally,
the relative salience of the other features—especially insults
and curses—determines whether an observer or a participant
describes the event as either altercation or reprimand. Thus,
while reprimand is a generic trait of any altercation, not every
reprimand constitutes an altercation.[1]

An altercation may occur at any time and in any place
between any two individuals or groups. A dispute between a
husband and his wife inside their family hut may concern
economic or sexual matters. Co-wives, particularly in the early
period of their marriage, frequently argue over alleged or factual
removal of sweet potatoes from each other's garden plots and, if
they live together, about their problems in dividing domestic
tasks. The Jalé actually describe the women's state of relative
amity by qualifying the frequency and intensity of altercations
between them. Thus, there are pairs of co-wives who never
squabble, others who occasionally quarrel, and those who brawl
often.

Whenever an altercation develops between two or more
persons belonging to different wards, the principal parties on
either side regularly receive support from their ward members.
Women participate very rarely in an inter-ward dispute even
though the altercation may follow the complaint of a woman to
her husband about a man's attempt to seduce her. Still another
kind of altercation may involve groups from different villages
vehemently arguing over compensation for an abduction.

Most altercations between wards that I observed took place in
the early evening. They began just before or shortly after sunset
and continued until dark. The timing relates both to daily work
routine and to strategy. An incident that has occurred during
the day may not become known to the person who later will
launch the complaint until he returns from his garden. Even if
the aggrieved person learns about the incident before getting
back to the village, he may need to wait until his opponent has
come home if, indeed, he has decided to rebuke him publicly
rather than resort to immediate, violent retaliation.

This delay provides the time necessary or desirable for

discussing the affair in the men's house. In such a session the aggrieved person's co-residents make a joint effort not only to piece together available information about the incident but also to recall troubles that the offender, his kinsmen, or members of his house group have caused for any of them in the past. Knowledge of previous cases greatly helps a speaker in the altercation to formulate his complaint and to parry counter-accusations. If the original complainant is an older boy who has not yet reached adult status, an older co-resident—usually an elder agnate—opens the altercation. Whenever the grievance concerns the whole men's house group, a "big man" frequently presents the initial statement.

A typical inter-ward altercation goes through certain patterned phases. The initial speaker leaves his men's house and positions himself near the entrance, facing the ward that he will assail. Several co-residents stand around him from the beginning, others step out of the house when the altercation is under way. As soon as he has finished his opening statement, anyone may

17 Scene of an evening 'shouting match' between two wards in the village of Pasikni

start shouting. They often have reiterated their complaint several times and have already referred to past incidents before the accused party begins to answer the charge.

Whether or not the accused person responds himself seems to depend on how much he feels inculpated. If, for example, the complaint concerns an attempted seduction and witnesses to the culprit's unsuccessful advances make an outright repudiation impossible, one of his elder kinsmen or co-residents will usually launch the counteroffensive. On some occasions I have heard the other side enter the 'shouting match' with a bawling in unison of "ha-ha-ha" or "ho-ho-ho." This special clamor temporarily silences the opponents, who realize that they would "waste their voices" if they continued the dispute. Subsequently, as the shouting resumes, either party may resort to this deafening howl whenever the noise level drowns all articulate speech. After a while some of the howlers manage to end the chaos by encouraging one another to listen to the other side: "Let us hear! Let us hear!" My impression is that exhaustion and tedium terminate an altercation. The participants become tired of repetitive speech and one by one drift back to the fireplaces of their men's houses.

A 'shouting match' never fails to create or enhance hostility toward one's opponents. My observations suggest that if the parties confront each other in daylight and in one place their encounter often leads to a scuffle. The evening altercation reduces the chances of combat within the village, especially by rendering arrow shots intractable. Significantly, the men who shout at a hardly visible opponent make typical threatening gestures used in the context of a scuffle, such as thrusting one's bow and arrow bundle toward the opponent and impetuously flinging out one's arm with extended index finger pointing at the adversary.

An altercation is always a public affair. Everything said provides information available to all people in the village. Furthermore, because it is an outdoor event, people from other wards have access to the scene and often render support to relatives among the disputing groups.

Songs represent another way for a men's house group to make

a complaint against another ward. While these songs technically are not an altercation but a form of reprimand, their "message" differs from accusations during an altercation mainly in style and in the use of circumlocutory references instead of outspoken and insulting attacks. The songs communicate a grievance in a way that obviates the necessity of a face-to-face confrontation. Since the texts and tunes conform to traditional stanzas and compositions, to sing them together with other well-known songs subdues their potentially offensive content even more, especially because some verses change only the names of localities, which then alone give the clues to their interpretation. Almost all the songs of this kind I recorded express a group's dissatisfaction that another men's house had either failed to provide adequate reward in pigs for its support in warfare or arrogated success on the battlefield.

The men sing these songs always in the evening while sitting around the fire of their men's house, and often a dispute about the delayed or insufficient reward or some altercation about a different matter precedes the occasion. Apparently, the Jalé accord the singers a kind of ceremonial indulgence. Their opponents would probably never attempt to disturb the singing group but, as several cases brought out, they always rebuke them in a later altercation or by reciprocating the complaint in songs on a subsequent evening.

The Scuffle or Minor Fight

Whenever participants in a face-to-face altercation resort to physical force, the encounter turns into a scuffle. As reprimands are an integral part of a 'shouting match,' so do altercations usually precede, accompany, and follow a scuffle. Typical features, in addition to (a) altercation are that (b) two parties actively engage in the encounter who (c) may push, beat, kick, or bite each other, wield and throw billets, stones, or burning logs, and in extreme situations may injure an opponent with stone adzes, digging sticks, or bow and arrow bundles. However, as in altercations, participants and observers may differ in their definition of a scuffle. If the victim of an attack, for example a wife or a child, does not fight back, they may describe the event simply as a "beating."

Like an altercation, a scuffle may occur at any time and in any place except the sacred men's house, whose ritual status does not suffer such outrage. Violent fights among boys, a married couple trading blows, a girl forcefully resisting an impetuous suitor's efforts to drag her toward his ward in an attempt to elope with her, women beating each other with digging sticks, two groups of men engaging in a mêlée—these are typical scenes that the Jalé describe as scuffle. Occasionally, someone may shoot an arrow toward his opponent but avoid hitting him. The Jalé use such "missing" arrows, as they are called, deliberately to defer a violent escalation of the confrontation when the parties belong to the same men's house or live in the same village. But even if a man does take aim, the encounter remains a scuffle as long as the other party does not immediately retaliate the attack by shooting back. A single aimed retaliatory shot changes a scuffle into "war."

Several features, apart from the use of physical force, distinguish scuffles from altercations. A men's house group never contemplates a scuffle when they discuss a grievance that requires concerted action. Only in rare cases will a man or a team of two or three plan an assault upon someone as a spontaneous act of revenge. Usually a scuffle either arises from an incidental encounter between two people who already maintain an inimical relationship or develops when hostility explodes into action through an aggravating altercation. However, while a "big man" usually exercises some control over an altercation, especially when whole men's house groups oppose each other, he rarely participates in a scuffle. If elders have a chance to interfere at all in such fighting, they attempt to halt it rather than to direct its course.

Because any injury sustained in a scuffle can lead to revenge— in the form of a pig seizure or a retaliatory assault—the fear of an eventual war exerts far greater pressure to terminate a scuffle than to end an altercation. For example, a 'shouting match' between wards may follow its course without anyone attempting to stop it; but during a scuffle within the ward or between men's house groups, observers intervene by pleading for an immediate cessation of the fight or even by separating the combatants. Their exhortations always emphasize the need of living together peacefully and in harmony. When members of the same men's house get into a fight, their co-residents remind them of their common residence. If a confrontation between men from different wards leads to a scuffle, people from both sides urge restraint. Elders inevitably lament about past wars that occurred within their village and forced whole lineages into exile; and they warn that their common enemies in other villages will exploit their enmity and launch an attack.

An elder, even if he is a "big man," can only manage to break up the scuffle. His influence in such a situation does not give him any authority to arbitrate or even mediate other conflicts. The exigency of a particular case prompts his action, and his position in intersecting networks of kin and debt relationships between the opponents rather than formal status decides the success of his intervention in the dispute.

Like grand altercations, scuffles are public events. Every major fight quickly becomes known throughout the village or a garden area by relay message shouting. The cry "People are fighting!" brings men and boys from nearby places running to the scene. Often they do not learn the cause of the confrontation before arriving at the spot, although sometimes people, mostly women who have passed by, may shout bits of news to the men rushing along. Regardless of the nature of the initial conflict and a man's relationship to the parties involved in the fight, he seldom fails to come with his bow and arrows, because he recognizes that any scuffle can escalate into armed combat.

Sorcery as Magical Attack

One method of retaliation for injuries or killings that does not require open warfare is sorcery. A sorcery rite differs from altercation and scuffle in that one party directs a hostile action against the other, who remains unaware of its performance. Although the secrecy that surrounds the rite obstructed my investigation of the whole complex, the infrequent references to this practice in pertinent contexts convince me that the Jalé seldom resort to this form of ritual redress. I have recorded only six cases of death by sorcery which occurred during the past three decades in Pasikni, and my informants knew only one medicine man in the neighboring village of Savilivi who was a specialist in curing sorcery victims. In all instances the rite employed food scraps or cigarette butts, which explains the expression "mouth thing" as a cryptonym for any kind of sorcerous matter.

In every case my informants either were unable to identify the victim when they knew who had performed the rite, or did not know who had performed the rite when they knew who the victim was. I believe that this ambiguity in matching a person's death with a rumored rite or a particular rite with someone's death explains why the pragmatic Jalé seldom use this method of obtaining redress.

Avoidance

The lack of any aggressive action—except when suicide occurs —defines an avoidance relationship, a state of mutual shunning in which the opponents suspend all modes of normal communication.[2] This behavior demonstrates anger and communicates grievances, but reduces the danger of a violent confrontation that may permanently sever the residential association and kin relations of people who have a common interest in continuing their amicable cooperation. Avoidance most often involves the dyads of brother-brother and father-son, but it may occasionally also occur in mother-daughter and husband-wife relationships and, though rarely, even between members of a men's house who are not kinsmen. When two agnates shun each other, a lineage may divide with some members associating with either principal. Typically, the parties no longer speak to each other, cease to share food, and avoid sitting or sleeping close to each other. Often, the aggrieved person temporarily leaves the common domicile. Usually avoidance follows an altercation or a scuffle that failed to remedy the initial grievance, but an aggrieved party may also prevent a fight by spontaneously shunning the person who infringed upon his rights.[3]

An avoidance relationship may last from a few days to several years. Its termination depends entirely upon the readiness of both parties to restore amity. As long as the opponents continue to live in the same ward, their agnates and other members of their men's house try to mediate through friendly exhortations. If, however, one party moves away, either to a neighboring ward, to another village, or to his garden hut, the chances of an early reconciliation diminish. After some time—which my limited case data cannot specify—good words no longer suffice to bring the opponents together again, and one must present a pig to the other, who later returns the gift. I thought that the aggrieved person would expect the pig from the offender but my informants denied that they adhere to any rule for this exchange. They explained that "what one feels in one's heart" and "whether one has a pig to give away" determine a decision to end the avoidance.

Suicide is the most extreme manifestation of avoidance. The Jalé distinguish three kinds of suicide: suicide in anger, suicide from fear, and unintended death caused by one's own action. The last category refers to what we would call an accident, like falling from a cliff. Suicide from fear may occur when a person expects violent punishment, as would a woman whose husband has discovered her adultery. Only suicide in anger dramatizes avoidance.

Four of twelve recorded cases happened in Pasikni over a period of twenty-five years, the last one during my stay in the village. All involved old people who felt neglected by their children. One man and two women set fire to their huts during the night, and the other man drowned himself in the Jaxólé River.[4] The Jalé believe that such suicides mean to hurt the guilty, who afterward suffer feelings of regret and self-reproach. One finds this conception of post-mortem revenge in many societies and, as among the Jalé, it is often associated with a jurally recognized claim for indemnification against the responsible party by the victim's other kinsmen—consanguineal and affinal, respectively. However, fear of the deceased's ghost, frequently found elsewhere, appears to be rather tenuous in Jalémó.[5]

Warfare

By Jalé definition war means any overt hostility that entails the use of bow and arrow in a combat situation. The Jalé expression "making war" denotes only the actual fighting and different expressions define distinct phases in a conflict involving armed confrontations, but I extend the meaning of the term "war" to include also the state of hostility existing between the belligerents until the termination of the conflict. Warfare, a catastrophic phase in processes of Jalé conflict management, indicates the absence, inadequacy, or breakdown of less violent procedures to resolve disputes.

The histories of Jalé wars fought over a period of two generations in the Jaxólé and Ovaxak Valleys show that among these people the cause of the initial attack is virtually always a bodily injury or the killing of a person in the course of retaliatory actions. Retaliation may follow an offense like adultery and theft or the breach of an obligation such as the failure to provide compensation in pigs under customary law.

Once somebody has been killed, the "men of knowledge" among his agnates or non-kin co-residents fashion a special arrow. The ritual attachment to this arrow of skin torn from the victim's body when it lay on the pyre expresses their intention to revenge the killing. To ensure revenge a small group of warriors then attempts to approach the hostile village in order to shoot the device toward or, if possible, even into the ward of the enemy. Members of the men's house group who scored the initial killing prepare a different kind of arrow and shoot their contrivance, which carries pig fat, into the bush to keep the ghost of the slain enemy away from their home.

Jalé warfare does not mean continuous day-to-day fighting. In prolonged wars between villages belonging to the same region actual combat takes place on a few consecutive days perhaps for as long as a week or two. Periods of daily skirmishes alternate with times when patrols of warriors escort groups of women to the gardens. Since all belligerents need to harvest food, the principal parties to the conflict often agree on a temporary cessation of the fighting in a shouted exchange at the close of a battle.

After several weeks of intermittent skirmishes, anxiety that the long neglect of garden work will lead to famine militates against continuing open warfare. An indefinite extension of a harvesting recess then constitutes a kind of armistice. This truce is a rather perilous affair, because now small bands of men from the men's house of a victim whose death has not been revenged on the battlefield make occasional clandestine expeditions across the demarcation line in search of a chance to ambush an enemy. On these forays the raiders capture pigs from the foraging grounds of the hostile village if they perceive no risk of immediate discovery. Since a revenge action of this kind often leads to a resumption of open warfare, vengeance expeditions increase in frequency and audacity when new gardens are ready for harvest. In an effort to defend against raids and to reduce the danger of revenge attacks, all wards of the belligerent villages evacuate their garden hamlets once they have met in battle.

Fighting on the battlefield follows a loosely coordinated pattern of individual engagements. The techniques of arrow warfare, terrain conditions, and the greater peril of getting hit if the warriors form attack units make dispersed fighting positions a tactical expediency but they also impede any ready coordination of movements. Fighting on open land, a warrior looks for vantage ground from where he can attack with a shoot-and-run technique. He advances as far as the topography affords him cover, quickly discharges one or more arrows, and then hurries back to escape the reach of enemy shots. I have seen warriors band together only after their side had already pushed the enemy back to defensive positions on the edge of their village. The belligerent men's house group formed a compact cluster and staged a series of dance-like movements that ended in a wild rush toward the beleaguered enemy. This move signaled their determination to attack the village.

In the course of a day's battle the fighting deteriorates several times into phases of relative tranquillity with both sides exchanging arrows only sporadically. Small groups of warriors then gather around fires to smoke and to discuss the fortunes of the battle. They enumerate wounds suffered and inflicted and describe in detail the circumstances and anatomical aspects of a hit, count the arrows lost to the enemy and those picked up, and trade news about alliance relationships with individuals or men's house groups from other villages. Some may even visit with friends or distant relatives among the spectators, who have come from all over the region to watch the battle from safe uphill places. Before going back into action the warriors adjust their cuirasses and the protective nets wrapped around their necks.

If one side has succeeded in driving the enemy into his village or in surprising him before he builds up a defense line around the settlement, the battle becomes a sniping war fought around

18   A man killed from ambush

the huts and in the surrounding gardens. Women and children
always leave their homes if an invasion is imminent and, taking
the family's pigs along, seek refuge with friends and relatives in
other villages. In a defensive action of last resort the men retreat
into a sacred men's house which a tabu protects from being
burned down. When that happens, the victorious warriors often
begin to plunder and burn family huts. My case explorations
discovered that the scope and randomness of destruction
depends on how extensively the various wards of the defeated
village have become directly involved in the war by their
participation in past vengeance actions and on the intensity of
rancor and rage that sustained the battle. The defeated wards
commonly emigrate to allied or friendly villages during the
night after the raid. Their escape results in a permanent cessation
of battle warfare, but hostilities linger on until a peace ceremony
has reconciled the principal parties.

Cannibalism is an integral part of a particular kind of war.
The Jalé distinguish between a *wim* war and a *soli* war. Only

19   —relatives carry his body to its cremation

soli warfare ideally features anthropophagic revenge. While a *wim* war always ends within a few years and may last only for a day or two, a *soli* war usually endures for a much longer time and may extend over the period of a generation. Other differences are even less precise but have, nevertheless, some empirical validity. *Wim* warfare occurs between two or more wards of the same village, between two segments of the same ward living temporarily at different localities such as garden hamlets, or between two or more villages in the same district or adjacent districts. *Soli* wars, on the other hand, are usually waged between two villages separated by a wide river or by a mountain ridge, a geographic condition that puts them in different districts or regions.

Informants repeatedly stated the maxim that "people whose face is known should not be eaten." In practice immunity from anthropophagic vengeance derives from the nature and relative frequency of affinal links between two villages. Since in most inter-village marriages the wife comes from a settlement in the same or an adjacent district, geographic distance determines the precarious *soli* boundaries in this sense. Informants confided to me a few cases of secret cannibalism,[6] but the only intra-regional war with open anthropophagic vengeance occurred when the fathers of the oldest people were young men. In all other wars within a region cannibalism was restricted to sporadic revenge actions during a truce and involved special circumstances that greatly reduced the probability of retaliation because of the victim's social and political position in his community. Generally, this means that the victim had no autochthonous agnatic kinsmen at his place of residence.

However, since warfare cuts off all direct communication between inhabitants of the belligerent villages, including visits between affines, prolonged hostility may bring about a redefinition of "people whose face is known." This happened, for example, in a conflict between the Jaxólé and Sévé Valleys which had lasted for two decades at the time of my fieldwork. In this war people in the originally neutral Jaxólé village of Hompokéi accepted the leg belonging to a man who lived in another Jaxólé village from the Sévé people and subsequently suffered horrendous vengeance.[7]

The Jalé modify their strategy of military operations in *soli* wars. Warriors from several wards or even different villages often join in a revenge expedition into enemy country. A raiding party seeks to avoid battles on open ground, the typical pattern of *wim* combat, because the distance between the hostile villages favors the men who fight on their own familiar territory. Furthermore, *soli* raiders exact their vengeance indiscriminately upon anyone whose natal or current residence in an enemy village defines that person as a suitable victim. Consequently, the kinsmen of people killed in a war sometimes execute women from an enemy village who have married into an allied ward or village. As in *wim* wars, the boundaries separating hostile villages change with the extension of the conflict to villages not engaged in the original dispute between two lineages or men's house groups. However, while *wim* alliances form according to existing consanguineal and affinal links to the belligerent wards, *soli* warfare may induce men living in a previously uninvolved region to kill a person from one side and present the victim's body to the other for a reward in pigs and in return for relative trade advantages. In general, *soli* wars favor the formation of multi-village alliances; *wim* hostility strengthens traditional bonds between lineages and establishes new amity relationships between particular wards.[8]

In every war the Jalé recognize one particular person on each side as "man of the arrow's stem," whom they hold responsible for the outbreak of hostilities. These men are the parties to the original disputes that ultimately escalated into armed combat, although neither need have inflicted the injury that precipitated the initial skirmish. A "man of the arrow's stem" is liable for the compensation of all injuries and deaths suffered by his supporters on the battlefield as well as by anybody who is victimized in enemy revenge actions executed before a peace settlement.

Case histories suggest as a general rule that the principal parties can terminate a war by mutual agreement anytime after

the first battle as long as nobody has been seriously hit. Once a
warrior has been wounded or killed, especially if he does not
belong to the lineage of the arrow's stem, his kinsmen seek
revenge. They will advocate a continuation of the war unless
they receive immediate, satisfactory indemnification in pigs from
the "man of the arrow's stem" and his agnates. However, while
compensation may induce the victim's kinsmen to refrain from
further fighting, every killing ultimately demands blood revenge.
Consequently, they will attempt to exact vengeance either by
ambush or in the course of another war in which they align
themselves with groups who fight against their enemy. Since
these uncertainties make Jalé military alliances highly precarious,
the "men of the arrow's stem" always seek to avenge the death
of a supporter lest the ill-feeling of his kinsmen jeopardize their
own safety.

Nothing but the payment of a 'wergild' pig can prevent blood
revenge. This pig must be given by the killer or his kinsmen to
the agnates or maternal kinsmen of the victim. Apparently, the
Jalé conclude such arrangements very seldom because my informants knew of only six 'wergild' transactions since ca. 1930.
If these cases are representative, only parties who live or once
lived amicably in the same village succeed in the necessary
negotiations, and only men who cannot rally support for a
revenge attack and refrain from solitary vengeance accept a pig
as death indemnification.

A formal peace ceremony requires the ceremonial slaughter
of a "kidney" pig, so called because the carcass is cut into two
halves along the spine leaving one kidney attached to either
half, while normal butchering leaves the thoracic section undivided. The "men of the arrow's stem" receive one half each
and share it with their men's house group and allied lineages
in other wards. The pig need not be provided by either of the
principal parties. For example, a man from an allied ward who
has a personal interest in a settlement of the conflict may furnish
the animal. My records include one case where a man, whose sib
brother was killed in an inter-regional war, supplied a "kidney"
pig to terminate an intra-village conflict in which his ward was
not a principal party so that neighboring men's house groups

could resume concerted warfare against their common enemy.

If minor wars do not result in a killing—and especially if no people are forced into exile—mutual assertions of the house groups responsible for the conflict that they have "laid down the arrows forever" can end the hostilities. When a truce has begun, both sides may initiate and maintain contacts with each other through their wives whose kinsmen live in the opposite village. I have never witnessed a whole round of communication in this delicate trucial diplomacy that helps the Jalé to sound out the intentions of a hostile group, but I listened to several discussions in the men's houses dealing with the observations, messages, or allusions heard from visiting women.

Apparently, the group fearing a revenge killing usually makes a formal peace offer. Group members perform a dance within shouting distance of the enemy village and sing a series of traditional peace songs. These songs bemoan the loss of men and pigs and express regret over the cessation of trade between the two sides, and they often blame a third group or a particular man for the hostilities. For example, in a war between the Sévé and Jaxólé Valleys (Case *53), the Sévé men sang the following message toward their enemies in the Pasikni district:

> Weli,* it is your fault!
> Weli, it is your blame!
> That fire ate the Rivers' water,†
> That fire ate the Sévé River,
> That fire ate the Jaxólé River,
> Weli, it is your fault!
> Weli, it is your blame!

* A man from the village of Wanjok who started the war.
† Meaning: many people and pigs were lost in the war.

A standard stanza, which all peace messages include, said:

> Fighting is a bad thing, so is war.
> Like the trees we will stand together,
> Like the trees at Fungfung.*
> Like the trees at Jelen.*

* Place names on the ridge between the hostile valleys.

If the opponent "men of the arrow's stem" accept the offer, both sides may arrange the "kidney" pig ceremony. But whether or not they hold this ritual, each side invites the other to dance in its village. The visiting group stages the dance from afternoon to early morning, when people of the host ward or village give pigs to their relatives and trading friends among the dancers. These pigs represent gifts made in the context of existing exchange relationships. Therefore, the occasion and the scale of the prestations rather than a specific category of pig mark the whole event.

Every war in turn creates diverse debt relationships that prescribe certain pig transactions. The "men of the arrow's stem" must compensate their allies from other wards and villages with "parsley" pigs and they receive in return "stump" pigs. All men who have suffered serious injuries, which require the slaughter of a pig for the curing ceremony, expect a whole animal, the "guilt" pig, that must be reciprocated with a special kind of "stump" pig called "spleen" pig. The transfer of most "parsley" and "stump" pigs follows existing exchange lines between members of the belligerent ward and their allies from other villages. Usually these prestations, too, are made after dance performances at the donating group's ward, but portions of "parsley" pork go to the members of an allied men's house as a group on various occasions after the war has begun. Pigs captured on clandestine raids, for example, are always shared in this way.

Avenging the death of a person who does not belong to the killer's agnatic or maternal relatives entitles the killer and his lineal kinsmen to "head" pigs from the agnates of the victim. As their "head men," they return "stump" pigs to the donors of the "head" pigs, upon whose unmitigated support they can rely in their own future conflicts. These transactions create contingent exchanges between the victim's agnates and their maternal kinsmen or sister's children, but gaps in my data preclude a meaningful analysis of these reciprocal pig movements (see Figure 6).

Songs heard at every dance keep alive memories of battles and ambush killings. Many stories are cast into a traditional syntactic frame, often changing only the names of people and places to describe similar events that occurred in different wars. The verses exalt the valorous feats of one's own side and deride the enemy's recreancy and humiliating defeats. Several songs I heard frequently at dances celebrated killings in a war between the villages of Pasikni and Savilivi that occurred during my stay (Case *50). One verse jeers the death of a man by the name of Wempa in these words:

> The man Wempa will never eat again,
> Nor will Alavóm* ever eat again.
> But we live [to see] the sweet potatoes roast,
> The sweet potatoes from Wongele and Tukui.†

* Wempa's sib brother.
† Names of garden areas near Savilivi.

Another verse tells of the fate of a little boy who was shot on the path outside his besieged village as he tried to escape with his elder brother's wife:

> When your father told you "go!"
> You did not get far.
> When your mother told you "go!"

6 Pig exchanges in warfare

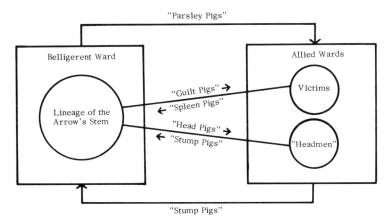

You did not get far.
Your body writhed and swayed
At the Tukui stream, at the Wongele spring.

One popular song in the Jaxólé Valley commemorates a past war
which featured cannibalistic revenge:

The men who ate your younger brother
Will not eat your elder brother.
The leaves will fall on their own,*
The leaves at Somókt will fall on their own,
The leaves at Alovamt will fall on their own.
The men who ate your elder brother
Will not eat your younger brother.

* Meaning: the victim's kinsmen will die a natural death.
† Look-out places.

As part of the people's oral tradition these songs help to preserve
their knowledge of events in the long history of warfare in the
Jaxólé Valley.

Liability and Retaliation

The preceding analysis of methods of conflict management
shows that the Jalé rely to a decisive degree on coercive retaliation. To understand their ideology of retaliation as jurally sanc-
tioned redress, one must know how the Jalé assess liability for
injuries and death suffered by one person as a consequence of another's action or neglect. Since my analysis of conflict cases in
the following three chapters will deal with several disputes that
arose from a refusal to provide "guilt" pigs, I want first to
elucidate the concept of liability by describing situations where
people were killed outside of warfare and without malicious
intent.

Jalé reasoning deduces jural liability from a doctrine of effective action that does not distinguish between intent, negligence,
inadvertence, and accident as aggravating or extenuating circumstances. In evaluating only the consequences of the injurious act,

the Jalé do not question a person's guilt or innocence—his psy-chological state—when they establish his formal liability, that is, his obligation to provide restitution or indemnity to the injured party. The recognition of personal responsibility influences only the procedure by which the injured party seeks to obtain redress.[9]

For centuries in the history of Western thought, philosophers, legal scholars, and judges have examined similar ideas as a problem of jurisprudential analysis, public policy, and moral culpability. Few anthropological studies on customary law, however, have dealt with the problem in a systematic way. Many have distorted the content of native concepts by uncritically categorizing them in terms of Western legal and ethical ideology and by failing to recognize the contextual significance of specific social relationships between the parties involved in a case.[10] In Jalé society those relationships determine whether and how a person's responsibility for causing harm is translated into liability for providing redress.[11] A few examples may help to explain these principles.

In one case Telféokné, a young man, was buried by a land-slide along with Majuangken, his maternal kinsman, whom he was helping to build a fence in his garden when the accident occurred. Majuangken's son promptly delivered a "guilt" pig to Telféokné's eldest living agnate, the son of his elder brother.

The significance of this case concerns two important jural aspects: the attribute of the pig and the extension of liability. My informants thought that Telféokné's agnates would probably have received a "lung" pig, the customary condolence gift, if he had worked on land that Majuangken might have given him for his own use. The payment of a "guilt" pig, however, signified that Majuangken's kinsmen held him responsible for his nephew's death and accepted the obligation to indemnify the victim's lineal kinsmen.

The Jalé do not limit joint liability to cases where the responsible person is dead or has absconded; instead they apply this principle to every situation in which one member of an agnatic descent group injures or kills an outsider. In times of war, re-

venge—a form of compensation obtained by forceful self-help—
widens the circle of people who may become victimized to include
all residents of a ward, a village, or even a group of allied villages. The next situation accentuates the irrelevance of intent
and negligence in assessing a person's liability.

In this case Kevel became liable for the death of a woman in
spite of his efforts to prevent the accident. Kevel was cutting
down a large branch of a tree that grew close to a path when
the woman approached. Disregarding both the markings that
Kevel had placed across the path to warn people of the danger
and his furious shouts, she hurried on. As the woman passed
the tree, the branch broke and killed her and a child she was
carrying on her shoulders. My informants insisted that Kevel
had to indemnify the woman's relatives because "the branch fell
down by his hands," even though the accident occurred through
the woman's own fault.

The last example involves a man's liability to indemnify his
affines upon the death of his wife in childbirth, a circumstance
that conspicuously evinces the principle of absolute liability.
According to Jalé reasoning, the husband had incurred liability
for his wife's death "because she died by his penis." This
rationalization substantiates particularly well the doctrine of
effective action, for had the man not impregnated his wife, she
would not have died in childbirth.[12]

What the Jalé consider an effective action need not be the
cause of a person's injury or death. In a purely logical sense
we can see some, albeit remote, causal connection between death
in childbirth and impregnation and a more proximate connection
of action and effect in the case of the falling branch. But the
Jalé extend the causative link even further. For example, if
someone invites another man to join him on a hunting trip or a
ratan-collecting expedition across the Central Range and this
man suffers a fatal accident, the initiator of the venture must pay
a "guilt" pig to the deceased's agnates. Refusal to comply with
this obligation creates a grievance which may lead to forceful
retaliation.[13]

While all these examples involve physical injury and death,

a person may suffer loss or damage in many different ways. Somebody's pig may destroy his fence and uproot his crops, another's disregard of pollution tabus may endanger his health, and malicious or careless gossip may harm his reputation. Unfortunately, the limited information contained in my case records about the jural implications of such wrongs prevents any inferences concerning the extent and enforcement of joint liability for damage of this kind. It appears, however, that property damage—including the wounding of dogs and pigs—initially calls for repair or restitution by the responsible party. If such claims remain unsatisfied, the grievance can precipitate a confrontation that may lead to injuries and even killings. As the scope of a conflict enlarges, support and alliance structures determine the involvement of more people in the dispute and lead to the participation of the parties' kinsmen, men's house groups, neighbors, and trading friends from other villages.

Although the doctrine of effective action disregards the circumstances of a person's injurious conduct, it does admit circumstantial variables for determining the magnitude of compensation and the time of providing the pigs. As a rule the urgency of providing compensation increases with diminishing contact and amity between the parties. As I have explained in the preceding section, the possibility of negotiating 'wergild' compensation after intentional killings also depends largely on the social distance between the parties. The use of a special term denoting the 'wergild' pig clearly indicates that the Jalé recognize the mental element in evaluating a man's responsibility for another person's death. However, since in very few cases did a party accept a pig in lieu of a revenge killing, my data are inconclusive as to how acceptance of a 'wergild' pig affects a kin group's demand for a "guilt" pig if the casualty represents a revenge killing and an allied village is responsible for the hostility. I suspect, however, that receiving the one does not cancel a claim to the other.

The observed relationship between political organization and the concept of liability in Jalé society suggests the following general hypothesis. In societies with localized descent groups lacking permanent superordinate political integration and without jural authorities, liability tends to be joint and absolute. Both attributes of liability tend to correlate with the necessity of solving disputes by self-help. If in the absence of jural authorities abscondence and alleged or actual accidents were to confer immunity, the maintenance of regulated social life would become a precarious enterprise. The following analysis of actual dispute cases will explain the conditions that prevent or promote the escalation of conflicts among the Jalé given their reliance on coercive methods to obtain redress.

IV Conflict between Relatives

The preceding chapters have provided the bare ethnographic background one needs to know to understand the ways in which the Jalé handle conflicts. In the foregoing description of their methods of conflict management I have stressed the fact that in their society the political implications of kin relationship and residential association determine the patterns by which the parties to a dispute manage to work out an agreement or fail to reach a settlement. Therefore, I will discuss these patterns in the political context in which the cases arose.

I distinguish three main ranges, so to speak, in accordance with the way the Jalé themselves view the political reality of a case. The first range delineates disputes between people whose primary relationships are defined by their relative positions in the kinship network. These positions may derive from their common membership in an agnatic lineage, or from their husband-wife relationship, or from their roles as affinal relatives.

The second range involves people who consider themselves neighbors. They may live either in the same ward or in different wards of the same village. The third range includes people whom the Jalé call "strangers." While they recognize pragmatic differences between strangers living in neighboring villages and those from distant places, these differences become very subtle in conflict situations, so that residence in the same or a different region marks the only major distinction and impinges upon the chances of a peaceful settlement and the conduct of warfare.

Disputes among Agnates

The co-resident, agnatic descent group is the most inclusive corporate unit in Jalé society. Agnates have common economic interests ranging from coordinated cultivation of their land to shared participation in affinal exchange relationships. Furthermore, the joint jural liability of a lineage correlates with its obligation to render support to its members who fight with people belonging to other lineages and local groups. Since agnatic solidarity constitutes a prerequisite for concerted defensive and retaliatory actions against outsiders, I must analyze disputes among agnates before treating the patterns of conflict management involving other kin relationships and territorial groups.

My case records contain six cases of conflict between agnates. They involve four different kinds of offenses: stealing garden produce (*1 and *18), jeopardizing the safety of kinsmen by adulterous conduct (2), withholding an invitation to a purification rite (15), and failing to share food (16 and 17). Although the particular cases concern only a few dyads, any pair of agnates may fight over any of these grievances.

The first case describes a situation which illustrates very well how the Jalé respond to a minor transgression by an act of retaliation.

No. *1. The Case of the Rancorous Brothers (January 1965)

Place: Nelelum ward in the village of Pasikni
Principals: Avele and his younger brother, Selon

Amenteruken owned a banana tree which had grown two clusters. He gave one to his oldest son, Avele, to harvest, the other to Avele's younger brother, Selon. On January 25, Selon took four fruits from his brother's cluster which he openly shared with two young Nelelum boys. When Avele heard what Selon had done he said nothing, but retaliated the violation of his property rights a week later, on February 1, by taking a taro tuber from a plot belonging to his brother.

As soon as Selon was told about Avele's action, he cut down his brother's banana cluster. That afternoon an altercation between the brothers developed into a scuffle. Two men from their ward who happened to be present finally succeeded in separating them. While Selon retreated inside the men's house and wept, Avele cut down his brother's banana cluster and gave it to a friend in a nearby village.

For almost a year Avele and Selon did not speak to each

other and no longer shared their food. Their co-residents deplored the hostility between the two, but they failed to persuade them to terminate their avoidance relationship. Finally,
in December, Avele gave Selon a pig. This gift reconciled the
brothers.

Informants explained that there was a marked difference between Selon's initial offense and Avele's reaction. Although Selon
should not have taken his brother's bananas, Avele should have
scolded him instead of exacerbating the situation and thus pro-
voking him to do further harm. In order to understand Avele's
response one must know a few things about Jalé property rights.
Apart from the settlement site, the corporate estate in garden
land, the men's house, and public utilities such as bridges and
fences around the foraging area, everything grown or manu-
factured is individually owned. Ownership, in turn, entails an
exclusive control over plants, fruits, and objects.

The Jalé distinguish between two types of unauthorized harvesting. Taking crops from a co-resident relative without his
prior permission has different jural implications from taking
crops belonging to someone else. In the first situation the person
who helps himself to his relative's garden produce must inform
the owner of his transgression and explain the circumstances that
made it necessary if he wants to avoid a quarrel. The owner,
in turn, is expected to approve of this infringement of his rights.
This conditional privilege excludes all fruits, but the most
stringent restrictions apply to all pandanus varieties. On the
other hand, any outright theft from a non-relative warrants
retaliation, which, as the "Case of the Pilfered Crops" (*14)
shows, may escalate the conflict into a war.

To some extent, however, social context and economic conditions modify this distinction. Not only do elusive factors such
as temporary strains in a relationship influence a person's response to a kinsman's transgression, but the relative abundance
of a particular vegetable also impinges upon the owner's reaction.
In one case (*18), for example, a father reprimanded his son for
having plucked some Hibiscus manihot leaves from his bush.
When in the course of the altercation the young man hit his
father with a stone, he was attacked by his father's brother's

20 Pakóak, a reputable medicine man, who treated the author after a bad fall

son and his own younger brother. Other members of their men's house soon separated them. Although the incident did not harm the young man's relationship with his other agnates, he henceforth maintained an avoidance relationship with his father.

In other cases spontaneous avoidance behavior constitutes a nonviolent response to a kinsman's transgression. Occasionally a ritual curse that calls upon the bones of a deceased relative and is often followed by a withdrawal of the curser from his common residence with the cursed aggravates the avoidance state.

This happened in a case (17) where a man failed to share with his son a piece of pork that his daughter's husband had brought. Since the lineal kinsmen of a woman who have contributed to her 'dowry' pigs hold a joint claim to the gifts coming from their affine, the father had deprived his son of his rightful share. Their fight, in which the father suffered a broken rib and imposed a curse on his son, led to an avoidance relationship that could only be terminated through a special reconciliation rite conducted by a medicine man.

In a cursed avoidance relationship one party may urge other consanguineal relatives who were not involved in the original dispute to avoid his opponent. Usually a man asks his sister's children for this demonstration of support against his agnates. This extension of avoidance then requires that all persons involved must participate in the reconciliation, at least by eating some consecrated pork if they are absent from the ceremony.

Like all rituals that validate a change of a person's status, this reconciliation rite, which mends the agnatic tie between the parties, requires the transfer of a pig from one side to the other. Either party may present the animal to his opponent, but the donor is usually the person who would have furnished a pig to the other if their relationship had remained amicable. In the case just mentioned, for example, the son gave his father a "spirit-nourishing" pig. This special pig represents a man's customary gift to his old parents. Since a medicine man employs blood of a freshly slaughtered pig in the rite, the presentation both facilitates the reconciliation and, at the same time, signifies the resumption of appropriate role performances between the parties as defined by their particular kin relationship.

Occasionally, the blood may come from pigs that both sides exchange. In one case (16), known as the "pandanus war," an agnatic descent group split up in the course of a conflict that began with a man's anger over his son's improper sharing of pandanus nuts with him. This dispute led to retaliatory actions which precipitated a war involving several villages. A few years afterward, another war forced the father to leave his exile residence and seek refuge with his estranged sons. Since the Jalé exchange pigs in any situation which brings relatives together after a long period of separation, the medicine man could use blood from these pigs in his treatment. The son who first fought with his father refused to take part in the ceremony and thus perpetuated the avoidance.

On the whole, residents of a men's house succeed in preventing agnates from resorting to violence as long as both live together in the same men's house. In the following case, which informants remembered as the "teaching war" because the conflict started with an exhortation, the antagonists lived at different places when the trouble began.

No. 2. The Case of the Defiant Adulterer (1962)

Place: Seleriek ward in the village of Savilivi
Principals: Antoxalem and his agnatic cousin Óngkómpé

Antoxalem of Seleriek had acquired a reputation of seducing other men's wives. When indignation over Antoxalem's conduct grew, his father's brother's son, Óngkómpé, one day publicly scolded him. As his cousin came along a nearby path, Óngkómpé shouted at him in a loud voice from his homestead at Hevikaxak, located close to the village. Although, as informants explained, Óngkómpé meant only to warn his kinsman because he feared that his offenses might cause serious trouble, Antoxalem was so furious that he killed one of Óngkómpé's pigs, which he found in the foraging area.

That evening the people living at Hevikaxak searched the fields and soon found the dead animal. Once an examination of the arrows had established the identity of the killer, Óngkómpé's younger brother, Sónmó, went over to the village pretending to have come to stay overnight in the Seleriek adjunct men's house, where Antoxalem lived. After everybody had fallen asleep, Sónmó took Antoxalem's cymbium shell necklace, stole out of the house, carefully replaced the door boards, and ran back to Hevikaxak. Antoxalem woke up shortly afterward and discovered that both his shell and Sónmó had disappeared. When he could not find Sónmó outside, he went over to his cousin's nearby family hut, sneaked up to the sleeping floor, and copulated with his wife in retaliation.

Still during that night, someone told Sónmó about the incident. Early in the morning he waited in ambush for Antoxalem to come to the defecation place at a nearby stream and shot a well-aimed arrow into his buttock. Antoxalem extracted the arrow and, together with a few men coming to his aid, pursued Sónmó who, however, reached Hevikaxak unharmed. After shooting a series of arrows at the men who showed themselves outside, Antoxalem and his supporters returned to the village.

Antoxalem's co-residents decided to avenge the injury. Contingents from other Savilivi wards and, later, men from the neighboring villages of Pasikni and Tengkeléi joined the battle on either side. Although the fighting had already started again the following morning, Óngkómpé succeeded in halting the skirmish and urged the combatants to "lay down the arrows." Antoxalem, in turn, announced that he, too, wished to end the fighting. The following day both sides cooked three pigs and delivered the pork as compensation to their allies.

Informants explained that the Savilivi people were especially adamant about ending the conflict, because they had never forgotten the tragic outcome of a fight between a group of agnates in their village in which one of them lost his life (Case 15). In that situation only the transfer of a 'wergild' pig and a permanent termination of communication between the principals prevented further bloodshed.

The disputes described above elucidate several important points. A person's right to exclusive control of his property coexists with a strong emphasis on solidarity among agnates involving an obligation of sharing food with one's kinsmen. The Jalé have solved this apparent paradox by distinguishing in jurally relevant terms between conditional theft and theft proper. If a person steals garden produce from a kinsman, he can

expect a sort of retroactive authorization from the owner provided he explains the necessity for his transgression. If someone ignores this responsibility, or, on the other hand, if he fails
to share garden produce with his kinsmen, he breaks a customary
norm of good conduct and can expect reprimands at least and
possibly retaliation.

Although disputes over such matters among agnates may
escalate into warfare, formal avoidance tactics often provide
an alternative method of conflict management. The Jalé have
firmly institutionalized this procedure only for agnatic kinsmen.
But it is precisely this group where avoidance can have its great-
est effect, because it negates the very nature of their collective
existence. The requirement of a special rite to terminate a formal
avoidance relationship clearly shows that a dissolution of lineal
ties has occurred and subsequently demands a reaffirmation of
the role relationships between the estranged kinsmen.

Conflicts among agnates not only weaken the solidarity of a
kin group, but also reduce the political strength of their men's
house vis-à-vis other wards or villages. For this reason, their
co-residents always attempt to prevent a dispute from reaching
a phase where a break-up of amicable relations becomes inevitable. But since they lack judicial procedures to decide a case,
their influence remains limited to persuasion. Obviously, such
informal pressures are most effective when both opponents live
together with them. Consequently, a dispute between agnates
who live in different places at the time of their quarrel tends to
create partisan factions in their separate residence groups. Once
such factions have been formed, the dispute has extended beyond
the range of a kin group, and the political contingencies of territorial association then increase the chance of violent confrontations. I shall discuss these contingencies in the next chapter.

Disputes in Marriage

Unlike conflicts among agnates, which threaten the solidarity
of a lineage and weaken the power of their men's house group in
any current or potential enmities with other wards or villages,
disputes between husband and wife constitute primarily a threat

to the maintenance of their marriage. This threat, however, has crucial implications for the exchange relationship linking the affined lineages. The eleven cases of marital conflicts included in my records had a variety of causes. Three were precipitated by quarrels between co-wives (*3, *22, and *28), two by the wife's unauthorized harvesting of her husband's crops (*4 and 19), two by the wife's refusing sexual intercourse (*20 and *21), and four by the wife's adultery (*12, *30, *31, and *40).

Although most disputes between co-wives involve young women in the early years of their marriage, older women do occasionally quarrel. For example, in one of the fifteen polygynous marriages in Pasikni, the senior wife at first had not only welcomed her husband's second wife, but even provided one of the 'marriage' pigs for her co-wife's agnatic kinsmen. After several years of peaceful co-residence the two women had a fierce fight because the junior wife had harvested from her co-wife's gardens without permission. Subsequently the senior wife asked her sixteen-year-old son to build a new hut for her, revoked her husband's cultivation rights to her own gardens, and transferred the land to her son. Informants claimed that this case was uncommon and that more often co-wives who first lived separately agree to establish a joint household after both have children. Generally, however, co-wives continue the initial residence arrangement throughout their marriage. In Pasikni, where in six of the fifteen polygynous marriages the wives live in one family hut, they have always kept a joint household, while in seven of the remaining cases the women never lived under one roof.

The most common grievance leading to disputes among young co-wives issues from the senior wife's fear that her husband might neglect to prepare sufficient land for her after he has acquired a second wife. However, in one case (*28), one of the three marital disputes that arose from a conflict of interest between co-wives in their husband's labor, it was the junior wife who felt neglected, left the joint household, and went back to her ward of natal residence.

Although it is difficult to decide from the cases how often these anxieties are justified, many discussions of this matter have convinced me that the nature of exchange relationships between the husband and his two sets of affinal kinsmen may determine an uneven allocation of his labor to preparing plots for either wife. The more extensive the flow of reciprocal gifts between the husband and his affines, the stronger is his motivation to prepare land for their sister.

A wife's sexual recalcitrance may also relate to the balance of affinal pig exchanges. A young wife's refusal to bear a child before her husband has delivered a sufficient number of 'marriage' pigs to her kinsmen is a generally recognized sanction. A woman may also avoid sexual intercourse for more personal reasons. In Case *20, for example, the woman deserted her husband after frequent quarrels over the issue allegedly because his pig gifts were insufficient. However, her father, the person most interested in these transactions, spontaneously brought his daughter back to her husband after she had fled to her sister, who was living in another village. The fact that the woman went to her sister instead of returning to her mother, as most young wives do in similar circumstances, indicates that at least in this case delinquent gifts were the pretext rather than the cause of her objections to cohabitation.

Different norms attach to a man's and a woman's adultery. While a wife always risks being punished by her husband, I heard no case where a husband's adultery resulted in marital conflict. In addition to the absence of women among my informants, three factors account for this discrepancy. First, Jalé marriage rules prohibit a married woman from sharing her sexual activity with more than one partner and permit a man to have more than one wife. Second, the belief that an adulterous wife endangers the health of her husband by contaminating the food she prepares for him with a maleficent ingredient has no parallel applying to a husband's adultery. Third, the prolonged lactation sex tabu prohibits coitus only for the mother, but allows the husband at least the risk of seeking sexual satisfaction with other women. In sum, institutional arrangements and ritual sanctions discriminate against women by allowing the men a relatively greater opportunity for sexual activity.

A similar asymmetry exists regarding the control of property. Although a woman has nominal rights to pigs and the crops she has planted herself, she can do little more than rebuke her husband if he violates these rights—and provoke his anger at that. Yet, as the "Case of the Delinquent Husband" (*4) described below shows, a man may severely punish his wife if she dares to harvest his crops. In another case (19) a woman harvested sweet potatoes from her husband's plot to prepare a meal for him, but she received a thrashing nevertheless.

A wife who has been injured by her husband in a marital dispute may leave her family hut and return to her ward of natal residence, where she stays with her mother or her brother's wife. Although a woman may also seek temporary refuge with other relatives, such as a married sister in a distant village, most often she turns to her father or a married brother after deserting her husband—a move that has certain consequences for her marriage. As the recipients of her 'marriage' pigs and donors of her 'dowry' pigs, her agnates can best decide how to negotiate a reconciliation of the spouses.

Cases show that a young childless woman tends to leave her husband more readily than a mother. However, a woman's kinsmen are more eager to reconcile her marriage if she nurses a child because the lactation sex tabu greatly reduces her chances of getting abducted soon and thus prolongs her dependence on their support. The attitude of a woman's agnates toward reconciliation also depends on the status of their exchange relationship with her husband. The following conflict, precipitated by the husband's second marriage, elucidates this issue.

No. *3. The Case of the Unruly Wife (1966)

Place: Seraxanpini ward in the village of Pasikni and its garden hamlet of Pue-Ikma
Principals: Óngkólili of Seraxanpini and his wife Lilen
Other Participants: Taling of the Nelelum ward in Pasikni, Lilen's father, and his son Wali

In early January, several Seraxanpini families moved to their gardens at Pue-Ikma to prepare new fields during the coming season. Some of the men, including Óngkólili, who married the Nelelum girl Lilen, left their wives in Pasikni because their family huts in the hamlet needed repair or reconstruction. At

Pue-Ikma Óngkólili soon acquired Heriek, a girl from a nearby village, as his second wife.

On January 15, Óngkólili brought Heriek to Pasikni, where he gave her some plots in his garden to harvest. Taling, Lilen's father, happened to do some clearing work nearby. After a while Lilen walked by, pretending not to notice her husband and his new wife. Taling called after his daughter and told her to harvest from the plots in Óngkólili's garden that she had planted herself. Lilen began digging up sweet potatoes a few plots away from Heriek.

Since Óngkólili and Heriek did not take the direct path when they left for Pue-Ikma, Lilen followed them to see if her husband would give his new wife plots that she had planted in his gardens outside the village. Although her suspicion was wrong, she continued to go after them, apparently to find out what had happened to the plots Óngkólili had prepared for her at Pue-Ikma. Before long, Óngkólili told Heriek to go on alone, turned around, and came back toward Lilen, who immediately ran back to Pasikni, where she resumed harvesting. She did not look at her husband or speak to him when he squatted down sixty feet away from her.

At this point Taling stopped his work and told them to stay together in Pue-Ikma. Lilen angrily shouted that she wanted to know if "that bad short-short woman" would get any of the plots she had planted. Her father replied: "My son-in-law did well to take another wife. If he had a pig, he would have killed it for her agnates already. For you he has given enough. Another man would have given only one pig. My son Wali ate pigs from my son-in-law; I ate some, too."

Óngkólili said nothing and soon left for the Seraxanpini men's house. When Lilen went to her hut a few minutes later, she hurled away tabu marks her husband had placed on his own plots with her digging stick. Early next morning Lilen went to Pue-Ikma. At the hamlet she threw away all of Óngkólili's marks that tabued the plots which he had originally prepared for her. She returned to Pasikni in the afternoon.

After a while Lilen's initial anxiety subsided; she moved to Pue-Ikma and her relationship with Heriek became quite amicable. Both women occasionally visited Pasikni together, and at my house Lilen even mediated Heriek's barter of vegeables for salt and cowrie shells. A few weeks later their cooperative spirit waned.

In the afternoon of April 19, Lilen arrived in Pasikni crying aloud. Since her mother was dead, she went to the family hut

of her elder brother, Wali, and informed Taling and other
Nelelum people who gathered around her that she had come
"because they have beaten me." She explained that during the
past weeks Óngkólili had prepared garden plots for his two
wives, allotting them equal shares. That morning, after
finishing her own plots, she had planted some left-over sweet
potato vines on a bed belonging to Heriek. She had intended to
tell her co-wife that she would not care to harvest the crop
from these vines. However, Óngkólili had pulled the vines
from Heriek's plot and had scolded and insulted Lilen, who
had then torn out vines planted by Heriek. Then Óngkólili
had shot a five-pronged bird's arrow into Lilen's arm. Both
her brother and her father urged Lilen to go back to her husband, reminding her of the six pigs they had received from
Óngkólili. Lilen stayed overnight and returned to Pue-Ikma
the following day.

Two days later she was in trouble again. As they were
planting new plots, Heriek suddenly inquired why she had
bothered to come back. Lilen retorted by asking whether
Heriek had not seen her pigs, alluding to the fact that unlike
herself Heriek had not yet brought 'dowry' pigs into the marriage. When Óngkólili, working nearby, rushed up to his
wives and tried to calm their altercation, Lilen felt that he
sided with Heriek. She ran to the place where Óngkólili had
left his bow and arrows and cut the string with her teeth.
Enraged by his wife's pertness, Óngkólili attacked her with his
digging stick. Lilen beat back with hers, but retreated when
her husband's parents approached loudly denouncing her
mischievous conduct. She ran back to the hamlet, grabbed one
of the piglets from her 'dowry' sow, placed it in her net, and
started for Pasikni. Since people quickly reported the incident
by message shouting to Óngkólili, she freed the piglet, but
went to Pasikni nevertheless, where she stayed with Wali's
wife.

The next day Óngkólili came to Pasikni, where he found
both Taling and Wali in the company of a few other men at
my fireplace. He squatted down and lit a cigarette. Taling
initiated the conversation by asking his son-in-law whether
he kept beating his daughter because he had come to dislike
her. Óngkólili defended himself and listed several instances of
Lilen's insolent conduct. In reply Wali indirectly warned his
brother-in-law of common consequences from strained marital
relationships by mentioning a number of recently abducted,
young childless women who had deserted their husbands. At

this point Óngkólili changed the subject by asking me for tobacco; shortly afterward he left.

Lilen stayed in her elder brother's family hut for a whole week. On April 26, Taling sent his daughter back to Pue-Ikma with one steel axe, one lump of salt, and two nets.

This case reveals a typical strategy employed by a woman's agnates when they mediate in her marital conflict. They seek to reconcile the couple in an attempt to promote both the woman's well-being and their interest in a continued exchange relationship with her husband. Therefore, if the woman's grievance stems from her aversion to a junior co-wife, they defend her husband's right to acquire another wife, but urge her to assert her rights to gardens that he prepared for her use. If a woman seeks refuge with her kinsmen after being maltreated by her husband, they still try to induce her to go back. However, if her predicament does not ameliorate, they may reprove his conduct and warn him of a possible abduction. In the case just described the woman's father facilitated a reconciliation of her strained marriage when he succeeded in persuading his daughter to return to her husband with gifts for him.

Informants, including Taling himself, explained the choice of this strategy. Since their exchange balance was even when the trouble started, Lilen's agnates interpreted Óngkólili's conduct according to the general rule that "whenever a man beats his wife and makes her go back to her kinsmen he want another 'dowry' gift." A comparison with other cases makes the social importance of obligatory pig exchanges even more obvious. In a similar dispute (*22), which involved Lilen's elder sister, the woman's agnates refused to mediate a reconciliation because their affine owed them a pig at the time of the dispute. This procedure probably reflects a common strategy in the management of marital conflicts, but other factors complicate this pattern, as the next case will explain.

*No. *4. The Case of the Delinquent Husband (1962–1965)*

Place: Villages of Pasikni and Klengleng
Principals: Féré from Klengleng and his wife, Lulupik of the Seraxanpini ward in Pasikni

Other Participants: See Figure 7; numbers refer to persons named in the text

Background: After a war had forced Senalék (1) to leave his native village of Sangkalpunu, he fled to Pasikni, where his daughter Ampukatok (9) was married to Hélémó (2) of Seraxanpini. In time Ampukatok's sister, Lulupik (8), married Féré (10), who lived in the nearby village of Klengleng, but whose natal ward was Kénanghólómó in Pasikni. Because Senalék made his gardens on land belonging to Hélémó's lineage, he promised part of the 'marriage' pigs due from Lulupik's husband to Hélémó, who thus acquired an interest in the pig exchanges between Senalék and Féré.

One day when Ampukatok visted Lulupik in Klengleng, her sister prepared a meal from two yam tubers which Féré had planted on one of the plots he had tilled for her. In the evening she offered the remainder of the food to her husband. Féré, however, refused to eat and beat his wife for having harvested the tubers without his permission. Lulupik defended herself by reminding him that he owed two 'marriage' pigs.

When Féré had left her hut, she hid a bundle of tobacco leaves that her father had recently asked her to bring to her husband. Next morning Féré noticed that the tobacco had disappeared. He searched the hut and found it behind a board in the wall. Enraged by her mischief, Féré began to beat Lulupik, who struck his face with a stone adze but then suffered severe injuries from the burning sticks that her husband wielded against her. Lulupik went back to her mother at Seraxanpini, where Féré's mother, Uoxe (5), visited her twice to persuade her to return to her husband. But Lulupik refused and reminded Uoxe of her son's debts to her agnates.

7 Participants in Case *4

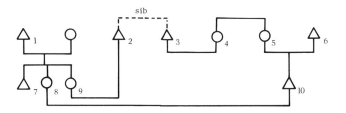

Several months later the Seraxanpini people moved to their garden hamlet Pue-Ikma, where they were one day invited to dance in a neighboring village. Together with a few men from Klengleng, Féré went there to watch the performance and visit friends. He returned home with his wife Lulupik and three 'dowry' pigs. Senalék had given him two, one cooked and one alive. The third, a live animal, came from Hélémó, who had eaten Féré's only 'marriage' pig. The two men told Féré that they expected him to give pandanus, yam, bananas, and other food to Lulupik's sister Ampukatok, her mother, and her brother's wife, when the women would come to visit Lulupik in Klengleng.

My discussions of this phase of the conflict with informants brought out two factors which account for this unusual step taken by the woman's father to reconcile her marriage. One relates to Senalék's position as an immigrant. Having only a limited amount of garden land to cultivate, he was anxious to have his daughter leave his household again. The other factor has a more incidental but nonetheless decisive importance. A Jalé always attempts to invest pigs received on a particular occasion in an existing exchange cycle, even if the balance is already in his favor. By accumulating credit a man increases his chances of obtaining a pig from his exchange partner if a sudden need arises which obligates him to furnish a pig he may not have at that time. Senalék, therefore, seized the opportunity provided by the gifts received at the dance to indebt his son-in-law even further. I believe that his readiness to choose this option also relates to his refugee status. For men like him, the absence of any kinsmen at his place of residence leaves a daughter's marriage as the only real way to enter into an exchange network.

Hélémó's contribution to Lulupik's 'dowry' gifts is more difficult to explain. Anyway, it was he who planned to disrupt the marriage, when Féré failed to reciprocate the gifts in due time.

After the Seraxanpini people had returned to Pasikni and several occasions had passed where Féré could have given a 'marriage' pig to Senalék, Hélémó began complaining about his stinginess. One day when he and Senalék's son, Sintuk

(7), discussed the matter, their talk was overheard by their co-resident Kerewarek (3), whose junior wife Esele (4) is Féré's mother's sister.

Kerewarek realized that Hélémó and Sintuk were already considering a proposition by one of Hélémó's sib brothers from their own ward to abduct Lulupik, so he decided to intervene. He had maintained a good exchange relationship with Féré as well as with Féré's father, Esalu (6). Therefore, he had a personal interest in a continuation of the exchange cycle that linked him via Lulupik's agnates to Hélémó, who also happened to be his younger sib brother. Knowing that Féré possessed only one pig in addition to the two received at the dance, he asked his wife, Esele, to let him give a sow and a piglet of hers to Sintuk as a 'marriage' gift on behalf of her "son," Féré. Esele agreed on condition that she would obtain other pigs from Féré.

Esele discussed the matter with her sister, who then went to Klengleng to inform her son of the plan. Fearing Lulupik's imminent abduction, Féré immediately took his three pigs to Kerewarek's family hut, and gave Lulupik's two 'dowry' pigs to Esele. Then, he took her sow and piglet together with his third pig to Senalék, who kept the piglet and gave one pig to Sintuk and the other to Hélémó.

Féré still owed two pigs when Senalék and Hélémó each gave Lulupik a live pig at a dance of the Klengleng men at Seraxanpini on December 5, 1965. Again he failed to reciprocate these gifts when the Seraxanpini men danced in Klengleng a few days later. Hélémó complained about Féré's deplorable attitude in the men's house and mentioned the problem to his wife. As soon as Lulupik's mother heard about the talk, she informed her daughter, who, in turn, warned her husband. Féré excused his delinquency with the smallness of the two pigs he owned at that time, but had his wife take these to her mother and sister the same day.

The interesting points in this case concern the involvement of persons who are only indirectly linked to the disputing spouses. Hélémó's interest in the pig exchanges connected with Féré's marriage to Lulupik explains both his initial participation in the reconciliation of this marriage and his subsequent search for a new and potentially more cooperative husband—a reasonable alternative because Lulupik was still without child. Kerewarek mediated in this conflict because he believed that a break-up of the marriage would hurt his own trade balance, which was tied to Féré's exchange relationship with his wife's agnates.

The obsessive concern of Jalé men with pig trading also influences the strategy of an adulterous wife. An adulteress prefers to suffer a beating instead of returning to her natal family. She tends to seek refuge with her kinsmen only if she has been seriously wounded (Cases *30 and *40), because she must expect severe reprimands from her agnates for jeopardizing their exchange relationship with her husband. Furthermore, since great wars in Jalémó have resulted from adultery (Cases 32, *50, and *51), they will also consider her offense a threat to peace.

Nevertheless, as Case *31 shows, an adulteress, especially if she is an older woman, may abscond from her conjugal ward for a few days, the time she estimates her husband needs to lose his anger. Under these circumstances, however, a woman prefers to seek refuge with relatives who are not directly involved in the exchange cycle established by her marriage. If the wife does return to her ward of natal residence, an interest on both sides to continue the affinal relationship promotes a settlement of the conflict through the provision of a pig or other gifts by one party to the other within the context of the existing exchange pattern.

The function of pig exchanges has such a critical influence upon the management of marital disputes that any serious quarrel between spouses necessarily concerns their whole lineage and may, in fact, be the beginning of a conflict between the affined kin groups. The fate of a marriage, especially during its early years, depends to a decisive degree upon the relative exchange advantages that the woman's agnates and her husband perceive for themselves. This means that both sides will adjust their efforts to reconcile a marriage according to its benefits for each party's wider exchange network. These considerations imply that marital stability in Jalé society is primarily linked to the exchange balance maintained by the affined lineages.

Disputes among Affines

Not all troubles between affinal relatives derive from an unresolved family dispute. Pigs, however, figure prominently also in those cases that begin with a confrontation between affines. In fact, all seven recorded cases except one—which concerns a dispute over a stolen fruit (27)—deal with pig debts (5, 23, 24, 25, 26, *28). The causes as well as the consequences of these disputes vary widely. In one case (24) two men, Alóat and Sineng, who had married Alóat's uterine half-sister, quarreled over a piece of land. Further exploration revealed, however, that the original grievance resulted from Sineng's failure to give Alóat a pig after the birth of his first child. As the child's closest maternal kinsman, Alóat had a claim to this special pig, particularly because he had generously provided his old stepfather with a "spirit-nourishing pig." In retaliation, Alóat appropriated a stretch of garden land that his half-sister had inherited from her father and that Sineng had cultivated in the past. The parties finally negotiated a compromise. Sineng delivered a pig to Alóat, who in turn retained only a small portion of the garden he had seized.

In two other cases, the aggrieved parties resorted to pig seizures after their opponents had rejected their demands to satisfy their rightful claim to compensation. In both cases, however, the linking marriage had been terminated, either by the abduction of the wife (23) or by the death of the husband (26).

In these situations, forceful self-help against affines has a far greater propensity to exacerbate the conflict than a similar action when the marriage continues. This difference has a simple explanation. As long as both parties perceive some shared advantage in a continuation of their exchange relationship, they are prepared to settle their dispute by a negotiated compromise. When the value of this relationship diminishes with the break-up of the marriage, the parties' interests tend to become antagonistic and their insistence upon obligatory pig payments less flexible. Simultaneously, each party's reliance on the support of his men's house group pulls them even further apart. The following case shows how easily a grievance between affines under these circumstances can lead to hostile encounters between factions from different wards. The dispute also elucidates the intricate relationship between loyalties based on co-residence and those deriving from affinal ties in conflict situations.

No. 5. The Case of the Angry Affine (1953–1964)

Place: Village of Pasikni

Principals: Kepolok of Longkopini and Selelemangke of Nelelum

Other Participants: See Figure 8; numbers refer to persons named in the text

Background: The original settlers at Longkopini were two different lineages who seceded from Seraxanpini, another Pasikni ward. When the Pasikni people abandoned their village during an influenza epidemic in the early 1920's one of the lineages resettled in the village of Savilivi, the other joined their former ward at a different place. Only one of the Savilivi settlers, Ngóróné (1), later returned to Longkopini, after the other lineage had reoccupied the site.

After Ngóróné's wife had died in childbirth, Kepolok, who belonged to the woman's sib, gave him a 'condolence' pig. When Ngóróné failed to share the meat with his wife's deceased father's brothers, Amenteruken (2) and Selelemangke (3), they openly complained about his greed to the other residents of their men's house.

Avele (8), Amenteruken's fourteen-year-old son, and his cousin Pavéon (9), Selelemangke's ten-year-old son, decided to help themselves to some of the meat that Ngóróné had stored in his family hut. They were discovered by a man from a neighboring ward before they had succeeded in their venture. Avele escaped to hide in the hut of his mother, and Pavéon fled to a garden hamlet where he stayed with a sib brother, who belonged to his men's house.

8 Participants in Case *5

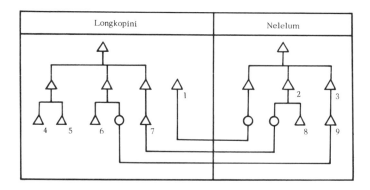

The altercation which Ngóróné started in the evening led to a scuffle between the two men's house groups. In this fight, the Nelelum men were supported by Kepolok, who had married Amenteruken's daughter, and his agnatic cousins Hesum (4), Hónómó (5), and Avalék (6).

The following evening Kepolok publicly demanded a pig from Selelemangke as compensation for the pain he and his kinsmen had suffered in the brawl. The Nelelum people rejected this claim, and another altercation ensued.

Next morning Kepolok, Avalék, and Hónómó waylaid Selelemangke on his way to his gardens. They seized one of his piglets that he had taken along and cooked it in front of their men's house.

Later that day Selelemangke was invited by the husband of a distant cousin of his wife to settle in his village, located an hour's walk north of Pasikni. Selelemangke accepted the offer, dismantled his family hut in Pasikni and rebuilt it at his host's ward, where he lived for six years. In 1959 he returned to Nelelum.

Selelemangke and Kepolok settled their dispute not before early 1964, although Pavéon had married Avalék's sister in the meantime. At the initiation of Kepolok's son, Pavéon claimed and received three pigs: one in return for the pig he had given the boy's agnates in his role as his mother's "brother," the second for a steel axe he gave to the initiate, and the third for the piglet once seized from his father.

I have selected this particular dispute for discussion because it illustrates some general features of Jalé conflict management. One aspect concerns the influence of affinity on alliance relationships. In this case, for example, a men's house group split up in a fight with a lineage in a neighboring ward. This happened when one member, Kepolok, supported by his agnates, sided with the kin group from which both he and their antagonist in his own men's house had taken wives. An interpretation of this choice must consider both residence and customary norms of redistribution.

Pigs received as condolence gifts upon the death of a relative should be shared with others who mourn the death. Kepolok, who furnished the pig, expected Ngóróné to distribute some pork to their common affines at Nelelum. Their participation in its consumption would have meant that Kepolok could exploit his generosity in future disagreements with his wife's kinsmen. His subsequent seizure of a pig from his wife's "father" demonstrated his eagerness to obtain a pig from his affines.

Residence always figures in decisions on alignment strategies. The long years of separate residence had alienated Ngóróné's lineage from their former co-residents. Ngóróné's ties to Longkopini were personal and with men in his own generation. Their sons, Kepolok and his cousins, preferred to support their affinal kinsmen in a neighboring ward rather than Ngóróné, whose own kin group could not provide effective assistance should they need help in future conflicts.

While diverging loyalties can sometimes deter the escalation of a dispute by preventing retaliatory actions (see Case 25), this situation may also leave the aggrieved party without any support at all. If a man cannot rely on the undivided support of his agnates in a dispute with their common affines because of several marriage links to the affinal lineage, he may leave his ward and take up residence with distant relatives in another village. But as long as the affinal relationship has not been severed by the death or abduction of the linking woman, the dispute can ultimately be settled. As in cases of marital conflict, pig prestations in the context of obligatory exchanges then serve to reconcile estranged affines.

The main difference between the management of conflicts in marriage and those among affines lies in their relative propensity for escalation. Marital conflicts, even if they result in serious injuries, apparently never result in warfare. The mutual interest of both sides in the preservation of their exchange relationship prompts the husband and his affines to handle the dispute by peaceful means. An equalization of the balance of pig exchanges, or new gifts if the balance is even, usually facilitates a reconciliation. In conflicts between affines, however, especially if these follow the dissolution of the linking marriage, the aggrieved party tends to resort to force in the pursuit of his interests.

The Jalé must always reckon with situational variations in the network of dyadic ties that determine the power balance in a particular conflict. Apart from an individual's past experiences with neighbors and affines, the territorial range of the conflict influences the composition of factions engaged in a confrontation. As a general rule, the importance of group membership—descent or residence—as opposed to individual ties increases with the social distance among the parties. This distance is a function of the volume of affinal exchange transactions and other forms of economic cooperation as well as relative geographic propinquity. This means that the fewer the affinal ties between the descent or residence groups of the principal opponents and the greater the distance between their place of residence, the smaller is the chance that a group will divide its support between both sides.

In a society that lacks procedures facilitating the intervention of a third party, this state of affairs has serious consequences for the settlement of disputes. When the parties' interests in obtaining redress are no longer balanced by an overarching concern of their kinsmen or co-residents for an amelioration of the strained relationship, resort to retaliation becomes the preferred strategy.

V Conflict between Neighbors

Inasmuch as both the agnatic descent group and a family are co-residential units of a ward, my discussion of disputes among agnates and between marriage partners has already dealt with several intra-ward conflicts. Since almost every men's house in a Jalé village includes more than one lineage, disputes among residents of a ward frequently involve parties who belong to different descent groups. The Jalé concept of ward membership applies to a societal segment that consists of a men's house group and their families who live in huts built on ward territory. Temporary absence from the ward during a seasonal stay at a hamlet or a prolonged homestead residence does not alter a person's ward membership. But, as I have explained, spatial separation has a detrimental effect upon the peaceful management of conflict between parties belonging to the same ward.

Disputes in the Ward

All intra-ward cases that I recorded concerned either women or pigs, which, indeed, seem to be the main bones of contention in Jalé society. Two of the five cases in my sample involved adultery (*30 and *31); the others dealt with a person's failure to pay a compensatory pig (*6), an abduction (7), and the theft of a pig (29).

The following story of a conflict is rather difficult to recount. Nevertheless, I have chosen to discuss it in detail because it deals so clearly with three important aspects of Jalé conflict management. First, it explains how a particular dispute generates new grievances between parties who were not involved in the original dispute. Second, it outlines the process by which the alliances are created that draw other people into a conflict. And third, it elucidates the mediating effect of cross-cutting affinal relationships.

*No. *6.* The Case of the Thwarted Sib Brother (1965)

Place: Womikma ward in the village of Pasikni and its hamlet
Suaxéi, located in the Walingkama area (see Map 3)
Principals: Ngajóxók and his sib brother Nalek
Other Participants: Men from the wards of Womikma, Hale-
pini, and Nelelum in the village of Pasikni; numbers in
Figure 9 refer to persons named in the text
Background: This dispute arose from a conflict between Lóló
(1) of Womikma and his son Wielu (7) that is described in
Case 16. Their quarrel over a few nuts escalated into a war
between several villages, in which Pové (9), another
Womikma man, lost his life. Since Pové had fought on
Wielu's side, Wielu became liable to pay a "guilt" pig to
Pové's half-brother Ngajóxók (10). When six years after
the war Wielu still owed the pig, Ngajóxók decided to seek
redress by force. At that time Lóló was staying with his son
Nalek (8) at Suaxéi. Wielu, who had never terminated the
avoidance relationship with his father, lived by himself at a
nearby homestead.

On July 29, 1965, Ngajóxók went to Suaxéi and seized a
small pig belonging to Nalek. He was already cooking the
animal inside his garden shed, located approximately halfway
between Suaxéi and Pasikni, when Nalek began searching for
it. Later that day someone told Nalek that, some time ago,
Ngajóxók had stolen and eaten another one of Nalek's pigs.
(The Suaxéi people had always thought that this pig had
drowned in a river or fallen off a cliff.)
    Nalek set out for Pasikni accompanied by his father-in-law,
Muriek (3) of Halepini, another Suaxéi resident. On their way
they discovered thick smoke emanating from Ngajóxók's shed.
While Nalek stayed behind, Muriek approached the place.
Squatting down near the shed, Muriek asked Ngajóxók for a
piece of ember to light his cigarette. Ngajóxók told him to
wait a moment as he was just taking sweet potatoes from the
oven. After a while Ngajóxók handed some of the food to
Muriek through the entrance and gave him the desired piece
of ember. Muriek pretended to walk off, but soon sneaked
back to the shed and, peeping through an aperture in the wall,
watched Ngajóxók remove meat from the oven and hide it on
the logs stored above the fireplace. He walked back to Nalek
and told him his discovery. Nalek now went straight to the
shed, entered it, grabbed a pig's leg from the hiding place, and
left without speaking a word to the surprised Ngajóxók.

9 Genealogical relationships of participants in Case *6

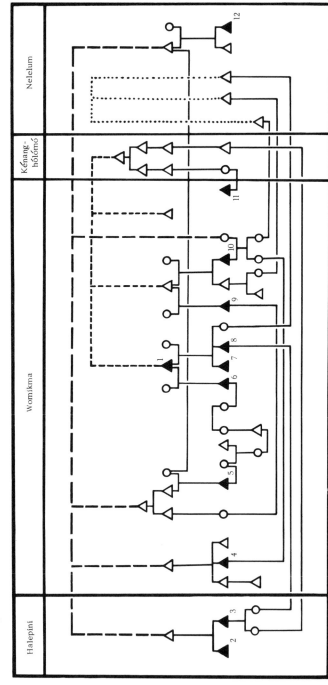

Halepini | Womikma | Kénang-hólómó | Nelelum

Broken lines indicate common sib membership

Solid symbols mark persons named in the case

The two men continued toward Pasikni, where they arrived in the late afternoon. Near the Womikma ward they found a pig that belonged to Ngajóxók. As Nalek struggled to tie a rope to its front leg, he was discovered by a small boy, whose father's brother had married one of Ngajóxók's daughters. The boy immediately informed Ngajóxók's wife, who rushed to the place where the two men were still struggling with the pig and attacked Nalek with her digging stick. Muriek pushed the woman to the ground. Attracted by her screams, several Womikma people came to her help.

The noise of the fight drew men from other wards to the scene, among them Muriek's younger brother, Kuron (2) of Halepini. Soon the brawling had developed into a tumultuous fight, with bows and arrows being used as lances, between Womikma men and their supporters from the Nelelum ward and several Halepinians who assisted the two Suaxéi raiders.

As I watched the medley and listened to the altercations I could not detect any reason for the particular composition of the two factions. However, a clear pattern emerged when I later discussed the case with informants and examined the genealogical relationships among the participants.

The most active fighters on Ngajóxók's side were his son-in-law, Silóxóp (4), and his brother, both of whom actually injured Muriek and Kuron. Affinal links also called for his support by Nelelum men. One of them was betrothed to Ngajóxók's second daughter and another had married the daughter of his deceased brother. Although Ngajóxók's wife came from Halepini, she had been the adopted daughter of a man who himself had settled there as a war refugee. Therefore, the Halepini men aligned themselves with Ngajóxók's opponent Muriek. The decisive role of affinity in conflicts extending beyond ward lines becomes even clearer during the next phase of the conflict.

The scuffle was still going on when Nalek suddenly ran away. When someone shouted, "He is going to kill Ngajóxók," many of the men pursued him. His opponents wanted to prevent the suspected action, his supporters to come to his defense. At this point Ngajóxók, who had observed the fight from a ridge bordering the village, decided to return to Womikma. When he reached the path leading to the village,

Ésangko (11), another Womikma man, attacked him. The fight between the two men ended when Silóxóp and his brother intervened to escort Ngajóxók home.

Ésangko came late to join the scuffle because he happened to be visiting another men's house in the village when the fighting started. He had two reasons to side with the Suaxéi party. He had married the agnatic cousin of a man from the ward of Kénanghólómó, who was the husband of one of Muriek's daughters. These links involved him with Nalek in one intricate exchange network. Moreover, Ésangko held a grudge against Ngajóxók because he had never reciprocated a pig that he had once received from Ésangko's father.

Muriek and Nalek soon heard that Ésangko was in trouble because he had sided with them. They returned to Womikma and the inevitable altercation again evolved into a scuffle. Several elders from Halepini and Nelelum urged the fighters to stop and reminded them that Nalek was, after all, a Womikma boy and not just some stranger. They also warned that the dispute might turn into war. None of the men engaged in the scuffle heeded their admonitions.

Finally, Uluon (5), a Womikma resident and a sib brother of both Muriek and Silóxóp, ended the fight by a dramatic show of anger. Keeping his bow at the ready, he pointed the arrow toward the opponents as he stepped rapidly between them in repeated back-and-forth movements. His uterine half-brother, Jénguruk (12) of Nelelum, whose father had married Uluon's widowed mother as his second wife, joined him in this performance. At the top of their voices the two men shouted again and again, "Stop the scuffle, don't go on!" They reprimanded the Womikma men for beating each other in front of their own men's house, for which Jénguruk's elder brother had killed an enemy in revenge for the slaying of a Womikma man (see Case *53). Now that their brother himself had been eaten by the enemy, they should seek to revenge his death and bring a body to Nelelum instead of fighting among each other.

Meanwhile it had become dark and everybody drifted back to his ward. Ésangko, who had stood aside from the scuffle weeping and complaining that nobody else from Womikma had helped Nalek, went to Kénanghólómó, his wife's natal

ward, where he had built his family hut. He slept in the
Kénanghólómó men's house for several weeks. When he returned to Womikma, his co-residents welcomed him and called
the incident "something that has always happened."

Given the failure of the elders to end the scuffle, the successful
intervention of Uluon and his brother, Jénguruk, both younger
men, needs to be explained. Certainly the unrevenged death of
their brother gave their complaints a considerable weight. However, I believe that Uluon's position as an affine to both parties
was a more important factor. Pové, whose killing created the
whole conflict, had married the daughter of Uluon's father's
brother; and Uluon had generously invited his widowed cousin
to live with her two children in his family hut. His relationship
to Nalek derived from the betrothal of his adopted daughter,
the child of his second wife, to a sister's son of the wife of
Jóxóliangke (6), a uterine half-brother of Nalek. Since Jóxóliangke had adopted the boy after his father's death, he participated in the affinal exchanges between Nalek and his agnates
and Uluon.

Jóxóliangke's position in the conflict prompted him to intervene when he heard of the fight after Nalek and Muriek had
returned to Suaxéi late in the evening. At that time he happened
to be at his garden hamlet, located near Suaxéi, but he was the
only member of Lóló's lineage who had retained his permanent
residence at Womikma. Therefore, he had a personal interest in
a settlement of the dispute. He could not defy his brothers, nor
could he afford to jeopardize his place in the Womikma ward.

The following afternoon, Nalek returned to Womikma together with Jóxóliangke and Wielu. A discussion took place
inside the men's house and lasted for several hours. Ngajóxók
defended his seizure of the pig with his rightful claim to
compensation for the death of his brother and refused restitution. In vain Jóxóliangke and Wielu urged him to return a
pig to Nalek. The three brothers left with the threat that they
would harvest Ngajóxók's garden near Suaxéi.

A few days later Nalek delivered portions of a "parsley" pig
to Halepini. Ésangko received the largest share. Ngajóxók
shared the meat of Nalek's pig, which he had hidden in a

thicket near the village on the day of the fight, with his
Womikma men's house group.

On December 20, 1965, the Womikma men initiated the
son of Ngajóxók's deceased brother into their men's house.
Ngajóxók, who had adopted the boy, gave one of the pigs he
received from the initiate's maternal kinsmen to Nalek. This
gift settled the case.

To understand the obstacles to a settlement of disputes without fear of a violent confrontation requires a comprehension of
two critical problems in Jalé conflict management, which the
events in this case and its pre-history (Case 16) elucidate with
particular clarity.

The first problem is the "snowball effect" of inadequate procedures to deal with grievances. The absence of an authority
capable of adjudicating disputes creates situations in which even
minor disagreements among agnates, such as a quarrel over a few
nuts, may result in a war between whole villages. The second
problem is the potential of every retaliation to generate new
grievances. Since a "man of the arrow's stem," the party responsible for the hostilities, incurs a liability for compensating all
injuries and deaths suffered by his supporters, he may, by
refusing to comply with this obligation to pay "guilt" pigs to the
agnatic kinsmen of the victims, create a conflict between himself and his allies. This new enmity, in turn, entails a definite
chance that forceful seizure of pigs will lead to further violence.

Whether or not one side resorts to armed combat depends
entirely on the outcome of the confrontation following the
seizure. As long as nobody is seriously injured in an ambush or
a scuffle, an intra-ward conflict can still be settled in face-to-
face negotiations between the principal parties. In the original
dispute between Lóló and his son Wielu, the possibility of a
peaceful settlement was eliminated when one of Lóló's friends
wounded Wielu with an arrow. By contrast, in the case just described a fierce fight did not prevent a meeting of the opponents
on the day after the brawl. Although the discussion failed to
achieve an immediate settlement, the aggrieved party abstained
from executing the threatened retaliation. Undoubtedly this

restraint influenced the other side to make the demanded restitution. Significantly, the initiation of a boy into their common men's house, a ritual act that reaffirms and consolidates the unity of its membership, provided the occasion for the settlement.

Other important aspects of Jalé conflict management evident in the "Case of the Thwarted Sib Brother" concern the influence of sib affiliation, affinity, and common residence in dispute processes. In intra-ward conflicts, the main support lines to residents of other men's houses follow affinal links rather than sib affiliation. The reason for this predominance of personal linkages through marriage over putative kinship through descent is obvious: interests in the maintenance and enhancement of affinal exchange relationships have no counterpart in the mere recognition of common sib membership. The intervention of the men who terminated the fight also reveals the influence of conflict with an outside enemy on the management of local disputes. Their reprimand reminded the opponents of their collective duty to avenge the death of their own sib brother and appealed to their sense of solidarity in the presence of an ongoing *soli* war with villages in a distant region. The Jalé always recognize that conflicts within a group—in a ward as well as in the village—increase the danger of its defeat in wars against a common enemy; and this threat, as several cases reveal, may mitigate the violence of these conflicts.

Finally, this case adds more evidence for my conclusion, already derived from the analysis of disputes among agnates, that residential separation of the parties to a conflict implies an increased tendency to forceful self-help against a wrong and thus enhances the chances of further violence (see also Case 29). All types of serious disputes in Jalé society have one conspicuous trait in common: at one point either in the etiology or in the management of a conflict a real or alleged pig debt becomes an issue. Several cases suggest that compliance with a demand for payment or acquiescence to seizure by the aggrieved party can prevent perilous scuffles and even wars. The next case exemplifies how this alternate response avoided the escalation of an intra-ward quarrel about a woman.

No. 7. The Case of the Competitive Abductors (1963–1964)

Place: The Tangkema hamlet of the Seraxanpini ward in the
village of Pasikni

Principals: Hampok and Walusa

Background: In 1963 Hampok began an adulterous affair with
Wampexasa. One day the woman's husband, a man from
the Angkuruk district, discovered Hampok as he was leaving her hut in his garden hamlet. The enraged man
pursued the intruder and hit him with three arrows.
Hampok got back to Seraxanpini, but he needed a month's
rest to recuperate from his injuries.

A few months afterward Hampok made an unsuccessful attempt to abduct Wampexasa when she was at the Pasikni
ward of Nelelum on a visit to her father's sister. Some time
later, following a fight with her husband, Wampexasa decided
to desert him and let herself be taken by Hampok. She appeared in the Seraxanpini garden hamlet of Tangkema, where
she stayed with the wife of Hampok's agnatic cousin Sóxól.
(Wampexasa could expect this hospitality because her deceased
father had been a close friend of her host's father, a man
from the Pasikni ward of Longkopini, and he had years ago
sponsored the initiation of her host's elder brother.)

Since Hampok was still in Pasikni, Wampexasa accepted
a proposal by Walusa, another Seraxanpini man who lived at
a nearby hamlet, to stay with him. Walusa's natal ward is
Womikma in Pasikni but he had settled with his elder sister's
husband at Seraxanpini, his wife's natal ward. When
Wampexasa's mother arrived the next day to look for her
daughter, Walusa gave her a live pig. She brought it to her
daughter's closest consanguineal kinsman, a son of her
father's sister, who later gave a 'dowry' pig to Walusa.

At Seraxanpini Hampok complained about Walusa. He
claimed that Wampexasa should have been for him to marry,
not only because she had come to Tangkema but also because
her husband had injured him rather than Walusa. A month
later he 'eloped' with Wampexasa to the village of Waléi,
where he found refuge with his sister's husband. In retaliation Walusa seized a sow and a piglet belonging to Hampok
and another pig belonging to his younger brother. The two
sons of his sister's husband helped him in the raid. They appropriated the second pig because Walusa had restituted a
pig to a Nelelum man whose pig had been seized by mistake

after Wampexasa's abduction (see Case 35). After a week or so Hampok returned with Wampexasa to Tangkema. A year later, in early 1965, she deserted him.

This case adds a new dimension to the influence of separate residence of the parties on the settlement of a dispute. The "Case of the Defiant Adulterer" (2) is typical of situations in which residential distance deters peaceful procedures in intra-ward disputes, even among agnates, and instead promotes forceful retaliation. On the other hand, as the "Case of the Competitive Abductors" shows, temporary withdrawal of one party from the place of common residence with his opponent may also prevent violence and thus eliminate the "snowball effect" of escalation.

Abscondence of the guilty party from his local group in fear of punishment probably prevented an armed combat in the two intra-ward disputes over adultery. In one case (*31), a man committed adultery with the junior wife of a sib brother. His transgression was particularly severe because the woman's husband had taken care of him and his younger brother after their father's early death; worse yet, the offender had only recently caused an inter-village war in which a member of his own men's house was killed (see Case *50). The man who surprised the couple in the act and threatened to shoot the offender merely demonstrated that public opinion regarded this behavior as an outrageous violation and a menace to peace within the village, for no kinship links to the woman's husband prompted the intervention. The adulterer escaped to a distant village, where he could stay with his sister's husband. Later he took up residence at the garden hamlet of a man from a neighboring ward, where he could stay until his offense became "a thing of the past."

The second case (*30) shows that even attempted adultery entails the risk of severe punishment. A young man tried to seduce the wife of one of his co-resident sib brothers. Although the woman had acceded to his propositions in the past, she feared that the circumstances of the new encounter had led to a discovery of her liaison and she informed her husband of the young man's overture lest she be accused of complicity. In retaliation, the husband, together with his brother and a few other members of his men's house, injured a pig belonging to the offender's father in an unsuccessful attempt to seize the animal. No further violence occurred, because the young adulterer fled from his ward and sought refuge in another village, where, as their maternal kinsman, he could rely on the hospitality of the sons of his father's sister. His father left the ward as well and took up residence at the homestead of his wife's sister's husband.

To summarize, all these cases exemplify great difficulties in settling disputes within the ward. In the absence of a judicial authority an aggrieved party can choose between three courses of action. He may either abstain from seeking redress altogether, claim restitution or compensation in the form of pig payments through negotiation, or retaliate the offense and thereby risk an aggravation of the conflict if his opponent does not acquiesce in this action. If the principals live together when the dispute arises, withdrawal of one party favors an ultimate reconciliation through informal mediation of their men's house group. If, however, the principals live at different places, even when their separate residence is temporary, retaliation tends to be the prevalent method of obtaining redress. This procedure frequently divides their local group into partisan factions and thus aggravates and extends the conflict (see Figure 10).

Thus, as in disputes between agnates, the strategies of intra-ward conflict management depend largely on the residential proximity of the parties. Spatial distance increases the propensity of an aggrieved party to resort to forceful retaliation and hampers a remedial intervention of other members of the local group.

10 Residence and conflict management

Residence of Parties	Probable Reaction	Probable Result	Probable Consequence	Participation of Men's House
Common	Quarrel	Avoidance	Reconciliation	Mediation
Separate	Retaliation	Counter-Retaliation	Escalation	Divided Support

However, a temporary separation of the opponents in the course of their dispute may also alleviate, but will not eliminate, the danger of violent reactions against wrongs. On the other hand, since the offender's withdrawal from his ward threatens group solidarity, it improves chances for ultimate reconciliation.

Disputes between Wards

It is obvious from the preceding analysis that disputes between relatives and among non-kin residents of a ward very frequently entangle people from other wards. Neighbors participate in the management of an intra-ward conflict either by promoting negotiations between the parties or, more often, by supporting retaliatory actions. Thus, many intra-ward conflicts expand across ward boundaries and generate hostilities in a wider realm. A parallel expansion of conflicts occurs when people from other villages are drawn into disputes between neighboring wards.

Several cases reviewed in this section document the patterns of their involvement. Of the fourteen inter-ward disputes I recorded in reasonable detail, six cases deal with adultery or attempted adultery (32, 33, *39, *40, *41, and *42), three involve killing or wounding of animals (34, 36, and *38); two quarrels concern garden land (*8 and 9), two the mistaken seizure of a pig from an innocent person (35 and *37); and one case concerns bodily injury (10).

The outcome of these cases differs not only from one type of dispute to another but also for disputes involving the same kind of grievance. Two main factors account for this variation; the contingencies of political alignments and the more incidental results of the initial confrontation. A comparison of the two land disputes exemplifies the effect of these variables on the management of inter-ward conflicts.

*No. *8. The Case of the Stubborn Gardener (1965)*

Place: Village of Pasikni
Principals: Selelemangke of Nelelum and Herin of Seraxanpini
Background: A generation ago Selelemangke had acquired
    ownership to a tract of land adjacent to the Seraxanpini

ward by initial cultivation. Konu of Seraxanpini owned a small plot in that area. Both men had not made a garden there for many years, because the rocky ground had a very low yield.

Around the middle of March, Selelemangke began cutting down the brushwood. Konu, who wanted to reserve his rights but found the job too laborious, urged Herin, another Seraxanpini man, to make a garden on his part. In the afternoon of March 17, 1965, Herin started clearing the thicket and continued his work despite Selelemangke's objections that he was trespassing on his garden land. Nightfall ended their altercation.

The following morning Herin came to the site accompanied by about two dozen men and boys from Seraxanpini. He had just resumed his work when Selelemangke arrived with a few Nelelum men. The inevitable 'shouting match' quickly led to a brief scuffle between the younger men. Disapproving shouts from older men, including Selelemangke, halted the fighting, but the altercation continued for almost an hour.

A central issue in the dispute was a pig that Selelemangke had received from Walusa, the brother of Herin's wife. Two years before this incident, in the context of the "Case of the Competitive Abductors," Walusa had restituted a pig to Selelemangke after men from another village had seized one of the latter's pigs in a retaliatory action against the former (see Case 35). Since he could have refused the demand for compensation, Walusa assumed that Selelemangke would one day reciprocate this 'gift.'

Herin offered to leave the whole area to Selelemangke if he delivered a small pig to his brother-in-law. As the dispute continued, it became clear that the real grievance arose in the context of a recent inter-village war between Seraxanpini and a ward in the village of Savilivi (Case *50). In this conflict Selelemangke's eldest son had fought on the Savilivi side against his neighbors even after a Seraxanpini warrior had died. In the 'shouting match' both parties frequently called the land "an utterly bad garden not worth the complaints [by the other side]" and warned of the deplorable consequences their fight would have in the face of the unsettled conflict with their common enemies from Savilivi.

The dispute ended with a compromise: Selelemangke retracted his claim when Herin promised to cultivate Konu's land for one season only. Halfway through the dispute, several men and boys had uncovered remnants of the old stone wall which marked the boundary between the two parts of the land.

My analysis of the preceding cases has stressed the tendency of conflicts within a local group to involve people from other localities. Usually their involvement reduces the chances of a peaceful settlement, because it increases the strength of one or both parties to coerce the other. The "Case of the Stubborn Gardener" illustrates other consequences of this involvement: in an inter-ward dispute a past alignment of one party with an outside enemy of the other impedes the settlement of the case. Moreover, this alignment may create grievances that turn a minor disagreement into a potentially violent conflict.

Informants with whom I discussed the case just described agreed that Herin or Konu would not have interfered with Selelemangke's work if his son had not persisted in supporting their enemies after a Pasikni man lost his life. The poor quality of the disputed land, and the smallness of Herin's plot—which measured only fifteen square meters—would not have warranted their unrelenting stand.

The following case deals with a similar dispute, but has a very different outcome, because the initial confrontation between the parties led to bodily injury.

No. 9. The Case of the Negligent Heir (1958)

Place: Village of Savilivi
Principals: Léong of the Usapini ward and Méléirek of the Longkopini ward

Léong of Usapini owned a piece of land in a garden area near the village. One day when he and his son had started to prepare new plots, Méléirek of Longkopini came up to them and claimed that part of the land belonged to him. Léong's father had indeed permitted Méléirek's father to cultivate this part, but Méléirek had neglected to give Léong a "Cordyline" pig, which would have established an inheritable property right to the disputed ground.

The quarrel between the two men developed into a scuffle that turned into a skirmish in which both sides were supported by their co-residents and relatives in other wards. After an arrow had hit one of Méléirek's allies from the ward of Seleriek, both sides announced their intention not to continue

the fighting. However, when the victim's condition deteriorated, his father Selexenéi threatened to avenge the injury.
Although Méléirek refused to pay a "guilt" pig, Selexenéi encountered strong public opposition to his threats. Therefore,
he went to Pasikni and solicited help for a revenge battle from
the Serexanpini ward.

Particular historical circumstances explain this move. Selexenéi's
ancestors had originally lived at Seraxanpini, from where they
had moved to a new ward in Pasikni two generations ago. During an epidemic in the early 1920's, they abandoned their new
homes and settled in Savilivi. Since part of their land lay in an
area belonging to Seraxanpini, several men, including Méléirek,
had in recent years lived in the garden hamlet that the
Seraxanpini people had built there. It was this continued residential association with Seraxanpini that allowed him to ignore
the warnings of his neighbors.

Early one morning Selexenéi led a large party of warriors
toward his own village. Some Savilivi men, among them some
of Selexenéi's own agnates, tried in vain to stop the attack
force before it reached the village. After initial skirmishes the
Usapini men retreated inside their house, from where they
continued to shoot arrows through loopholes made by pulling
ajar planks in the wall. When Selexenéi was fatally hit in the
throat, the fighting ended. For the rest of the day, the Seleriek
men stayed inside their house mourning the death of both
Selexenéi and his son, who died from his wound the same
day. Fear of revenge kept the Usapini men hidden in their
house. The Pasikni warriors went home and prepared themselves for battle on the next day.

The battle did not take place. Aware of their predicament,
the Usapini men left the village in the middle of the night,
some of them fleeing to the Helók Valley south of the Central
Range, others to friends and affinal relatives in Wanjok, on the
west side of the Jaxólé River. Two boys who did not want to
leave hid themselves underneath the ground floor of a neighboring men's house where they had sib brothers. In the
morning enraged Seleriek men discovered and killed them
on the spot. Later that day two more Usapini men were
killed: one man who had stayed in nearby gardens until
sunrise because he wanted to harvest potatoes before making
his way over the Range, and another who had lingered behind

the main group and was hunted down by a pursuit party of Seleriek and Seraxanpini men. About a week later, Selexenéi's kinsmen ambushed a fifth victim near the Jaxólé bridge to Wanjok when he returned from the Helók Valley.

The Usapini people resettled in Wanjok, where they had once lived after their exodus from their original home at Wisalek, near the present village of Tuluk-Ikma, in a war with Pasikni that took place several generations ago. Women and small children continued to stay in Savilivi for about a week after the fighting and then moved with the family chattels across the river to join the men. Méléirek, the "man of the arrow's stem," emigrated to Waléi, where he settled permanently with a trading friend.

Several conclusions emerge from a comparison of the two land disputes. The original quarrels are very similar and the main arguments of the parties differ only with regard to the demanded pig. A grievance over an unreciprocated pig induced the "Stubborn Gardener" to interfere with his opponent's customary privilege to appropriate a brushwood-covered tract of rocky land through recultivation. Léong merely refused to extend gardening privileges to Méléirek, who had no claim to the land because he and his father had failed to convert the usufruct granted by Léong's father into ownership rights.

The essential difference between the two cases lies in the outcome of the initial confrontation. While the parties reached a compromise in one dispute, the injury of a man blocked a peaceful settlement in the other. One can assume that a state of war with another village exerted considerable pressure on the opponents in the "Case of the Stubborn Gardener" to cool their fight, especially since the Jalé themselves recognize this effect of inter-village hostilities on the management of local disputes. Nevertheless, I believe that the general validity of this interpretation is too simple to account for the outcome of any particular dispute. Apart from the structural constraints exerted by overarching enmities against a common outside enemy, much more elusive conditions and incidental factors determine to a degree the fate of an inter-ward dispute.

Bodily injury in the course of a scuffle is a decisive though most unpredictable cause for the escalation of a conflict, especially if the victim does not belong to a principal's kin group. As in conflicts among agnates or within the ward, the victimization of people outside the principals' lineages creates a new grievance that must be solved independently of the original dispute. The victim—or his agnates in case of his death—have a claim upon the "man of the arrow's stem" for a "guilt" pig, and its payment may prevent revenge. If they receive no compensation, they resort to retaliatory measures, either by seizing a pig from the delinquent party, as in the "Case of the Thwarted Sib Brother" (*6), or by seeking revenge in battle.

The Jalé recognize the danger of bodily injury to the maintenance of peace. Therefore, an aggrieved party will often seek redress by clandestine pig seizures that reduce the chances of a violent confrontation at least temporarily. This course of action produces a new grievance if the seized animal belongs to a person who is not directly involved in the conflict. In this situation the residence of the three parties determines the strategy of the innocent victim.

Let us assume two cases where A and B are the principals in a dispute and B steals a pig from C in a retaliatory action against A. If all three parties belong to the same village, C tries to negotiate restitution from B. If, on the other hand, A and C belong to the same village and B to a different village, C demands restitution from A. A man follows the same strategy in his attempt to obtain the customary compensation from the abductor of his wife. He will demand a pig from the woman's agnates if they live in a neighboring ward and if a state of hostility with the abductor's village or an expected violent confrontation makes direct negotiations with the abductor a perilous endeavor.

I call this choice of action the strategy of minimal risk (see Figure 11). The Jalé view any inter-village confrontation as a precarious enterprise for the person claiming restitution because of his residential association with one of the parties to the original dispute. In contrast, they regard inter-ward negotiations following the seizure of a pig from a man of the wrong ward as entailing little danger for the claimant because he can expect sympathy from both parties to the original dispute.

There is a peculiar difficulty with a settlement in which C

receives compensation from A. While A would be liable to compensate any injury suffered by his supporters, he is not responsible for the loss of a pig incurred by a nonpartisan resident of his village in the course of his conflict with B. However, according to Jalé notions of liability, C nevertheless blames A for the seizure and resorts to retaliation if he is unable or unwilling to claim restitution from B. If A accedes to C's demand for compensation, this arrangement merely serves to eliminate the imminent danger of a new conflict. As the "Case of the Stubborn Gardener" shows, a pig paid in this fashion represents little more than a gift that should be reciprocated at a future occasion. The uncertain nature of a settlement of this kind then creates a new grievance that may aggravate any future dispute between A and C over an issue entirely unrelated to the original problem.

The outcome of the inter-ward disputes dealing with the killing, injury, and seizure of domesticated animals shows that cases of this kind can usually be settled by peaceful procedures (Cases 35, 36, *37, *38). However, in the absence of standardized and predictable modes of obtaining redress, such conflicts between members of neighboring wards may also result in violence, which in turn may precipitate a war (Case 34).

In a war between neighboring wards the power resources of the principal parties largely control the magnitude of violence. As long as either side estimates their relative strength to be in balance, an equalization of killings tends to promote a readiness

11 The strategy of minimal risk

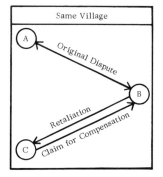
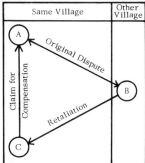

of both to end the fighting. There are also other factors that
favor an early termination of hostilities: for example, the status
of a victim within a local group. The next case gives some in-
sight into how such circumstances influence the politics of intra-
village conflicts. The war in this case ended by mutual agreement
before killings were equalized. This case also shows that the
event precipitating a war between neighboring wards need not
be an offense as serious as the killing of a pig; even a quarrel
among boys can generate a state of enmity that leads to a series
of violent revenge and counter-revenge actions.

No. 10. The Case of the Quarrelsome Boys (1956)

Place: Homaxavak hamlet of the Usapini ward in the village
of Savilivi
Principals: Hóvóló of Usapini and Iknielek of the Seleriek
ward in Savilivi

One day Hóvóló, a twelve-year-old Usapini boy, was preparing a garden at Homaxavak not far from a field where fifteen-
year-old Iknielek of Seleriek was working. When it started
to rain a little, Hóvóló jokingly chanted some rain-making
stanzas. Iknielek did not like this because he had a long way to
go back to his village and asked him to stop the chanting.
When Hóvóló continued his invocations, Iknielek hit him with
a stone. Hóvóló ran home to Homaxavak and complained
about Iknielek's attack. His two elder brothers decided to
avenge his wound.
    On the path to Savilivi they met the wife of Iknielek's elder
brother and struck her several blows with their stone adzes.
Iknielek's kinsmen decided to retaliate the injury, walked to
Homoxavak and killed a woman by the name of Nóuilélang.
Her death resulted in open battles between Seleriek and
Usapini. The war, in which contingents from the other
Savilivi wards fought on either side, ended after two days by
mutual agreement.

The choice of the victim in this case followed a strategy of
revenge that has certain consequences for the management of
conflicts in Jalé society. Nóuilélang was a "stranger" in Savilivi.
She was born in the ward of Seraxanpini in Pasikni and had
married a man from another ward of that village. When her

husband fell ill with some protracted and incapacitating disease, she deserted him and took up residence with her elder sister, who was married to an Usapini man.

As informants explained, this man, though obliged by custom to seek revenge for the killing of his guest, had no interest in a prolonged war within his own village over the death of a foreign woman. Moreover, his supporters could not expect any compensation if they suffered injuries because the woman had no agnatic kin in Savilivi except her brother. The latter lived there as an immigrant himself, and he advocated a cessation of the fighting when his former co-residents in Pasikni refused to rally to his help.

Although I suspect that the killing of a woman tends to generate less vindictive furor than the slaying of a man among either her husband's group or her own lineage, the woman's fate clearly relates to her status as a foreign resident. In fact, the deaths of immigrants in two other inter-ward conflicts indicate that the strategy of minimal risk applies also to a calculation of the potential consequences of revenge killings (Cases 32 and 33). The killing of a stranger reduces the danger of violent retaliation or, at least, increases the chance of a settlement through 'wergild' indemnification.

A preference for the killing of a foreign resident in inter-ward conflicts generally corresponds to a reluctance to avenge his death upon an autochthonous person. Nevertheless, in any particular situation, the reaction of the victim's residence group cannot be predicted, since affective bonds may outweigh considerations of local politics (see Case 32).

A man's assessment of his chances to get the support of his men's house group also influences his strategy in inter-ward conflicts dealing with adultery. The Jalé typically handle an attempted seduction in public altercations or by retaliatory pig seizures. Adultery commonly elicits a violent response, and only extraneous circumstances can prevent an escalation of the conflict into war.

One affair that occurred in Pasikni during my stay in the village illustrates these constraints. In this case (*40), the aggrieved husband himself discovered the adulterous couple in the act. He let the man escape but nearly killed his wife. Particular circumstances determined his reluctance to punish the offender. His sister's betrothal to the brother of the offender's wife blocked his revenge. In addition, as my informants emphasized, he could hardly expect the support of his men's house group if a violent retaliation had caused a war with a neighboring ward because the group had recently fought a prolonged war with Savilivi, his wife's home village, following the killing of his elder brother in battle (see Case *50).

The aversion of the husband's co-residents to new enmities became evident when they reproached him for the excessive punishment of his wife. They were especially angry because her death would have diminished the chances of an early peace with her lineage, which had already lost two members in the recent war. In order to prevent a wrong and undesirable interpretation of the incident by the woman's kinsmen, a sib brother of the aggrieved husband declared in a shouted address to the whole village that the woman was wounded solely for her misconduct and not because her kinsmen were responsible for her husband's brother's death, and that the adulterer should provide a pig for the woman's relatives if they demanded compensation.

Several distinctive features emerge from a comparative view of the cases dealing with inter-ward conflicts. The principals to disputes over land and accidental seizures of pigs in retaliatory actions directed against a third person tend to seek a settlement in face-to-face negotiations. A peaceful conclusion is then possible as long as nobody suffers an injury in the process. Similarly, wounds inflicted upon a person's domesticated animals by other people's dogs or pigs constitute grievances amenable to peaceful settlement by negotiation. Even if the owner of a pig bitten by another person's pig has injured or killed the attacking animal, the parties can still reach an agreement without resorting to retaliation.

An attempted seduction of a married woman usually results in verbal confrontations in which both parties receive support from their co-residents (Cases *39, *41, and *42). Men from neighboring wards may join either side and complain about any past grievances they might hold against the opposing house.

Occasionally the woman's husband may seek redress by seizing a pig from the would-be adulterer, an action also taken in intra-ward conflicts over the same issue. Violent retaliation tends to follow adultery, but in intra-ward cases abscondence of the guilty man may prevent retaliation, and since bodily injury regularly exacerbates a conflict the flight of the offender greatly reduces the chances of armed combat. Whether or not the aggrieved husband decides to revenge the offense in inter-ward cases depends largely on the strength of estimated support for both parties. Regardless of the offender's place of residence, an aggrieved husband always, of course, has the choice of abstaining from any action against him altogether and punishing only his wife. In fact, several inter-ward disputes that occurred during my stay referred to past cases where the aggrieved husband refrained from retaliation to avoid the risk of a war.

Regardless of the nature of the original dispute, bodily injury demands revenge in kind and often generates a chain of coercive actions that end in open warfare. Since amicable relationships among the wards of a village enhance their security against attacks by other villages, a foreign resident tends to be a pre-ferred victim in a retaliatory killing because his death involves a diminished risk of revenge. Furthermore, as absconding often prevents an escalation of conflicts within a ward, emigration of the "man of the arrow's stem" reduces the possibility of new violence in inter-ward conflicts. Finally, a state of hostility with other villages, requiring cooperation in defense and revenge, influences the opponents in an inter-ward conflict to refrain from forceful retaliation and to seek instead a peaceful resolution.

On the whole disputes between wards entail even greater difficulties for an amicable settlement than disputes among people of the same ward. If the principals belong to different wards, factions need not be created; they exist already in the politically autonomous men's house groups, which constitute a permanent power base for either party. The mitigating effect of individual links of affinity between wards may not be strong enough to prevent violence. In such a case, only the disastrous consequences of intra-village warfare and unresolved conflicts with a common enemy can deter an escalation of local disputes.

VI Conflict between Strangers

The cases so far analyzed have shown how kinship links and residential association determine the alliance structures that draw people from other villages into intra-village disputes, especially after a conflict has escalated into warfare. Their participation not only widens the range of enmity, but also creates the conditions that engender new disputes between groups from different villages. Revenge killings and pig seizures represent typical reprisals that extend an original local dispute across village boundaries. Most inter-village conflicts, however, concern offenses that a person committed against a resident of another village outside of any existing hostilities. Six of the fifteen inter-village conflicts in my records involve an abduction (*12, 44, 45, 46, 48, and *52) and three the seizure of pigs (13, 47, and *49). The other cases deal with adultery (*50 and *51), the wrongful appropriation of land (*11) or pilferage of garden produce (*14), and the killing of visiting trading partners (43 and *53).

Before analyzing these conflicts in their political context, I want to return to a vexing problem that I have already mentioned. This problem concerns the high incidence of warfare in memory cases. It is all the more disturbing because this book advances the thesis that the frequent use of coercive and violent methods of conflict management in Jalé society results from its fragmented political structure and a correlated absence of third-party institutions. Since the data which suggest this hypothesis are the histories of disputes collected in my records, I must raise the crucial question of how representative these cases are given the fact that some disputes are settled peacefully.

Unfortunately, I cannot give a wholly satisfactory answer. The realities of ethnographic fieldwork on conflict in a society like that of the Jalé excludes the ethnographer from information about many disputes that the parties settle by quiet negotiation. Long residence in a particular village greatly increases his knowledge of alternate procedures taken to remedy a wrong within the community. But disputes between residents of different villages remain unnoticed, unless they gain at least some degree of publicity or incidentally involve people whose daily life the ethnographer can regularly survey.

In the absence of formal forums at which disputes are discussed, past cases settled by peaceful means are even more elusive. People tend to remember conflicts more easily if they involved violent confrontations. Under these circumstances recorded cases necessarily represent a skewed sample. This inherent bias would distort a sociological explanation of conflict management only if it derived from a quantitative analysis. I am indeed unable to say which kinds of inter-village disputes tend to be settled by negotiation and which end in warfare. Since, however, inter-village relationships lack many of the structural constraints on forceful retaliation that common residence and denser exchange networks provide for the local community, the untempered violence evident in conflicts between strangers certainly reflects greater impediments to their peaceful resolution. The available evidence clearly shows that in Jalé society even disputes over minor grievances can escalate into warfare; and this fact alone warrants the theoretical inquiry that my analysis pursues.

The only peacefully settled dispute over garden land that I collected occurred during my stay. Informants could not remember another dispute of this kind with the same outcome. Significantly, this particular case did not become generally known in Pasikni because the parties solved it by quiet discussion, and informants from wards not involved in the dispute first heard about the incident when I discussed it with them weeks after it occurred. Hence, I must assume that the agreement reached in the following case represents the kind of inter-village settlement that negotiation can produce but that for this reason does not come to public attention and falls easily into oblivion.

No. *11. The Case of the Forgotten "Cordyline" Pig (July
1965)

Place: District of Pasikni

Principals: Pólépóléjok from the village of Angkenteng and
   Wéak of the Kénanghólómó ward in the village of Pasikni

Background: Two generations ago Wéak's grandfather had
   granted usufruct to two neighbors living at the ward of
   Heriekpini. Both men later paid a "Cordyline" pig and thus
   acquired title to the land which they had cultivated. One
   of these men was the maternal grandfather of Pólépóléjok,
   whose father, a native of the distant village of Nisikni, took
   up uxori-patrilocal residence in Pasikni. After his father's
   death Pólépóléjok cultivated the land which his mother had
   inherited from her father, including the plots originally
   owned by Wéak's lineage. In the course of an intra-village
   war Pólépóléjok resettled in Angkenteng (Case 46). The
   other Heriekpini man was the father of Wali, who lives in
   the village of Tuluk-Ikma.

In July 1965, Wéak began to clear Pólépóléjok's land. He
had already tilled several plots when Wali appeared and
demanded that he stop the work, because he feared for his own
land. After a prolonged altercation Wéak went home, where
his father, Pakóak, scolded him for having tried to reappro-
priate the garden. Soon afterward Pólépóléjok came to Pasikni
to defend his rights. A discussion took place inside the
Kénanghólómó men's house. Pólépóléjok first demanded a
pig, but Pakóak persuaded him to accept a compromise:
Pólépóléjok permitted Wéak to plant two of the beds for one
season in exchange for the labor he had already expended on
the rest of the land.

Without doubt the intervention of Wéak's father, who upheld
the validity of Pólépóléjok's claim, facilitated a peaceful agreement by which the owner granted the transgressor usufruct of
part of the land to compensate him for the improvement of a
larger area. I gather from informants' comments on this case
that an aggrieved party tends to seek a settlement in face-to-
face negotiations whenever an infringement of his rights has
caused no actual damage.

Generally, every dispute resulting from an abduction can also
be settled peacefully. Although a man suffers a loss by his wife's

abduction, the collusion of the woman rules out any restitution. However, the deserted husband has a recognized claim against the abductor for a compensatory pig. Informants cited several cases in which the payment of a pig to the deserted husband prevented open hostilities. During my stay in Pasikni I heard of a few abductions in nearby villages where the deserted husband, as in Case *51, had indeed no difficulty in obtaining a pig from the abductor. However, if this case indicates a general pattern, as I believe it does, successful negotiations between the parties depend on the presence of affinal relatives of the deserted husband in the ward of the abductor. Existing hostilities between the village of the husband and that of the abductor prevent negotiations and the husband has no chance to obtain compensation except by clandestine seizure, a particularly dangerous enterprise under these circumstances. But even if no enmity exists with the village of the abductor, a man may still seek to obtain a pig by stealth, a procedure of self-help also used in cases of intra-village abductions when the abductor is living in a garden hamlet at the time (see Case 23).

A man whose wife has been abducted and who cannot obtain a pig from the abductor may still receive compensation if he maintained a satisfactory relationship with his affines prior to the abduction. Especially when the exchange balance favored the woman's agnates, they tend to transfer to him the first 'marriage' pig received from the abductor (Case 48). Typically this procedure follows when the deserted husband and his affines are neighbors, while the abductor lives in another village. Such an arrangement ended Case 45, which, however, informants remembered for another reason: a man retaliated the abduction of his wife and the abductor's subsequent refusal to pay compensation by abducting the wife of a man from the abductor's village and likewise refusing to satisfy her husband's demand for a pig.

A different procedure to obtain pigs by peaceful means requires an unsolicited dance of the husband's kinsmen and other co-residents at the ward of the abductor. Informants said that this method was an "Eastern" custom which villages in the Ovaxak Valley had only recently adopted. In the following case, which occurred during my stay, the woman's kinsmen performed a dance soliciting the payment of pigs from the abductor. Informants agreed that this procedure was a novelty. I describe this case in detail because it exemplifies not only the consequences of a woman's adulterous conduct and the conditions that favor an abduction, but also the choices of procedure in negotiations with the woman's agnates and the difficulties and dangers entailed in a man's attempts to obtain compensation from an abductor living in a distant village.

*No. *12.* The Case of the Intrepid Cuckold (1965–1966)

Place: Villages of Pasikni, Kaliepini, and Hélariki
Principals: Sóxól of the Seraxanpini ward in the village of
    Pasikni and Wanénangéi from the village of Hélariki
Other Participants: Saxavak, Sóxól's wife, and her brother
    Malong from the village of Kaliepini
Background: After Sóxól had acquired his third wife, Saxavak,
    a woman from Kaliepini, by abduction in 1963, his first
    wife, a Pasikni woman, deserted him and married a man in
    another ward of the village. In August 1965 his second wife,
    a woman from the village of Savilivi, died. Saxavak, who
    had been known for her promiscuous sexual conduct before
    Sóxól brought her to Pasikni, continued to have adulterous
    affairs after her remarriage. She was, as informants
    explained, a woman "with an itching vulva."

On December 29, 1965, Wamné, Sóxól's mother's brother's son, who belongs to the Savéapini ward in Pasikni, observed Saxavak engaged in adulterous intercourse in the bush. In the evening he stepped out of his men's house and shouted reprimands at Saxavak, who was in her hut with her husband. He justified his public censure with the fact that he had provided a 'marriage' pig for Sóxól. Afterward Wamné went to Seraxanpini and talked with Sóxól's father in the men's house. He suggested that there be no fighting over the incident, but that Sóxól take care to guard his wife more strictly.

I was very puzzled by this attitude until informants explained Wamné's motivation. Wamné chose this course of action for the same reason that facilitated a meditation in the "Case of the Delinquent Husband"(*4). He was caught in the middle of a potentially serious conflict between two parties with whom he entertained exchange relationships. On one side, his status as maternal kinsmen tied him to Sóxól's exchange cycle. On the other, the adulterer happened to be the half-brother of his deceased elder brother's wife, whose children he had adopted. Therefore, he had a personal interest in a continuation of Sóxól's marriage as well as in perpetuating his relationship with the maternal uncle of his adopted children. Thus, while he warned Sóxól's kinsmen of the possible consequences of Saxavak's misconduct, he also advocated leniency toward the adulterer.

When Wamné had returned to Savéapini, a "big man" of Seraxanpini made a public speech in which he warned several young, still childless women married to Seraxanpini men to avoid adulterous encounters. Lamenting about a recent war over such an affair (Case *50), he denounced the prospect of another war. "We don't want to fight battles for what you might do. We still have arrows stuck in our bodies. That war has depleted our stock of pigs." Sóxól did not beat his wife for fear that she might run away to her married elder sister in the village of Hélariki, as she had done in the past after a beating. But he no longer ate the food she prepared.

Three weeks after the incident, on January 20, 1966, Saxavak deserted Sóxól. She left in the company of Wanénangéi from Hélariki, who had come to Pasikni to see trading partners at the Womikma ward two days before and with whom she had had an affair during past visits to his village.

Every day from January 21 to 25, Sóxól went to Kaliepini hoping that his wife might return to her kinsmen there. On January 24, Malong, Saxavak's elder brother, traveled to Hélariki to find out what his sister's plans were. People told him that Wanénangéi intended to keep Saxavak and had left with her for a distant hamlet. Malong's attempt to obtain a pig from Wanénangéi's kinsmen failed. On January 25, the Womikma men, who felt uneasy about the fact that they had housed the abductor of a local woman, discussed with other men's houses how they could get a pig for Sóxól from Saxavak's kinsmen. In the evening a Womikma "big man" announced their plan in a public speech. Referring to a recent inter-village conflict (Case *41), he urged the men's houses to quit being angry with one another and render support to "a man from our village" whose wife had been abducted.

This intervention of the Womikma house group once more exemplifies two important aspects of Jalé conflict management, the Jalé notion of absolute liability and the interaction of conflicts on different structural levels. Although Wanénangéi's hosts were not responsible for Saxavak's abduction, they realized that Sóxól and his kinsmen would ultimately blame them for their guest's offense and probably seek to obtain compensation by seizing one of their pigs. The possibility of such retaliation reflects the constant threat that the failure to settle an inter-village dispute will deflect the aggrieved party's effort to obtain redress upon neighbors, whom the doctrine of effective action will then implicate in the conflict. By their spontaneous show of support for Sóxól the Womikma men not only dissociated themselves from their troublesome trading partner but also expressed their determination to side with their neighbor in his quest for redress. This quest was particularly difficult, because many families who had been driven from their homes in the

21   A party of armed Pasikni men on the way to another village to negotiate compensation for an abducted woman

village of Savilivi in a recent war with Pasikni had found refuge in villages located near Kaliepini (see Case *50).

Early next morning about seventy Pasikni men from all wards except Kénanghólómó went to Kaliepini. The Kénanghólómó group refused to participate because they still held a grudge against Seraxanpini stemming from the recent inter-ward dispute. The party stopped at a distance of two hundred yards from the village.

Hesum, a "big man" from the Longkopini ward who had sponsored Sóxól's initiation, addressed Malong: "You, Malong, can go where your 'daughter' Saxavak now stays and get a pig. We cannot do that [because of the recent inter-village war (Case *50)]. Therefore, come to us and bring a pig of yours. If she [Saxavak] had gone to Nisikni, Sangkalpunu, Kévéangken, Waléi, Pinii, Pimtok, or Wanjok, we could have gone ourselves. To Hélariki we don't go, because enemies will cross our path."

Malong replied: "Saxavak did not come to me; she went to Hélariki. Her [new] husband, taking her along, did not come here either when he went home. I have no pig. For the pig that you [Sóxól] got as your sister's 'marriage' pig and then gave to me, I furnished a pig for your [recent] curing ceremony, when you lay ill. I, your brother-in-law, have remained with my lips closed [i.e., did not even eat your pig] since I left if for that injured man [his agnatic cousin who was seriously wounded in a battle with Seraxanpini (see Case *49)]. You come now and sit on my shoulders, on my shoulders I am going to get you there" [to Hélariki, implying that he could provide safe escort for Sóxól and his supporters].

Sóxól said: "Saxavak, who went to Hélariki, was forbidden [to leave again] by her elder sister. Because this woman did not say 'go back' but made her stay, he [Malong] should come to me and bring a pig from her. I have come to let you [Malong] know this."

The dispute lasted for about half an hour. Hesum and other Pasikni men, notably Wamné, repeated over and over again their demands for an immediate delivery of a pig. They cited past abductions of women married in Pasikni by men from Kaliepini and other villages in that district who had refused to pay the customary compensation. Malong reiterated that he had no pig but was ready to accompany the Pasikni men to Hélariki.

This phase of the conflict introduced a new idea into the negotiations. After Malong had repudiated Sóxól's claim for a pig on account of the even balance in their transactions prior to Saxavak's abduction, Sóxól blamed her sister for the break-up of his marriage. Rather than exonerating Malong, this complaint simply projected a different reason for his responsibility in accordance with the principle of joint liability of agnates.

When a rumor reached Pasikni the following day that people from Hélariki had brought a pig to Kaliepini, Sóxól, accompanied by his father and a few other Seraxanpini men, again visited Malong to ask for a pig. The rumor, however, was false, and they returned to Pasikni without a pig. Ignoring repeated admonitions of his co-residents not to go to Kaliepini alone, Sóxól visited Malong almost every day. In early February he even spent a week with a friend in Angkenteng, a village near Pasikni, to escape the constant complaints about his trips into dangerous territory. On Februay 14, he left Pasikni and took up residence with Malong. In the meantime he had cut off part of his left ear when he noticed that a banana shoot which Saxavak had planted had begun to sprout.

Neighbors commented on Sóxól's departure with a mixture of amusement and derision. Though they understood that Sóxól did not want to sever the good exchange relationship with his brother-in-law, they ridiculed his grief over the loss of a notoriously adulterous woman. They believed that he disregarded the danger of being killed "because his heart was hit and he threw it away." Sóxól did things that were still stranger. He not only collected most of the material for Malong's mother's new hut but even brought this woman to Pasikni and let her harvest from his village gardens. The Pasikni people talked incredulously about this demonstration of affinal devotion.

On March 11, Malong, accompanied by a small party of Kaliepini men, traveled to Hélariki, where he succeeded in persuading his sister to come back. In Kaliepini, Saxavak stayed overnight with one of her sisters. The following morning she refused to accompany Sóxól to the gardens under some pretext. Shortly after he came back, she sneaked out of the village and returned to Hélariki. Informants said that

Saxavak expected Sóxól to bring a pig for her kinsmen, but
they also saw her departure as an expression of dislike for
Sóxól, since Wanénangéi had so far not given a pig for her
at all.

Sóxól now asked Malong and his co-residents to get him a
pig through a dance. On March 13, most men from Kaliepini
and many from neighboring villages danced in Hélariki.
Wanénangéi presented a big live pig to Malong, who later
gave it to Sóxól, and two other men cooked a pig for him.
Following Sóxól's request, Malong's sister's husband, who
lived in Kaliepini, distributed the meat of one of these animals
among the dancers. The other pig was appropriated as a
"guilt" pig by a man from the village of Kéltémó whose father
had died a few years before from an injury suffered in an
inter-village war caused by a Kaliepini man (Case 46).

Sóxól had planned to accompany the dancers to Hélariki. It
turned out, however, that his disregard of his kinsmen's
warnings had indeed put him in great danger. During a
practice dance en route, some of the refugees from the recent
war against Pasikni who were living in that area (Case *50)
prepared an ambush attack on Sóxól to revenge their slain
kinsmen. But one member of the enemy lineage "of the
arrow's stem" signaled Sóxól to leave. When Sóxól ran away,
a few men from the village of Toxong, located near Kaliepini,
followed him. Led by the husband of Sóxól's mother's sib
sister, a Seraxanpini woman, they escorted him to their men's
house. Sóxól stayed there until the next day and returned to
Pasikni with the pig that Malong had brought him in the
morning.

The intervention of a man to save an enemy's life may appear a
peculiar move in view of the Jalé people's reliance on revenge
to requite a killing. However, the predicament of war refugees
explains this action. Having been forced to leave their homes,
these men depend entirely upon the generosity of their hosts.
Furthermore, they have had to give away most if not all their pigs
to their allies and often still remain indebted for a long time.
Consequently, their ability to rally support for a new round of
battles has been greatly impaired. A revenge killing under these
circumstances jeopardizes their safety to an extraordinary degree.
The threat of further violence thus deters the otherwise inevitable resumption of warfare.

The fact that co-residents and supporters from neighboring wards always accompany a deserted husband when he demands compensation from the abductor shows the inherent danger of inter-village negotiations for such payments. If the confrontation leads to a skirmish in which someone suffers an injury, the conflict tends to escalate into warfare (see Cases 44, 46, and 48). In one case an abduction led to the catastrophic devastation of two Pasikni wards after divided alliances turned inter-village hostilities into a war between neighboring wards.

While the payment of a pig can settle disputes over abductions, the Jalé have no institutionalized procedures that deal peacefully with adultery. Since every case of adultery may lead to war, it concerns not only the woman's husband but his whole men's house group as well. The public warning of the young, childless women to beware of extramarital adventures in the "Case of the Intrepid Cuckold" reveals how serious a threat to peace the Jalé view any adultery to be. In fact, two wars which occurred during my stay followed from an attack upon adulterers (Cases *50 and *51). The battles took the lives of several people and forced the defeated wards into exile.

Disputes over pigs that occur among agnates, affines, non-kin co-residents, and between persons belonging to different wards of the same village usually arise from injuries inflicted upon one pig by another, seizures of a pig from the wrong man, or forceful appropriation of outstanding pig debts. Wanton pig thefts and clandestine retaliation for a prior offense like abduction occur more frequently between villages. A comparison of the inter-village cases available for analysis reveals three factors that largely determine the reaction of the pig's owner: the distance to the offender's village, the degree of relative enmity with that village, and, as always, the support available from his men's house group.

In Case 47, for example, men from the Seraxanpini ward in Pasikni stole a pig in the neighboring village of Klengleng. Because emigrants from Pasikni had established that settlement and because the two villages had always maintained amicable relations, the owner of the stolen pig and his co-residents ventured to claim restitution. They managed to persuade the man who had actually killed the animal to give them an "ear" pig—as the Jalé call this form of restitution. However, because the "ear" pig was not of high enough quality to satisfy their demand, they seized another pig that belonged to a war refugee who lived at Seraxanpini and whose son had participated in the consumption of the stolen animal. Being a "lone man," without kinsmen at the ward of his residence, and because his own son had benefited from the theft, he received no support from the Seraxanpini group and had to resign himself to the loss.

Seizure of a restitutory pig constitutes also the only way to obtain redress if unresolved enmities between the parties prevent the owner of the stolen pig from claiming compensation through negotiation. Besides, the uncertain outcome of any inter-village confrontation is a recognized reason for dispensing with negotiations for an "ear" pig. In cases of inter-ward pig seizures an aggrieved party will at least attempt to get a pig from the person responsible for the trouble or from his agnates, but in similar acts of retaliation between villages anyone's pig may be

22   After a decisive battle Pasikni warriors have invaded the village of Savilivi and raid the deserted huts of their enemies. (Case *50)

stolen from the foraging areas. Consequently, anyone who observes the theft of a pig spontaneously initiates action to retrieve the animal before the raiders have reached their own village. A successful seizure always creates an inter-ward dispute if the pig belongs to a person from a ward other than that of the man responsible for the original trouble. The events of the following case document the diverse procedures taken under different circumstances to deal with pig seizures.

No. 13. The Case of the "Ear" Pig Raids (1961)

Place: The districts of Waléi and Pasikni
Principals: Molép from the village of Waléi and a lineage
   from the Seleriek ward in the village of Savilivi
Background: The war described in the "Case of the Negligent
   Heir"(9) forced Méléirek, the "man of the arrow's stem,"
   to leave his home village of Savilivi. Together with his
   daughter's husband, Molép, he settled in the village of
   Waléi. The kinsmen of two of his slain supporters, a father
   and his son from the Savilivi ward of Seleriek, never
   received the "guilt" pig that Méléirek owed them. In this
   war the Longkopini ward in the village of Pasikni had
   helped the Seleriek group.

One day some Seleriek people invited a few young Longkopini men to a picnic in their garden hamlet, which lay in the vicinity of Waléi. Gathering firewood, a kinsman of the two victims mentioned above discovered a sow with several piglets which he knew belonged to Molép. Since he did not dare to cook the pigs at the hamlet, he suggested to his guests that they take them to Pasikni instead. The Longkopini men succeeded in leashing the sow, after having assuaged it with sweet potatoes, and managed to lead it to Pasikni, the piglets following behind. Although some elders at Longkopini and other Pasikni wards disapproved of the magnitude of the loot, all pigs were cooked the same evening. The meat was shared with all men's houses in the village and several pieces were delivered to Seleriek in Savilivi.

By the next morning Molép had learned the identity of the raiders. He went to the Seleriek hamlet with a small group of supporters and seized a pig belonging to Ngalóló from the Savilivi ward of Hiktóxéi, who had just come to the hamlet to have his sow impregnated. Ngalóló, accompanied by two

other men, sought redress in Pasikni, where they captured
two pigs from the foraging area which belonged to a man from
the Womikma ward. They were observed, and a pursuit party
of Pasikni men succeeded in recapturing the pigs.

Later the same day, another raiding party seized a pig
belonging to a man from the Halepini ward and delivered it
to Ngalóló. When the news reached Pasikni, a large group of
men from several wards went to Savilivi. Their demands for
restitution precipitated a brief skirmish, but nobody was
injured. The Halepini men now demanded a pig from
Longkopini. The following day Kepolok, an elder brother of
one of the young men who had participated in the seizure of
Molép's pigs, brought an "ear" pig to Ngalóló. He returned
to Pasikni with the Halepini pig, which he handed back to its
owner, who happened to be the father-in-law of one of
Kepolok's agnatic cousins. The latter's brother, who had also
helped to capture Molép's pigs, later gave a pig to Kepolok,
whose intervention had settled the dispute with their common
affine at Halepini.

This case shows the effect of affinal bonds on the course of
inter-village conflicts. The chain of retaliatory seizures broke
up when the conflict had engulfed an affine of the party who had
started the trouble. Now that the conflict had jeopardized their
exchange relationship, restitution prevented further reprisals.
As long as such reprisals take the form of pig seizures between
neighboring villages, the parties need not resort to warfare
provided the raiders escape unharmed and a subsequent
confrontation does not result in bodily injury.

It appears that in cases involving pig debts the Jalé rely on
redress through pig seizure only if they see a reasonable chance
to retaliate in such a way. Since the danger of getting caught
with pigs taken in clandestine reprisal actions increases with the
distance between the parties' villages, a man has hardly a chance
to obtain redress should someone from a faraway village have
succeeded in seizing his pig. Therefore, in these circumstances
the offender may be killed if he later ventures into the vicinity of
the village of the aggrieved party (see Case *49).

In conjunction with its pre-history as described in the "Case
of the Negligent Heir," the "Case of the 'Ear' Pig Raids" also

reveals several features that have already emerged as the
principal determinants of Jalé conflict management. Every dispute
that cannot be settled by direct or mediated negotiation may
lead to forceful retaliation. This stage has two consequences. On
the one hand, it creates opposing factions composed of lineages,
whole men's houses, or villages, depending upon the territorial
range over which the hostility extends. These alliances enhance
the solidarity of the groups involved and may mitigate current
disputes among their members. On the other hand, any
vengeance suffered by supporters creates a new conflict between
the party responsible for the hostilities and those of his allies
who fell victim to enemy revenge. This situation may then lead
to a series of reprisals and counter-reprisals which rupture
existing alliances and realign former opponents.

   The same process occurs on every structural level. Consequently, as I have explained earlier, many disputes that I have
recorded as "cases" represent merely a distinct phase in the
history of a conflict. The "Case of the Thwarted Sib Brother"(*6)
is an example of an intra-ward dispute that arose in the context
of an inter-village war that, in turn, had developed from a
quarrel between agnates. Similarly, the inter-ward dispute
described in the "Case of the Stubborn Gardener"(*8) can be
understood only as a by-product of a previous inter-village war.
Thus, when a conflict has extended beyond the locality of the
two parties, every forceful retaliation against non-kin neighbors
of the "man of the arrow's stem" generates new hostilities
within smaller territorial ranges (see Figure 12).

   To break this vicious circle and thereby contain the escalation
of violence the Jalé seek to follow the strategy of minimal
risk that the "Case of the Quarrelsome Boys"(10) elucidated:
they revenge injury or death of one of their kinsmen or co-
residents by killing a foreigner living with their enemies. An
immigrant is more vulnerable to violent retaliation than
autochthonous residents because his hosts are generally more
reluctant to avenge his death. They cannot expect any compensation for possible injury or rely upon the support of neighboring
wards if their revenge precipitates a war. In fact, in cases where
an immigrant is himself the "man of the arrow's stem," he

and/or members of his family may be slain in revenge with impunity by the kinsmen of a person for whose death he is responsible. The following story gives an example of this kind of intra-village killing. It also describes an exceptional procedure that brought an inter-village war to a peaceful end.

*No. *14.* The Case of the Pilfered Crops (1964–1966)

Place: Villages of Kévéangken and Nisikni
Principals: Sangóvéng from the village of Kévéangken and
   several villagers from Nisikni
Other Participants: Saxal and Sómpé, two brothers whose
   matrilateral cousin, Woru, was killed in battle.

In November 1964, people from Kévéangken plundered Nisikni gardens located adjacent to their own village territory. Seeking redress, several Nisikni men went to Kévéangken and shot two pigs in the foraging area. A band of Kévéangken men pursued them and recaptured one of the pigs, which the fugitives had to leave behind. In the skirmish one man from Kévéangken suffered fatal injuries. The following morning an arrow carrying skin from the dead man's body was found in front of a Nisikni men's house, signaling the enemy's determination to avenge the death. A prolonged war ensued in which contingents from the neighboring villages of Sangkal-punu and Waléi fought on either side. Four men were killed: one Nisikni man, Woru from Waléi fighting on the Nisikni side, and two more men from Kévéangken. The last battles occurred toward the end of February 1965.
   The first to pilfer crops in the Nisikni gardens were a man named Sangóvéng and his wife. Being the "man of the arrow's stem" and having no agnates in Kévéangken, Sangóvéng feared the wrath of his own neighbors and fled to the distant

12 Extension and repercussion of conflicts

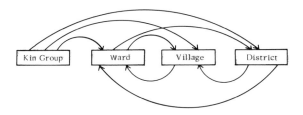

village of Wanjok. Several months later one victim's kinsmen indeed killed his wife when she returned to Kévéangken for a visit.

Particular circumstances facilitiated the revenge of Woru's death a year after the last battles. Two sons of Woru's mother's sister, Saxal and Sómpé, were living with their maternal kinsmen in Kévéangken. One of the latter had taken care of Sangóvéng's fourteen-year-old son and his little sister. On March 14, 1966, Sómpé moved his family to Waléi, where they were put up by Kaltong, Woru's younger brother. The following day he enticed Sangóvéng's daughter to accompany him to the gardens. At the Saruk River, which separates the districts of Waléi and Kévéangken, he shot her dead and threw the body into the river. On March 16—the Kévéangken people still did not know of the girl's fate—Sómpé asked her brother to help him harvest sweet potatoes. When they reached the bottom of the Saruk ravine, Sómpé severed the boy's head with his steel axe. [Informants emphasized the unconventional technique of the killing.] After hiding the body in a thicket, he went to Waléi and presented the victim to Kaltong, with these words: "The Hibiscus leaves I have put some place—are you going to eat them, or don't you want?"

Kaltong understood the message and replied: "I have been thinking of eating lizards, I have been thinking of eating frogs. I have been thinking of eating birds, I have been thinking of eating insects, I have been thinking of eating worms [i.e., tabued food for men]. As I have been thinking this, I am just going to eat!"

In the evening Kaltong, with the help of other men, carried the boy's body to the village and cooked it, spicing the meat, as informants who participated in the preparations repeatedly told me, "with the good salt you gave their wives when they came to trade vegetables." Kaltong and his kinsmen ate one leg and took the remainder of the meat to Nisikni in the early night hours.

After the party had reached the village and deposited the load in front of the men's house which had lost a member in the war, Kaltong addressed the group inside: "You, which son of yours is in Kévéangken? You, which daughter of yours is in Kévéangken? You, which elder sibling of yours is in Kévéangken? You, which younger sibling of yours is in Kévéangken? You, which mother's brother of yours is in Kévéangken? You, which father's sisters of yours is in

Kévéangken? You, which mother's sister of yours is in
Kévéangken?"
   A few additional cryptonymic phrases convinced the listen-
ing men that Kaltong had brought them the body of an enemy.
   In accepting the meat with the customary ceremonial
expressions of appreciation, a kinsman of the slain Nisikni
warrior replied: "The 'fathers' of Aphéra who settled in
Pasikni also ate one of their own people in lieu of a 'lung'
pig [condolence gift] before they went to Pasikni. I am a man
from Nisikni, a man who did this, I am a man of tradition."
   Three days after the killing of the boy, a group of Nisikni
men descended halfway toward Kévéangken and performed
a peace dance. Accepting their proposal to end hostilities, a
group of men from Kévéangken approached. The parties
assured each other that they had "laid down the arrows for
good" and promised mutual invitations to dances consoli-
dating the peace.

The quoted texts reflect the Jalé people's attitude toward
anthropophagy. While they talk freely about details of the
butchering and cooking process, they do not openly talk about
the matter when they present or accept a body. Instead their
speeches contain contextual clues and "hidden talk" that connote
the purpose of the transaction. Although they do not conceptualize anthropophagous revenge as a sacred act, their verbal
camouflage seems to betray some sort of awe. Be that as it may
—and I certainly have not fathomed their feelings about this
culinary predilection—the Jalé make fine discriminations between "edible" and "nonedible" people. Generally, as I have
mentioned, they draw a line between known people and those
"whose face is not known." But this ambiguous distinction is
only an ideal that roughly corresponds to geographic distance.
Traditional enmities make this line rather flexible, as the last
quoted speech fragment elucidates. The speaker referred to a
war that took place two generations ago, in which a lineage from
Nisikni, the agnates of the man named Aphéra, was forced to
flee to the village of Pinii. Before these people later settled in
Pasikni, they had eaten a man from their home village referred
to as "one of their own people." Since the founders of the villages of Kévéangken and Nisikni came from one original settle-

ment, in accepting the body of a Kévéangken boy from the Waléi men, the Nisikni speaker appropriately cited this case of anthropophagous vengeance against "their own people" as a precedent when he answered Kaltong's suggestion that nothing should prevent them from eating the body in the absence of any relatives in Kévéangken.

Informants agreed that fear of retaliatory cannibalism prompted the Nisikni people's hasty peace offer. They attributed its ready acceptance by the Kévéangken people to their reluctance to seek revenge for a "lone kid."

Just as an inter-village war may result in hostilities between wards of the same village, so can an inter-regional war lead to fighting between villages of the same region. In Case *53, for example, the village of Hompokéi, located in the Jaxólé Valley, had overtly remained neutral in a war between the Jaxólé and Sévé Valley regions. One day some men from Hompokéi procured a portion of a man from the Jaxólé Valley village of Savilivi, who was killed on Sévé territory, and ate it in revenge for the slaying of a relative in a past war with Savilivi. A strafing raid then destroyed Hompokéi, whose inhabitants fled to the Sévé Valley.

In another case (43), economic interests motivated Pasikni people to seek revenge for the killing by men from the nearby village of Kaliepini of visiting trading partners from the Helók Valley south of the Central Range, where they traditionally cut a lot of ratan. In this case, too, the avengers chose as their victim a foreigner living with their opponents. The reasons for refraining from a revenge killing of an autochthonous fellow villager in inter-ward conflicts and for exacting inter-village revenge for the slaying of foreign visitors appear to be similar. Inter-ward blood revenge not only jeopardizes the exchange relationships between the opposing men's houses but also entails the danger of a devastating war within the village, and the violent death of visiting trading partners may terminate all trade with the victim's region. Therefore, the desire to maintain an advantageous economic position largely determines the Jalé strategy of retaliation in both situations.

The cases discussed in this chapter reveal certain patterns of conflict management between strangers. Inter-village disputes, like any trouble among relatives or between neighboring wards, start with a grievance between two individuals or lineages. The absence of judicial authorities in Jalé society leaves self-help as the only method of gaining redress. Disputes over garden land, abductions, and sometimes even over pig seizures can be resolved by negotiation, especially if both parties participate in the same exchange cycle. Wholesale pillage of garden produce, adultery, bodily injury, and killing usually result in forceful retaliation and often precipitate a war. Whether or not an aggrieved party seeks a settlement through negotiation depends entirely on how that party perceives the risk involved in the confrontation. Generally, the greater the residential distance between the opponents and the greater the degree of relative enmity already existing between their villages, the greater is the risk of a violent encounter.

An important difference between inter-ward and inter-village hostilities is the range of potential victims. While disputes among neighbors tend to confine acts of retaliation to attacks on the principals and their kin groups, revenge against people from other villages frequently jeopardizes persons who are not involved in the conflict. Indiscriminate vengeance, in turn, creates new grievances and thus militates against the formation of enduring alliances between villages and perpetuates the political fragmentation of local communities. Consequently, apart from isolated links between affined lineages, only warfare against another region imposes temporarily effective constraints upon intra-regional conflicts, in the same way as inter-village enmities mitigate hostility among neighbors. This means that in the absence of political integration the chances of managing disputes by negotiation diminish with a decrease in routine contacts between the parties.

The Jalé recognize these implications of territorial separation and conceive of conflicts with villages in other regions solely in terms of war. Their idea of eating people "whose face is not known" supports the view that inter-regional *soli* warfare constitutes a distinct method of conflict management. Although anthropophagic vengeance has occurred in the context of intra-regional hostilities, in each instance—including the "Case of the Pilfered Crops"—the consumption of enemy bodies represented an exceptional revenge action. Inter-regional wars, however, feature cannibalism as a regular part of the conflict.

During the lifetime of the oldest men in Pasikni their village participated in only one inter-regional war (Case *53). This war, between the Jaxólé and Sévé Valleys, had already lasted for a generation when I arrived in the Jalémó. A comparison of this conflict with cases of intra-regional warfare elucidates the main aspects of inter-regional conflict among the Jalé. Although several villages of a region form an alliance and may even undertake joint revenge expeditions, the lack of political integration precludes coordinated procedures to resolve the conflict. While hostilities among neighbors and between villages of one region can be terminated by the original parties to the conflict if they have compensated their supporters for injuries and deaths sustained, the peaceful settlement of a *soli* war is a more difficult matter. The great distance between allied villages and the con-

23 Men from the allied village of Tengkeléi dance at the Seraxanpini ward in Pasikni to celebrate their victory over Savilivi. (Case *50)

comitant paucity of affinal links between their inhabitants reduce
the chances that people can obtain adequate indemnity from the
"men of the arrow's stem" and their men's house groups.
Furthermore, the longer a *soli* war lasts and the more people
from different villages lose their lives, the weaker become the
bonds of allegiance between the principals and the groups
that subsequently get involved in the hostilities. Consequently,
as the history of the great war between the Sévé and Jaxólé
Valleys shows, the kinsmen of victims from allied villages may
not agree to a peace treaty between the parties to the original
dispute.

I think it is significant that this war approached a settlement
when a rumor spread fear of an imminent attack by armed troops
of the national government and incriminated them with wanton
killings and destruction. In ignorance of their citizenship in a
nation that employs special agents of political control, the Jalé
people assumed that they were threatened by foreign invaders.
For the first time in their history people living in different regions

24   Pasikni men dancing in Tengkeléi a few weeks later

realized a common predicament: the potential intervention of an
outside power. This situation gave a new dimension to the
principle that mitigates conflicts among two opposing parties
if a common enemy puts both in equal jeopardy. The future pacification of the Jalémó will undoubtedly change many of the
indigenous processes of Jalé conflict management.

VII Conclusion: Theoretical Implications

My analysis of conflict management among the Jalé discovered that in their society very few and very ineffective methods exist to transform a dyadic confrontation into a triadic relationship which could secure a settlement by the intervention of the third party. Instead, the conditions that restrain an aggrieved party from seeking redress by retaliation depend entirely upon common interests of the opponents in a particular situation: (1) in conflicts among agnates and non-kin co-residents, the need to maintain the solidarity of a men's house group for the protection of its common political and economic interests; (2) in conflicts between spouses and affines, their mutual interest in the preservation of exchange relationships; and (3) in conflicts between wards or neighboring villages, the necessity for these local groups to form military alliances against an enemy from wider territories, other villages or regions. In addition, the liability of a principal and his agnates to compensate their supporters for damages or injuries suffered in the course of any conflict may dampen a party's desire for revenge. However, although kinship and residence provide certain built-in brakes that deter an escalation of disputes, these constraints are not strong enough to prevent forceful retaliation in any particular conflict. Especially if the parties belong to different villages, disputes often escalate into warfare.

Ethnographers have found similar patterns of conflict management throughout the New Guinea Highlands.[1] Why disputes in these societies tend to lead to war has remained an unsolved question. Although it has long been known that some societies handle conflict in conspicuously violent confrontations while others generally settle their disputes through peaceful procedures, anthropologists have only recently tried to explain this difference with more subtlety than Benedict's (1934) conjectural

4 Location of Peoples in Western Melanesia

WESTERN MELANESIA

0 20 40 60 80 100   150   200 MILES

1	Mejprat–Ajamaru Lake	
2	Biak Island	
3	Waropen	
4	Kaowerawédj	
5	Sarmi–Western Hinterland	
6	Tor	
7	Nimboran	
8	Sentani	
9	Kamoro–Mimika River	
10	Asmat	
11	Muju	
12	Jaqai–Mappi River	
13	Frederik-Hendrik Island	
14	Marind-anim	
15	Je-nan	
16	Kapauku (Ekari)	
17a	Dani–Swart Valley	
17b	Dani–Hablifuri Valley	
17c	Dani–Balim Valley	
18	Jalé	
19a	Ok–Star Mountains	
19b	Ok–Telefomin	
20	Duna	
21	Ipili	
22	Huli	
23	Mendi	
24	Kutubu	
25	Pole	
26	Kewa	
27	Enga	

28	Kyaka
29	Gawigl (Kaugel)
30	Mbowamb (Melpa)
31	Karam
32	Maring
33	Narak (Manga)
34	Kuma–Wahgi Valley
35	Chimbu (Kuman)
36	Gende
37	Gururumba
38	Siane
39	Gahuku-Gama
40	Benabena
41	Gadsup
42	Tairora
43	Usurufa
44	Jate
45	Kamano
46	Kukukuku
47	Fore
48	Gimi
49	Daribi (Mikaru)
50	Wiru
51	Keraki
52	Kiwai
53	Koriki–Purari River
54	Elema
55	Mafulu
56	Orokaiva
57	Motu

58	Mailu
59	Massim, Southern
60	Busuma–Huon Gulf
61	Wantoat
62	Ngaing–Rai Coast
63	Garia
64	Bánaro
65	Tangu
66	Mundugumor
67	Iatmül
68	Tchambuli–Chambri Lake
69	Kwoma
70	Abelam, Northern
71	Arapesh, Mountain
72	Boikin
73	Wogeo–Schouten Islands
74	Manam Island
75	Manus Island
76	Lesu
77	Tanga
78	Pala
79	Tolai
80	Baining
81	Maenge
82	Lakalai
83	Trobriand Islands
84	Goodenough Island
85	Dobuans
86	Rossel Island

Note: This list includes only those peoples whom ethnographers have studied. Their identification in the literature is very haphazard, deriving from geographic features or from linguistic traits, or from names by which peoples refer to themselves or from names that neighboring peoples use for them. Consequently, the names in this list may refer to a single village or a small island, a language area, or a "tribe," depending upon their ethnographers' onomastic preferences. Numbers 1 to 15 indicate peoples living in Irian Jaya, and numbers 16 to 86 indicate peoples in the Territories of Papua and New Guinea. Numbers 16 to 50 belong to peoples in the New Guinea Highlands.

distinction between a "Dionysian" and an "Apollonian" charac-
ter, for example, could achieve.

It is this problem that I will now pursue in a comparative
framework by examining the validity of five hypotheses for an
understanding of Jalé conflict behavior. The first hypothesis
postulates an ecological causation of armed conflicts. The second
attributes peaceful procedures of settling disputes to a type of
social structure that creates cross-cutting group affiliations. The
third hypothesis relates coercive methods of conflict management
to the formation of localized power groups. The fourth links the
absence of effective third-party institutions to a factional community organization. The fifth hypothesis deduces a propensity to resort to violence from certain patterns of socialization.

Since my conclusions differ from the views of anthropologists
who have cited ecological causes for the prevalence of warfare
in New Guinea, I begin with an examination of their ideas.
Meggitt (1965), Rappaport (1967), and Vayda (1971) believe
that among the Enga and Maring people, who live in the Highlands of East New Guinea, land shortage forced local groups to
conquer their neighbors' gardens. While I do not deny that
conflicting interests in land, especially in valleys without surplus
arable ground, may result in war, these writers' published
evidence fails to support their claim that land shortage itself
drove the Enga and Maring to seek new resources by conquest.
Meggitt (1965) derives his conclusion in part from a typological
tabulation of forty-one major fights between Enga clans over a
period of thirty years. But his data only show that about twice
as many fights occurred over "encroachment on land" as over
"theft of pigs" and "homicide." Since many fights, especially
those over land, favor the formation of military alliances of
neighboring groups, the relative frequencies of recorded conflicts may simply evince differences in their extent and intensity.[2]
My own critique of the reliability of Jalé memory cases for
quantitative comparisons leads me to suspect that these frequencies merely reflect a skewed sample, if not also the
ethnographer's special interest in the agronomic relationship
between Enga social structure, residence patterns, and land
tenure.

Rappaport's theory appears similarly tenuous. Writing about remembered cases of armed conflict among the Maring, he reasonably distinguishes between "proximate" and "underlying" causes of warfare. But then, in reviewing a war of "thirty to forty years ago," he sees land shortage as the real cause of conflict because "the proximate cause of the fight [bodily injury retaliating a theft of sugar cane] should have been easily resolved since it did not result in homicide" (1967: 115). But why should an intrusion of one group into the territory of its defeated enemy prove that the war was fought over land? And how can an ethnographer know that a dispute which happened many years before his study could have been easily resolved? There are numerous legal and political factors that influence the mode and relative success of settling disputes in Maring society, and old men's reminiscences hardly warrant Rappaport's inference.

Nevertheless, Rappaport proceeds to design something like an irritability model of conflict to explain how fights, triggered by population pressure, have led to a redistribution of people over available land. A mechanical concept of human behavior gives this model an odd simplicity:

> If twenty men, for example, each own one pig and have one garden, there are 400 possibilities for pigs to cause disputes between men by damaging gardens. If the number of men is raised to forty, each of which still has one pig and one garden the number of possibilities for disputes has increased to 1,600 other things being equal . . . Sources of irritation thus increase at a greater rate than popualtion size. If population increase were taken to be linear, the increase in some causes of dispute, if not actual dispute, might be taken to be roughly geometric. It might even be possible to find some way to express mathematically an "irritation coefficient" of population size. (1967: 116)

Other things hardly remaining equal during such enormous social and economic changes, this valvular model of demographic regulation makes no sense.[3]

Other New Guinea ethnographers have reached a less rigid but equally doubtful conclusion. Brown and Brookfield, for example, assert that among the Enga and Chimbu "population intensity [is] high enough for land shortage to be counted as an underlying cause [of warfare] and for the occupation of conquered territory to be a common outcome" (1959: 42). But their observations only show that "in Mae Enga as in Chimbu, loss of land was a *frequent result* of defeat in war" (1959: 74, emphasis mine). Indeed, the title of their book on Chimbu agriculture and demography, *Struggle for Land* (1963), is poetic rather than descriptive of constant warfare over a place to live, since "intratribal and intraclan fights, originating in any dispute, including encroachment, *sometimes led to* the acquisition of territory by force" (Brookfield and Brown 1963: 136, emphasis mine).[4]

There is a critical analytical flaw in what I call the "famine theory" of warfare. Its proponents believe that people seek to conquer territory in order to avert starvation. On the other hand they realize that wars result from a failure to settle conflicts—including disputes over cultivation rights—peacefully. Then they look at the observed consequence of a war, exploitation of land abandoned by vanquished neighbors, and declare the effect of the whole process to be its cause.

In short, the available evidence does not prove that an increase in population leads to war. Instead, it only indicates that when disputes escalate into warfare, the winning group may make gardens on land belonging to people who have fled from their settlements. Given the lack of historical records, one cannot know whether or not this change in occupancy represents conquest or temporary usurpation. In Maring society, for example, a particular rite imposes a tabu upon entering enemy territory except in anger. This tabu restricts territorial expansion. Thus, Rappaport reports that in a war between two neighboring groups, the victors were "restrained from reentering [their enemies'] territory by fear of both [their] ancestral spirits . . . who were thought to remain at least for a time on the ground lost by their living descendants, and also by fear of their own ancestral spirits from whom the injunction emanated" (1967: 144). Along with these and other ritual restrictions detailed by Rappaport, the frequent reoccupation of deserted territory by at least part of the defeated group and the apparently provisional status of ritually validated land annexations seem to weaken this author's hypothesis even further.

Even if the Enga and the Maring have fought more wars arising from disputes over land than other New Guinea societies, the frequency and the outcome of warfare in the New Guinea Highlands depend upon the *political* relationships between neighboring groups. For example, although both the Chimbu and the Enga suffer from a relative shortage of land, warfare leading to conquest appears to be much more frequent among the Enga. Kelly (1968), who compared the demography, ecology, and social organization of several Highland populations, could show that this difference relates, in part, to the political consequences of different rules of land tenure in both societies. While the Enga hold their land in corporate, agnatic estates, the Chimbu have a more flexible tenure system which promotes the dispersal of people along matrilineal and affinal lines. This situation creates divided loyalties in times of inter-group conflict and impedes, though does not prevent, the escalation of disputes into war.[5]

But the most convincing argument against the "famine theory" derives from a meticulous study of Maring ecology by the geographer Clarke, who concluded that "although warfare doubtless has recurrently resulted in deaths and caused migration in New Guinea, thereby slowing population growth, its population-limiting function has not been efficient enough to prevent the formation of immense tracts of anthropogenic grasslands" (1971: 192n). Clarke's observations prove, instead, that New Guinea people have responded to an increase in their populations with innovative agricultural techniques that entail a gradual shift from extensive to intensive cultivation. In sum, it appears that most Highland societies do not wage war to conquer resources, and that temporary or permanent exploitation of garden land belonging to defeated enemies occurs as a consequence of warfare precipitated by unresolved conflicts, including quarrels over boundaries.

The probably exaggerated view of killing as a way of life in the New Guinea Highlands[6] nevertheless reflects a general recognition that the cultural institutions which prevent the peaceful resolution of many conflicts are similar throughout the area. The specific aspects of Jalé society that in my view explain this situation are a political organization that prevents the institutionalization of third-party authorities and processes of socialization that engender a man's propensity to seek redress for a wrong by violence. Comparative anthropological studies have accumulated sufficient evidence to explain both the lack of an institutionalized intervention by judicial authorities in Jalé society and the bellicosity in Jalé procedures of conflict resolution. These studies suggest that the lack of a third-party institution and the correlated prevalence of violent self-help to obtain redress result from a combination of interrelated sociological and psychological factors; namely, the absence of cross-cutting group affiliations, the formation of corporate agnatic power groups, the existence of multiple, independent, political units within a local community, and patterns of socialization that develop an aggressive and vindictive personality.[7]

The second hypothesis to be examined here concerns the mitigating effect of divided loyalties. In a now classical study Colson (1953) analyzed the effect of cross-cutting group affiliations on the control of conflict among the Tonga of Zambia, who live in small villages, sometimes compact but more often scattered. An abundance of uncultivated land favors frequent changes in residence and thus villages and districts—a group of neighboring villages—contain people who belong to different exogamous matrilineal clans.[8] All residents of a local community must participate in rituals performed to ensure the productivity of the land. If a person fails in this obligation, his neighbors punish him because the Tonga believe that such neglect invites mystical sanctions endangering the whole community. Kinship determines other obligations. The lineal descendants of an ancestress constitute an effective kin group as long as they assume joint liability for the action of its members and, in turn, a responsibility to protect their interests and avenge their injuries. The group as a whole also provides bridewealth for its members and shares the bridewealth received for its women as well as the right to inherit the estate of its members. Mystical sanctions following offenses such as incest, suicide or attempted suicide, and physical violence against sisters and elders may strike any member of the group through illness or misfortune, but such sanctions can be averted and the group's integrity restored by a peace-making ritual in the context of an ancestral cult.

A person's economic and ritual association with his father's descent group further elaborates the network of cross-cutting affiliations to his matrilineal kin group on the one hand and within his local community on the other. Since marriage rules promote a maximal dispersion of affinal links, a particular marriage establishes a set of relationships between four distinct kin groups that share various rights and obligations created by the union. The resultant interaction of mutually incompatible loyalties in conflict situations produces an "entanglement of claims [that] leads to attempts to seek an equitable settlement in the interests of the public peace which alone enables the groups to perform their obligations one to another and a Tonga to live as a full member of his society" (1953: 210).

Conflicting loyalties also inhibit violent retaliation in societies that combine a rule of patrilineal descent with matrilocal residence. Murphy, who analyzed the relationship between inter-group hostility and social cohesion among the Mundurucú Indians of Brazil, discovered that this structural juxtaposition "made male solidarity on the village and tribal level not only possible but a functional necessity. Conflict had to be rigorously suppressed, for if men became arrayed in overt violence along lines of residential affinity, it would pit patrilineal kin against each other and destroy the very fabric of the kinship structure. And if the combatants aligned themselves according to kinship affiliations, strife could break out within villages and even within households" (1957: 1029–1030). Although Murphy, following Simmel (1908) and his exegete Coser (1956), believes that the Mundurucú kept peace among themselves because aggressive warfare against other tribes could release repressed hostility generated within the society,[9] he obviously recognized that the men's divided loyalties mitigated conflicts between neighbors.

Societies which, like the Ifugao of Luzon, have no form of

political government may settle disputes peacefully by strictly regulated mediation. According to Barton, among the Ifugao the bilateral family is an executive and a judicial body that includes the members of a person's own and his wife's natal families. Consequently, a conflict between the two groups tends "to make it a very complex and difficult problem for a man to decide to which opponent his obligation binds him . . . A man who finds himself in such a position, and who knows that on whichever side he may array himself he will be severely criticized by the other, becomes a strong advocate of compromise and peaceful settlement" (1969: 86). These cross-cutting loyalties facilitate the intervention of a mediator, whose office Barton considered "a whole court, completely equipped, in embryo" (1969: 87).

Divided loyalties inhibit the escalation of conflicts only when people share vital interests both with neighbors of their local community and with members of dispersed kin groups. Therefore, the absence of multiple *group* membership in Jalé society precludes the operation of similar constraints. In Jalémó, ritual and jural responsibilities coincide for the same group of co-resident agnates. Furthermore, since military contingencies largely determine transient alignments of local communities, isolated bonds between affines living in different villages effectively mitigate disputes only among themselves. Consequently, it appears that the theory of conflicting loyalties cannot apply to societies in which the corporate interests and obligations of a residential association remain without counterpart on an inter-community level.

The mitigating effects of conflicting allegiances have been observed in other societies as, for example, among the Bedouins of the Cyrenaica (Peters 1967). Gluckman, who recognized their importance for maintaining social order among the Nuer, has concluded that they secure "the peace in the feud" (1959).

My assumption that in Jalé society the prevalence of coercive methods of conflict management depends upon the formation of localized agnatic descent groups derives from the third hypothesis, which stems from a cross-cultural survey by Thoden van

Velzen and van Wetering. Their research followed up Murphy's hypothesis that matrilocal societies must repress open aggression to ensure their cohesion and continuity. Thoden van Velzen and van Wetering omitted the psychological component of Murphy's model and merely tested the relationship between matrilocality and intra-societal peacefulness with a large sample of unstratified societies.[10] The results of their study not only show a definite correlation between these two variables but also demonstrate that all patrilocal but very few matrilocal societies have "fraternal interest groups." Since these co-resident consanguineal power groups "share primary [especially economic] interests and . . . will attempt, forcefully if necessary, to defend or promote these interests," Thoden van Velzen and van Wetering concluded that "in societies with power groups every act of violence elicits a chain reaction and there is danger of any individual deed of aggression leading to group conflict" (1960: 180).[11]

The social organization of the Jalé, being determined by patrilineal descent and patrilocal residence, provides the conditions that most decisively favor the formation of power groups with a genealogical base. In fact, in its extended form the concept of power group applies to the men's house group as a whole, even if its members belong to several lineages, because all residents share some vital economic and political interests.

While this situation may explain the difficulties of resolving conflicts between villages, it alone does not account for the frequent occurrence of retaliation in disputes between neighboring wards. In this respect, a comparative study by Nader on the relationship between procedures of conflict resolution and community organization in a Muslim village in Lebanon and a Zapotec village in Mexico adds the fourth hypothesis. It supports my assumption that the segmentation of the local community into politically independent units prevents the institutionalization of third-party authorities that could facilitate alternative procedures of dispute settlement. In the Lebanese village a dual division into endogamous factions, lack of an effective local government, and the absence of any associations to which members of both factions belong have prevented the institu-

tionalization of judicial authorities capable of settling inter-
factional disputes on the community level. Since, in contrast, the
Zapotec village has various extra-kin associations, a working
government, and a court that facilitates the resolution of most
intra-community conflicts, Nader hypothesized that "villages
with dual organization are incompatible with village court or
council systems of settling conflict" (1965: 388).

This observation accords with Simmel's classical analysis of
the sociological requisites of the third party.[12] However, the
evidence from my study of conflict in multipartite Jalé villages
suggests a modification of both Nader's hypothesis, and Thoden
van Velzen and van Wetering's hypothesis. I maintain that the
consanguineal power group that studies have established as a
principal determinant of forceful self-help as a method of conflict management in unstratified societies represents only a conspicuous feature of a type of social organization in which small
residential associations constitute autonomous political units that
lack any effective superordinate government.[13] This conceptualization suggests a reformulation of the two hypotheses in order
that they read: political segmentation of local communities into
autonomous factions tends to inhibit an endogenous development
of a triadic system of conflict management.[14]

The correlation between the absence or inefficiency of third-
party authorities and self-help as an institutionalized method
of conflict resolution has been observed in many societies. Even
in industrial nations that have a bureaucratic court system,
conflict in local communities may show the same processes at
work, albeit with reduced prevalence. Brögger's study of a
peasant village in Calabria, southern Italy, provides a good
example. Unless the neighborhood council or a mediator succeeds
in resolving a conflict, an aggrieved party resorts to retaliation,
which commonly leads to counter-revenge. The consequences of
this escalation are similar to those described for the Jalé: "Once
the vendetta is started, the original issue at stake is almost forgotten and through revenge and counter-revenge an increasing
tension is built up between the parties. Unless the conflict is
somehow solved, blood-vengeance may be triggered off . . .
Revenge in some form or another is the sanction on which pub-

lic order rests" (1968: 231). As my hypothesis predicts, the
Calabrese villagers who resort to violent self-help to protect
their interests and to obtain redress have a weak local government; they constitute, as Brögger reports, "a fragmented community with feebly formalized institutions and are filled with
strife and conflict" (1968: 239).

At the beginning of this discussion I asserted that the structural constraints of Jalé social organization not only prevent
the institutionalization of third-party authorities but also—on the
individual level—create the conditions that produce an aggrieved
party's proclivity to resort to aggressive retaliation. This fifth
hypothesis derives from the results of comparative field research
that investigated the relationship between child-training and
personality in communities in Japan, the Philippines, India,
Kenya, Mexico, and New England. B. Whiting compared the
relative frequencies of assault and homicide in these communities
with critical aspects of their socialization practices. Her analysis
of the data derived from a theory which links a marked segre-
gation of men and women with male dominance and institutions
that accentuate the separation of the sexes in a psychodynamic
circle, in which "the separation of the sexes leads to a conflict of
identity in the boy children, to unconscious fear of being
feminine, which leads to 'protest masculinity,' exaggeration of
the difference between men and women, antagonism against and
fear of women, male solidarity, and hence to isolation of women
and very young children" (1965: 137).

This statement obviously applies to Jalé culture. The pervasive
male-female dichotomization reflected in the strict separation
of the sexes in public and ritual life finds its symbolic expression
in myths and its dramatic elaboration in the initiation complex.
In fact, all indices that account for the development of "protest
masculinity" appear in pronounced form in Jalé society. On the
basis of her sample, B. Whiting suggested a set of hypotheses
which, in part, can be summarized in the following proposition:
Societies whose social structure engenders "protest masculinity"
exhibit more violence in their patterns of conflict resolution, with

revenge as a typical form of punishment, than societies that do not engender this syndrome.[15]

Patterns of conflict in Jalémó conform to this prediction. Among the Jalé forceful self-help is, indeed, a common procedure of an aggrieved party to assert his rights. Since every violent retaliation tends to elicit a series of revenge and counter-revenge actions, available procedures to obtain redress frequently do not solve the trouble but confound it. Jalé patterns of warfare reflect a strong emphasis on revenge, for which vengeance rituals provide symbolic reinforcement.

Brögger's observations in Calabrese society further substantiate B. Whiting's research as well as the theory of cross-cutting intra-community ties. Among these peasants, "A man's ability to defend his rights is dependent upon his virility (*putenza*). This is negatively expressed by the derogatory term 'coward' (coglione, a man without testicles), a term which is used of someone who is reluctant to defend his rights . . . To a Calabrese peasant his virility . . . as a guarantee against an infringement on his rights by other men thus has a specific value, and may per se become a theme in a conflict" (1968: 232). Significantly, it is the young man who resorts to violence, while a man with a family tends to settle his disputes through the neighborhood council, since he has become "enmeshed in a system of reciprocal labour services with his neighbors who thus have vested interests in the maintenance of peace" (1968: 233).

I have shown that the initiation complex performs a key function in the structuring of Jalé social organization as well as in the sustenance of the male-female dichotomy experienced by an individual. As such, it implies an analytical link in a model that draws together sociological and psychological factors relating to inter-personal and inter-group conflict in Jalé society. The same conditions that correlate with the political fragmentation of the local community and, by preventing the establishment of third-party authorities, force an aggrieved party to resort to self-help also determine a mode of socialization that makes this procedure an especially violent method of conflict management (see Figure 13).

One may well ask what insights can be gained from an analysis of conflict among a small population in the Highlands of New Guinea for an understanding of those problems that throw whole countries into the turmoil of internal revolt and the atrocious devastations of international warfare. Certainly these conflicts appear to be of a different kind: Angola, Bangladesh, Biafra, Czechoslovakia, Palestine, Ulster, Vietnam, and Watts conjure up images of hostility and destruction quite different in scale from the quarrels among neighbors and the fighting between villages that I observed with the Jalé people. Yet, I believe that the intrinsic similarities are greater than the apparent differences. All warfare—whatever the cause and whether it involves violent confrontations between oppressed minorities and government police forces or battles between national armies

13 Conditions and consequences of Jalé conflict behavior

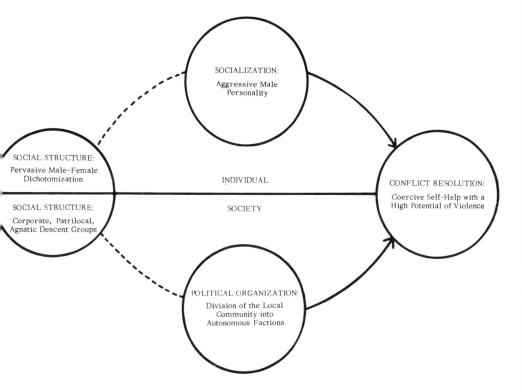

—follows from an absence or breakdown of peaceful means to settle the dispute.

In the past many scholars and politicians have suggested that the salvation ought to come straight from some "world law." The lessons of history expose their theories as pious incantations, notwithstanding the occasional success of the International Court of Justice, the United Nations, and other organizations in the management of international conflicts. Recent research on the matter evinces a more realistic view of the relationship between ideology, power, and conflict control.[16] As Corbett observed, "Though clearly essential to the organization, operation, and progressive development of community, law cannot create it. The indispensable beginning is a sense, however unreasoned and inarticulate, of common interest" (1971: 7). A political reorganization of the world community would require the formation of a supranational government along with the erosion and final elimination of social and economic goals in the name of "national interests," whether they emanate from capitalist or Communist, Christian or Zionist dogmas. Only when nations cease to play the role of Jalé men's house groups, and their "big men" begin to look upon international trade and the control of resources as a cooperative and distributive rather than an exploitative and acquisitive enterprise—in which success means having more pigs than someone else—can effective procedures of mediation and arbitration replace their parochial reliance upon coercion. "If the major concern of the statesmen of the world was to avoid conflict," writes Landheer, "we would already have a functioning international society" (1966: 49).

Unfortunately, good will may not be enough, because the present organization of international relations precludes the existence of effective institutions of conflict management. As Arendt recognized, "the chief reason warfare is still with us is neither a secret death wish of the human species, nor an irrepressible instinct of aggression, nor, finally and more plausibly, the serious economic and social dangers inherent in disarmament, but the simple fact that no substitute for this final arbiter in international affairs has yet appeared on the political scene" (1969: 5).

In an evolutionary perspective the development of a global community and the formation of triadic systems of international conflict management appear less utopian than the political realities of the "nuclear age" may suggest. The creation of regional and continental federations—preferably in the form of the European Economic Community rather than that of NATO—will probably constitute an intermediate phase in this process. However, as Mead has argued so persuasively, "as long as nation-states are the building blocks of international structures, regional organization, and non-localized power blocks must represent the weakness inherent in their component parts . . . The simple federation model is, for this reason, not a feasible alternative" (1968: 223). Neither, in her view, are alliances based upon political and religious ideologies capable of eliminating the threat of war. Workable constitutional arrangements require instead agencies for the administration of specific, interdependent programs such as the protection and management of the world's resources, the establishment and maintenance of communication networks, and the promotion and safeguarding of peaceful procedures to resolve conflicts.

Consequently, one can expect that the hegemony of sovereign nations—no doubt a necessary step in the unification of tribes and petty states in earlier periods and, true enough, often accomplished by wars of subjugation—will dwindle before the emergence of a higher political unity of mankind.

The unreasonable exploitation and corruption of the natural environment that industrial societies have perpetrated in a myopic quest for "progress" and their calamitous pursuit of international security by hoarding armaments that could work a global holocaust, may, fortunately, entail the very conditions that could reduce their arrogance so as to render their common ecological and social environment a healthier and peaceful place. Both historical developments and experimental social psychology[17] have shown the significance of common goals for the reduction of inter-group conflict. When countries define their common predicament as a common enemy, they may set the stage upon which conflicts find their resolution through mediation and arbitration rather than in war.

Appendix A Case Records

The sequence of the following sections follows the order in which they are discussed in Chapters IV to VI. Within each section the cases follow in chronological order. Case histories that contain disputes involving parties from different ranges are cross-referenced in parentheses.

Disputes among agnates: 15, 16, 17, and *18
Disputes in marriage: 19, *20, *21, and *22 (see also *12, *28, *30, *31, and *40)
Disputes among affines: 23, 24, 25, 26, 27, and *28 (see also *3 and *22)
Disputes in the ward: 29, *30, *31 (see also 2, 15, and 16)
Disputes between wards: 32, 33, 34, 35, 36, *37, *38, *39, *40, *41, and *42 (see also 2, 5, *6, 13, *14, 15, 16, 29, and 46)
Disputes between villages: 43, 44, 45, 46, 47, 48, *49, *50, *51, *52, *53 (see also 7, 9, 16, 27, 32, 34, and 35)

No. 15 (ca. 1940). When his father's brother's wife died, Osia of the Avirévam ward in Savilivi was the first of his lineage to cook a pig. Since all relatives who have shared food prepared or handled by a deceased person must participate in a brief purification rite before eating from their pigs, Osia should have asked the dead woman's sons, his agnatic cousins Lóló and Ójók, to attend the occasion. When he failed to invite them, they teamed up with their father's sister's son, Ngóróné of the Seleriek ward in Savilivi, and seized one of Osia's pigs, slaughtered the animal and used the meat for their own rite.

The following day Osia's son, Avésangéi stole a piece of pork which Lóló and Ójók had stored in their house at a garden hamlet and brought it back to his father. Accompanied by a few other men, Osia and Avésangéi then went back to the hamlet to demand restitution. The altercation ended in a skirmish in which Avésangéi was killed. After his funeral, battles raged for several days until Ngóróné decided to end the hostilities by providing the 'wergild' pig that Osia had demanded. When he accepted the pig, Osia declared his son to be avenged, but he moved to the neighboring ward of Ómpantopini and never terminated his avoidance relationship with Lóló and Ójók.

Informants explained that neither Osia nor his cousins could rely on unfailing support by local men's houses since their lineage had immigrated to Savilivi from the Helók Valley, south of the Central Range. Apart from a cultural norm that defines blood revenge among agnates as an odious offense, this situation certainly influenced Osia's decision to accept indemnification.

No. 16 (1959–1964). In 1959 Lóló of the Womikma ward in Pasikni lived at a homestead away from the village together with his third wife, Óngkómen. Nearby, at the Suaxéi hamlet, lived his sons by his deceased first wife, Wielu, Talala, Esetmena, and Nalek, and his son by his divorced second wife, Jóxóliangke. One day Wielu, Lóló's eldest son, returned to Suaxéi from a trading trip with pandanus kernels which he shared with his father and brothers. Lóló felt that Wielu had given him the less delicious marginal sections of the fruit. They had an argument about the matter and parted in anger.

The following day Wielu harvested a fruit from another kind of pandanus tree which grows locally. Since Wielu was still angry with Lóló, he did not invite him to the meal, even though he had received the tree from his father. This demonstration of filial neglect so angered Lóló that he cut down the tree from which his son had taken the fruit, together with two others that he had once given to him. He brought the remaining ripe fruits to his maternal kinsmen living in the village of Savilivi, who gave him in exchange the same kind of kernels that Wielu had obtained on his trading trip.

Back at his homestead, Lóló roasted the kernels in the company of a friend from Kaliepini, a nearby village. While the two men were busy at this task inside Lóló's men's house, Wielu appeared and rebuked his father for cutting down the trees "instead of just taking the fruits if you got 'cramps in your stomach' [a metaphor denoting extreme anger]." The altercation between father and son ended in an exchange of curses. Suddenly Wielu drew an arrow and shot at his father through the entrance of the house but missed him. Then, before Wielu could escape beyond the reach of the arrows of his father and his friend, an arrow shot by the latter hit his thigh.

Wielu told his brothers about this encounter and they decided to avenge the wound. At sunrise the following morning they hid in the vicinity of the homestead. When Lóló appeared outside to evacuate his bowels, his sons dashed forward and shot some arrows at him, forcing him to retreat into his house. Curious about the clamor, Óngkómen looked out through the entrance of her own hut. When she began shouting, Esetmena shot her in the arm.

When the brothers had walked off, Lóló and his friend, who was still with him, called for help from the nearby villages of Mere,

Toxong, and Sengfeng. Lóló had two main reasons to ask support from these villages: his long solitary homestead residence away from Pasikni had made him a frequent visitor at some of the men's houses of these villages and, as an expert hunter, he had provided a sacrificial marsupial for the initiation of several boys into these men's houses, upon whose help he could now depend as their "father." The same day the first battle took place between Lóló's supporters and his sons, whom a few kinsmen of Talala and Wielu's wives, both women from Toxong, assisted.

The following day Pasikni men joined the fight on both sides. The dispute between a father and his son had escalated into a war. On the third day of fighting Sangkéak, a man from Mere who fought with Lóló, was fatally wounded by an arrow shot by Jóxóliangke. When he died the following morning, the Suaxéi people immediately evacuated their hamlet and, carrying all their possessions, made their escape to Pasikni by a long devious trek through the forest. They had hardly reached the village when a war party advanced toward Pasikni along the Tuluk stream. While the Pasikni men banded together for a battle outside the settlement, a single man by the name of Pólépóléjok from the village of Angkenteng appeared in the village and shot dead the Womikma man Póve. With this killing Pólépóléjok avenged the death of Sangkéak, who had sponsored his secondary initiation. Except for a few men with affinal links to Lóló, all warriors who had originally supported him now helped to drive the enemy from their land. Póve's killing contributed to a fast retreat.

For several years an uneasy truce existed in the valley, but by 1964 Esetmena, Nalek, and Jóxóliangke had resettled at Suaxéi. Talala went to live with his wife's kinsmen in Toxong, and Wielu built his own homestead at a place not far from Suaxéi. Lóló moved to Savilivi, where he and his wife lived with a distant maternal kinsman. In early 1964 a new war broke out in the valley between the villages of Pasikni and Savilivi (Case *50). Lóló, as "man of the arrow's stem" and a resident in a hostile village, feared retaliation for the unrevenged death of Póve, and he returned to Suaxéi, where Esetmena, Nalek, and Jóxóliangke welcomed their father. They exchanged pigs and asked a medicine man to perform the reconciliation ceremony. Talala also participated in the rite, but Wielu refused to end his avoidance relationship, which had begun five years earlier with the pronunciation of a curse against his father during their ill-fated dispute.

No. 17 (1964). Wali of the Nelelum ward in Pasikni had given a pig to his sister's husband, Avésa, a man from the neighboring Kénanghólómó ward. Some time later, his sister brought their father, Taling, a large piece of pork from a pig slaughtered by Avésa. When

Wali found out that his father had eaten all the meat by himself, he rebuked him for his greed. During the altercation Wali pushed his father against a fence. Taling suffered a broken rib and cursed his son, calling upon the bones of his deceased father. They maintained an avoidance relationship for several months. Then Wali decided to present his father with a "spirit-nourishing" pig, whose blood could be used by the medicine man who performed the reconciliation rite.

Taling had told the children of his father's brother's daughter, who lived in another village, not to accept food from Wali or offer him food. Therefore, in order to resume friendly relations with Wali, the oldest of them took part in the ceremony and subsequently distributed ritually treated meat among his siblings. Wali's two sisters and his younger brother needed no treatment because they had remained "in the middle," or neutral, in this dispute.

*No. *18 (April 1966).* Pavéon of the Nelelum ward in Pasikni invited his wife's mother's sister's son, who had come on a visit from Savilivi, to a picnic at his father's garden shed. Pavéon's wife and his younger brother, Eneko, accompanied them. During the preparations for the earth oven Pavéon plucked Hibiscus manihot leaves from a bush that belonged to his father. Eneko objected to this and left the party.

In the evening Pavéon's father, Selelemangke, whom Eneko had told about the incident, shouted complaints from his own adjunct men's house toward the big Nelelum men's house where Pavéon lived. Pavéon thought that his father exaggerated the transgression and shouted back, demanding to know what else except a few leaves he had taken from "your hands, you old, senile man. If I took your potatoes, say so! If I took your yam, say so! If I took your taro, say so! If I took your pandanus, say so! What else have I taken?"

When Selelemangke continued his lamentations, Pavéon rushed outside, and threw a stone through the entrance of his father's house that wounded his knee. At this point Avele, Selelemangke's father's brother's son, came running from his family hut and attacked Pavéon. He was aided by Eneko, whom Pavéon forced to the ground with a blow in his stomach. Now other Nelelum men, who so far had only urged an end to the brawling, intervened and separated them. Although Pavéon had strangled Avele so fiercely that he required immediate treatment by a medicine man, they soon forgot about the incident; but with his father Pavéon maintained an avoidance relationship [which still continued when I left Pasikni two months later].

No. 19 (1960). Osalén, the younger sister of Somónak of the Seraxanpini ward in Pasikni, was married to Ómpalielek from the village of Klengleng. One day Osalén harvested sweet potatoes from her husband's plots without asking his permission. Although the woman cooked the food in her family hut and shared the meal with Ómpalielek, he nevertheless gave her a thrashing. He also reminded her that Somónak had given him only one 'dowry' pig in return for his own three 'marriage' pigs. Osalén left Klengleng and went to Seraxanpini, where she stayed with her brother's wife.

A week or so later, Ómpalielek came to Pasikni to get his wife back. Somónak invited him to stay at Seraxanpini overnight. Next morning he presented his sister's husband with a live sow and two piglets. Hóvólóngéi, Somónak's father's father's brother's son, who had received one of Osalén's 'dowry' pigs, killed another pig for Ómpalielek. Before their departure Somónak told Ómpalielek not to beat his sister and admonished the woman not to come back to Pasikni again but to stay with her husband through her old age.

*No. *20 (1966).* After her marriage to Móxóak of the Seraxanpini ward in Pasikni, Angke lived with her husband's mother. She stubbornly refused to have sexual intercourse and whenever her mother-in-law stayed overnight in Móxóak's elder brother's family hut, she escaped into the hut of a friend. Informants differed in their interpretation of Angke's behavior. Some thought that she was merely afraid; others believed that she wanted to force her husband to give her father more 'marriage' pigs because he had provided only one so far.

In early January neighbors repeatedly heard the couple quarrel over the issue. On January 10, after another fight, Angke left and went to stay with her elder sister, who was living in the village of Sengfeng. A man from the nearby village of Mere abducted her the next day. Móxóak had no chance to obtain a pig from the abductor because the presence of enemies in the area prevented all Seraxanpini men from traveling to that part of the valley (see Case *50). Worse yet, the abductor's younger sister happened to be married to a member of the enemy lineage "of the arrow's stem." Since Angke's father belonged to a different ward in Pasikni and had a married daughter in that district, he ventured to go to Mere, where he succeeded in persuading his daughter to return to her husband.

*No. *21 (1966).* Wamélangken of the Nelelum ward in Pasikni had repeatedly quarreled with his wife Ómpólók over her refusal to have sexual intercourse. On February 7 another quarrel led to violence:

when he came for his breakfast and saw that his children were already outside he grabbed his wife and tried to copulate with her. Ómpólók refused and shouted, "I am afraid of your fingernails, I have grown old. You still have an erection? My vulva is old!" When Wamélangken continued to force her to the floor she grabbed his penis and jerked it. Creeping outside the hut, Wamélangken lamented: "What was done in olden times, what old men used to do, what old women used to do as well—when I was doing it now, you ruined your thing [his penis]!"

For more than a week Wamélangken could barely walk and he had to restrict his movements to visiting the defecation place. Around the middle of March, their neighbors heard Wamélangken and his wife quarrel over the same issue on several occasions. When the men asked about the noise in his hut, he explained that he had fought with his wife over food. The Nelelum people reacted with amusement and behind his back derided Wamélangken's shameless conduct.

In the early evening on June 13, Wamélangken again got into trouble. People later heard that Wamélangken, after finishing his meal in his family hut, had shoved his hand under his wife's apron. Ómpólók had repulsed her husband and cried out, "Why did this man come here, to eat what?" At this point the couple's two children, who had been sitting at a place near the fire from where they could not see Wamélangken's motions, realized the situation. Ómpólók's daughter by her first husband, a sixteen-year-old girl, rushed outside and stayed overnight with a neighbor. Their seven-year-old son escaped onto the sleeping floor. Ignoring his wife's complaints and oblivious of the boy's presence in the hut, Wamélangken continued his efforts and, after much struggling, finally succeeded in subduing her. The following day informants remembered the following pieces of their altercation: Ómpólók: "This fellow! He is gluttonous for vulvae. Are you doing this thinking 'I eat that potato' [allusion to coitus]? This fellow is ravenous for vulvae! Go, cut out the vulvae of all and every woman around here, put them in your carrying net, in your head net, in your tobacco net, and then eat them while you keep running! You have done it enough! Is this something to be done where a girl who has just had her menarche is around?" Wamélangken: "Wife of Seéntéi [Ómpólók's father], you always say the same old stuff! You have committed incest and keep speaking up [a rhetorical insult]?"

Throughout the fighting, women in the surrounding family huts gave clamorous support to Ómpólók. An old man who sleeps in his family hut after his wife's death and some men in the adjunct men's house of the ward, including Wamélangken's younger brother, also voiced their disapproval, often in ironic and sarcastic terms. They particularly condemned the man's disregard of the children's presence. The residents of the big men's house, where Wamélangken sleeps, did not participate in the shouting. They pretended to slumber when he climbed up to them muttering, "Just because I ate a potato which my son was to have, Seétéi's wife scolded me."

No. *22 (1966). In June Avésa of the Kénanghólómó ward in Pasikni lived at the hamlet Élémó, near Pasikni, together with his younger brother, Wal, and their father's father's brother's son's son, Apering. They stayed in the men's house of Apering's father's brother, who lives there in a homestead. In Avésa's family hut lived both his own wife Mólaxe with her little son and Wal's wife.

For some time Avésa had been asking Apering to have his wife bring her mother's sister's daughter, a fourteen-year-old girl from the village of Savilivi, to Élémó, because he wanted her as a second wife. When the woman finally brought the girl to the hamlet, where she took up residence with Wal's wife, Avésa sent Mólaxe back to Pasikni. Two days later Mólaxe passed through Élémó on her return from garden work. Because it was late, Mólaxe decided to stay there overnight.

Next morning Wal's wife discovered feces on the sleeping floor. She angrily shouted at Mólaxe, who was about to leave for Pasikni, to clean up her child's droppings. Mólaxe excused herself for not having seen the feces before climbing down from the sleeping floor and immediately removed them. Nevertheless, Avésa scolded his wife and accused her of having left the feces deliberately because she was angry that he had taken another woman. Mólaxe replied, "If you think that we left the feces for you, why didn't you come and cook them?" Avésa drew an arrow and hit his wife's glabella, missing the eye by less than half an inch. Mólaxe left her son at Élémó and went to Nelelum, her natal ward.

Soon a small crowd of neighbors gathered around the bleeding woman. Her father, Taling, quietly squatted down and wept, and I treated the wound. The women lamented about Avésa: "Is his penis forked like the branch of a tree? Why does he have two wives? He who has no hand [which means no pigs to give] takes two women? Here where there are no pigs, one woman is enough. They don't give them [wives' kinsmen] pigs; but they give them [wives] their penes as if these were pigs! First the men make the women senile with their penes, then they beat them!"

Taling heard for the first time that Avésa had taken another wife. After his daughter told him what had happened at Élémó, he said, "It was my son who carried the corpse of Avésa's mother to the pyre [a few months ago], when her son [Avésa] was sick. He who should have cooked her himself [a contemptuous expression] has now injured my daughter, my heart."

However, the old man also scolded his daughter for having insulted her husband instead of keeping quiet. Several times he said that he would have crushed the child's head on a stone if Mólaxe had not left him at Élémó, and that he would have fought with Avésa if he had been present at the incident. [When I asked Taling whether he seriously meant to kill the child, he replied, "Of course I would have smashed that child, but tomorrow I would have wept about my grandson."]

After a while Taling and I returned to my house, where his son Wali later joined us. When Taling had informed him about the incident, Wali went to Élémó. He came back after one hour and reported that he had failed in his attempt to seize one of Avésa's pigs. Later in the afternoon Wali returned to within shouting distance of Élémó and assailed Avésa. His complaints repeated over and over again that he had carried Avésa's dead mother to the pyre, given him the "wood" pig, for which Avésa had not yet returned the "corpse" pig, and that he now demanded its immediate delivery. Avésa retorted that Mólaxe had railed against him and lamented that he had forsaken her and their child after he had taken another woman. When he came for his breakfast, she had thrown ashes at him and even hit him with a stone. Besides, he had used an arrow with a blunt point.

The following morning, before sunrise, Avésa brought his son to Pasikni, leaving him in Mólaxe's hut. Mólaxe had refused to stay with Wali's wife at Nelelum because she felt ashamed that her husband owed her brother a "corpse" pig. An hour or so later, Lilen, Mólaxe's younger sister, came to Kénanghólómó and delivered a long speech against Avésa and his kinsmen. She got into a fit of extreme anger and suddenly grabbed the little boy, shouting that she was going to crush his head on a stone. By that time, however, several Kénanghólómó women had appeared in front of Mólaxe's hut. One of them, the wife of Avésa's father's brother, took the child away from her. At this point both men and women began to shout at Lilen. The men blamed Mólaxe for her injury because she had complained that her husband had taken another wife. Crying aloud, Lilen went back to Nelelum.

Shortly afterward, Taling came to Kénanghólómó with Wali and his youngest son to demand a pig. They entered the men's house, where they found Avésa's father's brother, Pakóak, and two of his sons, and Avésa's younger brother, Esele, as well as Sineng, Apering's elder brother, and Óaklaxevak, a matrilocally residing Nelelum man. Pakóak and his sons defended Avésa. The other remained silent because particular kin relationships prompted their overt neutrality;

Sineng's mother is Taling's father's father's brother's son's daughter and Óaklaxevak's father married Pakóak's father's father's brother's son's daughter. Using customary rhetoric, the Nelelum men pressed their demand by suggesting the opposite of the intended message: "Are you beating our daughter because we ate your pigs for nothing? Do you keep scolding us because you think 'they don't give us pigs'?"

When Esele uttered a defense for his brother, the Nelelum men turned on him: "Did your 'father' Pakóak provide your [initiation] pig? Did your elder brother Hóló? Was it your brother Wéak who killed a pig on your behalf? It was we who gave Lilen the pig which she brought to your 'mother' [Mólaxe], who gave it up so that you could be placed into the men's house. Having forgotten this, you scold your 'mother' now?" Esele left without reply and went to Élémó.

The dispute brought out that Mólaxe had quarreled with Avésa not simply over her new co-wife but because he had acquired another woman before providing the "corpse" pig. Nor did Taling and Wali express any disapproval of Avésa's second marriage. On the contrary, recognizing that Mólaxe's poor health greatly reduced her capacity for good garden work, Taling and Wali maintained that they would have given Avésa a pig for his new wife if he had reciprocated Wali's "wood" pig. By early July [when I left Pasikni] Avésa had yet to furnish the "corpse" pig. He still lived at Élémó and had not visited Mólaxe again.

No. 23 (1958). Halim of the Seraxanpini ward in Pasikni had given five 'marriage' pigs for his wife Asivil. Although she planted, weeded, and harvested in his gardens, she continued to live with her mother at the neighboring Nelelum ward. One morning her father, Alóat, then staying with his family at a homestead away from the village, brought one of the pigs, a sow that had just littered, back to his son-in-law. Halim thought that he was to take care of the sow while the piglets, which Alóat kept, were being weaned. However, the same day he learned that Esetmena of the Womikma ward in Pasikni, who lived at a garden hamlet located near Alóat's homestead, had abducted Asivil. The following day Halim visited Alóat to find out about the situation. Since Esetmena had already left the area with Asivil and gone to the village of Waléi, where he had distant relatives, Halim demanded that Alóat either get his daughter back or return all 'marriage' pigs.

A few days later Alóat received a pig from Esetmena. He cooked it and took the meat to his uterine half-sister's husband, Sineng, a man from the village of Kaliepini, who lived at a small garden hamlet near Alóat's homestead at that time. Halim's younger brother,

Ovokéi, who had observed Alóat's movements from afar, exploited the opportunity by stealing the piglets of Halim's sow from Alóat's family hut. The next day a party from Halim's men's house went to Sineng and pressed him to give up the remainder of the meat, which Halim then had distributed among all Pasikni men's houses.

The same afternoon Halim surprised Esetmena and Asivil as they were working in a garden. He shot at Esetmena but missed him four times. A fifth arrow hit Asivil in the arm. Esetmena ran to his hamlet to summon help. Halim had just reached the vicinity of Kaliepini when he noticed a pursuit party trying to reach the main path leading to Pasikni. He therefore hastened to Kaliepini, where he entered the men's house of his mother's brother's son, Améelek of the Halepini ward in Pasikni, who lived there with his mother's sister's son. Améelek's brothers, Hilik and Wali, happened to be on a visit from Pasikni and joined the brief skirmish that began as soon as the pursuers had reached the village. After Améelek, who was married to Esetmena's elder sister, had persuaded them to go home, Hilik and Wali escorted Halim to Pasikni.

On different occasions during the following months, Halim clandestinely seized two pigs from Alóat and two pigs belonging to Esetmena. He cooked all four animals secretly with his kinsmen and a few trusted co-residents at a distant Seraxanpini garden hamlet.

No. 24 (1961). The widowed mother of Alóat of the Nelelum ward in Pasikni was remarried to Temek of the neighboring Womikma ward. They had one child, Filiken, who married Sineng from the village of Kaliepini. One day Alóat asked a few of his Nelelum neighbors to help him prepare a garden on land that had belonged to Temek and that Sineng now cultivated. Alóat decided to seize this land because Sineng and Filiken had failed to reciprocate his gift of a "spirit-nourishing" pig for Temek with a pig after the birth of their child. He had a claim to such a gift as the child's closest maternal kinsman.

As the Nelelum men were tilling the land, Sineng and his wife appeared and tried to persuade Alóat to leave. Oblivious of his sister's lamentations and disregarding her husband's objections, Alóat explained the reason for his action and continued the work. The following day Sineng and Filiken brought a pig to Alóat, who thereupon promised to leave the rest of the land to them. Both parties agreed to make the partition permanent, and Sineng later marked the boundary with Cordyline hedge. (See also Case 27.)

No. 25 (1963). Jóukmó from the village of Savilivi abducted the wife of Apjók from Tuluk-Ikma. The woman's elder brother, Amólé, who belongs to Apjók's men's house, was married to Jóukmó's elder sister. Amólé's residential association with Apjók and his double affinity with Jóukmó allowed him to prevent a perilous confrontation between the parties by assuring Apjók that he would receive a compensatory pig through him at a future date.

No. 26 (1963). Nengkesa of the Masaxavil ward in Pasikni disliked the looks of his old ratan dress and decided to get new vines from the groves in the Helók Valley, south of the Central Range. He induced his sister's husband, Fovole of the neighboring Savéapini ward, to accompany him on the trip. When Fovole died shortly after their return, people attributed his death to a mystical sickness that results from an attack of the female ghost guardian of the vine. Since Nengkesa had initiated the enterprise, he was held responsible for the death. Wamné, Fovole's younger brother, demanded a "guilt" pig, which Nengkesa refused to provide. After a prolonged altercation, the men severed their relationship, but Wamné continued to take care of his brother's wife and her children. (See also Case *37.)

No. 27 (1964). Alóat of the Nelelum ward in Pasikni had planted a pandanus tree on land which had come into his possession through his mother's second husband. In July 1964 he sent his son, Jóukmó, to harvest a large ripened fruit. Jóukmó discovered that the fruit had been cut down. He found out from people living in that garden area that Sineng, a man from the village of Kaliepini who was married to Alóat's sister, had eaten the fruit. Bringing his father the news, he suggested that they should seize one of Sineng's pigs in retaliation. When Alóat did not object to this plan, Jóukmó together with another Nelelum man set out to avenge the theft. They found a pig that belonged to Sineng, killed it on the spot, and later cooked it in a garden shed not far from Pasikni. In the evening Alóat distributed the meat among his co-residents. The following day Sineng appeared at Nelelum and accused Alóat of having stolen his pig. Alóat denied the charge, and Sineng left in great anger.

The next morning Sineng returned, accompanied by half a dozen kinsmen. A long altercation ensued in which both parties clung to their assertions. Threatening reprisals, the Kaliepini men went back to their village. Around noon they returned together with a large group of armed men from several villages of their district. While the main force stayed outside the village, Sineng approached Nelelum, escorted by a few of his kinsmen and his wife's father's brother's son, Ésangko of the Womikma ward in Pasikni. Holding up some remains from the cooking that he had discovered in the garden shed, Sineng demanded immediate restitution. No longer eager to deny the accusation, Alóat agreed to surrender a pig but insisted that his brother-in-law accept their reciprocal loss in lieu of the exchange that the future initiation of Sineng's son would have required.

The altercation between the parties had just ended when the warriors who could not follow the negotiations from where they stood became impatient and began to shoot sporadic arrows into the Nelelum ward, disregarding Sineng's shouts. When they continued their threats with further shots, the Nelelum men made a sudden sally and succeeded in driving the enemy from the vicinity of their village.

*No. *28 (1965).* After frequent fights with her co-wife, Óuilen, the wife of Hélémó of the Seraxanpini ward in Pasikni, moved into her brother's vacant family hut at the neighboring Masaxavil ward. A few months later when her husband came for his meal, she told him that there were no sweet potatoes left on the plots he had prepared for her in his garden and that she was now harvesting from land which belonged to her father. She would not give him any food, because he had prepared new plots in another garden only for her co-wife. Although Hélémó had tilled her father's land for Óuilen, he ceased to harvest the plots made there for his own use when he found out that she had placed tabu marks on the garden.

On December 8, Hélémó seized a pig that he had given Óuilen as a suckling from the foraging area. He needed a gift for his mother's brother in the village of Angkenteng, whom he expected among the people coming from Klengleng and Angkenteng to dance at Seraxanpini that evening. Óuilen was working on the Angkuruk mission station when other women informed her of Hélémó's action. She returned to Pasikni at once and complained to her father, Pisinangke, and her brother, Ólóvéng, who lived in the village of Tuluk-Ikma but happened to be in Pasikni on a visit. The men urged her to retrieve the pig. Óuilen walked over to Seraxanpini, found the pig tied to a fence near Hélémó's family hut, and brought it back to Masaxavil.

Hélémó heard what his wife had done when he returned from Angkenteng, where he and others had delivered a formal invitation to the dance. He went to Masaxavil and suggested that Óuilen keep the pig but that Ólóvéng bring him one of his instead. Hélémó left in great anger when his affines refused the proposal. After nightfall, Pisinangke and Ólóvéng took Óuilen's pig back to Seraxanpini. Believing that they had brought one of their own pigs, Hélémó "carried face" [a dramatic expression of gratitude]. The next morning, on presenting the pig to his mother's brother, he discovered the deception. He publicly called his affines "incestuous men." When

Pisinangke and Ólóvéng heard of Hélémó's insulting accusation, they threatened to shoot him if he ever attempted to approach Óuilen again.

No. 29 (ca. 1940). Nékak, a widowed woman at the Heriekpini ward in Pasikni, stole a small pig belonging to Puka, a Heriekpini man who lived at his homestead near Pamóxók, a hamlet of the Womikma ward in Pasikni. Informants did not remember the reason for this action. Investigating clues people had given him, Puka came to Pasikni. He searched Nékak's hut and discovered the remains of a recently cooked pig. When he later found Nékak in the gardens, he attacked her. The men in the Heriekpini men's house considered Nékak's three arrow wounds excessive punishment. A small party, including Nékak's three adolescent sons, went to Pamóxók and demanded compensation. The confrontation ended in a skirmish. A Womikma man, who as a resident in Pamóxók fought on Puka's side, suffered serious injuries and died a few days later. After his funeral an intra-village war started in which both sides received support from other Pasikni men's houses. The men fighting on the Womikma side very soon agitated against continuing the battle since they could not expect ample compensation because the victim had no agnatic kinsmen at this ward.

Several months after the last battle Puka and the Heriekpini man Pésak, with whom he shared a small men's house at Pamóxók, ambushed three Heriekpini men as they were returning to Pasikni from a picnic. They killed one of them, a man from the Seraxanpini ward who lived with his wife's kinsmen at Heriekpini. In the late afternoon of that day a combined force of Heriekpini and Seraxanpini warriors attacked Pamóxók. During the night the Pamóxók people fled to the village of Kaliepini, where Puka had maternal kinsmen. Since no kinship bonds existed between the dead Seraxanpini man and the "men of the arrow's stem," Nékak's agnates, his father's brother's son demanded, through an [unidentified] middle-man, 'wergild' indemnification from Puka. Although the delivery of a pig by Puka's mother's brother conferred immunity upon him and settled the conflict, Puka never returned to Pasikni.

No. *30 (1965–1966). In the early afternoon of December 18, a rumor spread through Pasikni that Heriek, the sixteen-year-old son of Kexewarek of the Seraxanpini ward, had copulated with Lilen, the wife of his sib brother Óngkólili. After sunset an altercation took place in the Élémó gardens, halfway between Pasikni and the village of Klengleng, which explained the circumstances of the dispute. The first part of the following account gives Heriek's version of the encounter, which he gave me after he had sought refuge in my house after nightfall. [Heriek had made several mats for my house and the people regarded him as one of my "sons."]

"I was sitting near the spring Hélampukaxak in the Kalésóntak gardens. I worked on this new nose plug [he displayed it]. I had planted potato vines. While I was just sitting there, Lilen, Óngkólili's wife—you know—came by on her way home. She had been weeding her husband's garden. When she bent over to drink water, I picked up a small piece of wood and threw it at her thinking, 'I am going to copulate with you.' [Heriek admitted this after considerable hesitation. Informants later explained that Lilen had told some Seraxanpini women that Heriek had copulated with her on several occasions in the past. They also maintained that Lilen had betrayed Heriek this time because she believed that some women had observed the encounter and wanted to protect herself against any accusation of complicity.] She became angry and scolded me a lot. She said, 'One shouldn't do this sort of thing with wives of elder brothers.' I got frightened and ran away. I hid myself in the bush. From there I could hear and see everything. Lilen went home.

"She [must have] said to the men, 'Heriek hit me with a piece of wood.' Then Talala, Óngkólili's elder brother, Somón, Hinók, Sakulu, Laxejek, Pintelu, Ómalo, Hélémó, Manték, Hampok, Koto, and some others went down to Élémó. Óngkólili was there, too. They looked for a pig of my father. I have no pig myself any more. They found my father's pig and Talala hit it with a steel axe. My father was baking sweet potatoes with Ésalu [a man from the Kénanghólómó ward in Pasikni who married the sister of Kexewarek's junior wife and had his homestead at Élémó]. When my father heard the pig shriek, he left the men's house. He saw what the Seraxanpini men had done. My father asked them, 'Why do you beat my pig?' They said, 'Your son, Heriek, has thrown a piece of wood at Lilen, wanting to copulate with her.' My father said, 'He has no pig. You should have given him a beating.' My father went away thinking, 'I am going to my friends in Klengleng, to Féré, the son of Ésalu.' He had provided 'marriage' pigs for him. The Seraxanpini men did not want him to leave. They scolded him. They said, 'Don't go there! You have not given them a pig when they came to dance.' The Klengleng people had heard the altercation. Some men came up. The Seraxanpini men looked for the wounded pig, which had run away. They said to the Klengleng men, 'We are going to cook Kexewarek's pig, because his son tried to copulate with Lilen. Pamóen [the wife of Pélavek of the Jekjekpini ward], Jéxék and Jesu [her sons], and Kamparing [another

Jekjekpini man] came. Because Pamóen and Jéxék and the Klengleng
men told the Seraxanpini men, 'Don't kill the pig,' they did not do it.
My father had received this particular pig from Pélavek. You were
there, too. You also know what happened there."

Kexewarek's co-residents had indeed some difficulty in persuading
him to stay and engaged in a long altercation with the Klengleng
men. Óngkólili and his supporters, however, kept silent throughout
the altercations. Kexewarek finally decided to take up residence with
Ésalu.

While the 'shouting match' at Élémó was going on, Lilen's father,
Taling of the Nelelum ward, visited the Seraxanpini men's house
and asked the men there to persuade his son-in-law not to beat his
daughter. Heriek, he said, would grow feeble anyway, because he had
copulated with his "mother's sister" [a threat nobody took seriously
because Heriek's mother and Lilen merely belong to the same sib]. In
the evening Óngkólili gave Lilen a fierce thrashing.

His elder brother, Talala, beat his wife, Sengkevin, as well. Earlier
Lilen had responded to Talala's reprimands by telling him angrily that
Sengkevin had copulated with his father's father's brother's son's son,
Sakulu, some time ago. As soon as Sakulu heard that Lilen had
betrayed him, he fled to the village of Toxong. There he stayed
overnight with the husband of his father's sister, who sent him away
the following morning because he feared that refugees from a recent
war against Seraxanpini would kill the boy (see Case *50). Sakulu
went to his sister's husband in Klengleng, where he lived for several
weeks before his father brought him back to Seraxanpini. The men
there did not scold him, because their realization that Talala might
have become responsible for his death "made the men's anger go
away."

Heriek fled to the distant village of Kévéangken before sunrise.
His whereabouts remained unknown only until December 20, when
a woman from Kévéangken reported to people in Pasikni that the
boy was staying with friends in her village. Three days later, three
Seraxanpini men went to Kévéangken and escorted Heriek to the
village of Angkenteng [where he still lived with his father's sister's
sons when I left Pasikni in July 1966]. For one month after the
incident Heriek did not visit Pasikni. In February both he and his
father met Óngkólili at a funeral, where the latter ignored them. When
others questioned Óngkólili about the boy's presence, he said, "What
he did happened a long time ago."

*No. *31 (1966).* Background: Kexewarek of the Seraxanpini ward in
Pasikni had taken care of his sib brothers, Axavéak and Pókné, after

their father's early death. In 1964 Axavéak caused a war with the Seleriek ward in the village of Savilivi in which a Seraxanpini man lost his life (Case *50).

On February 5, Nengkesa of the Masaxavil ward in Pasikni came upon Axavéak and Esele, Kexewarek's junior wife, as they were engaging in sexual intercourse in a bush near the Jaxólé River. He drew an arrow, took aim at Axavéak, and shouted, "We have fought a war for you. The Seleriek people were driven from their homes because of you. Have you been cooking pigs for us? Why are you doing this?" Axavéak ran away, holding his penis gourd in his hand. Esele got up and cried out, "This bad fellow has copulated with me!" [Informants said that a woman caught in adultery always blames the man for having assaulted her. They believed rumors that Esele had actually sustained her liaison with Axavéak for some time.] Esele continued her lamentations until she reached the hamlet Elémó, where she had lived with her elder sister since December 1965, when Kexewarek took up residence with her sister's husband following a quarrel with other Seraxanpini men (Case *30).

Upon his return to Élémó from a bird hunt, Kexewarek, already informed of the incident, scolded his wife, who countered his tirade with the kind of "bold speech" for which she was known. "They have not ruined me!" she retorted, "Your thing is still there; my vulva remains where it has always been." Very early the next morning, Esele went to a garden hamlet belonging to people from the village of Klengleng. She stayed there with the wife of Ésalu's son for a few days before returning home.

For two days Axavéak's whereabouts remained unknown to the Seraxanpini people, who expressed their outrage over Axavéak's behavior by describing the offense as "incest." They so frightened Pókné, a thirteen-year-old boy, that he escaped to the neighboring Longkopini ward, where he could expect protection because his father had sponsored the secondary initiation of two Longkopini men, Hesum and his father's brother's son's son Kepolok. Axavéak had fled to the village of Waléi, where he found shelter with the husband of his elder half-sister. When Hesum moved with his family and Pókné to a garden hamlet a few days later, Axavéak joined this group and gave Hesum the pig he had received from his brother-in-law in Waléi.

This angered Kepolok, who had often complained that Axavéak never helped him with his garden work although he had provided a "guilt" pig to the agnates of a slain Seraxanpini man for whose death Axavéak was responsible (see Case *50). When Kepolok came to the hamlet on February 20 to help Hesum rebuild his family hut, he reprimanded Axavéak: "What are you doing here? You, who doesn't prepare any gardens for me. After you had started a war, your sib brothers did not provide a 'guilt' pig for you when you had caused a man's death. As I killed a 'guilt' pig, I thought 'he is going to make gardens for me!' You have not done any work for me in my own gardens, nor have you prepared your land for me. You don't stay with me. Go away and stay in that shed up there [Hesum's crude cooking shelter in a garden near the hamlet]." Axavéak made no reply. He continued his work on Hesum's hut but did not participate in the picnic afterward.

About a week later Kepolok himself moved with his family to the hamlet. After a few days Axavéak and Kepolok resumed an amicable relationship. Half a year later [when I left Pasikni] Axavéak and Pókné were still living with the Longkopini people at the hamlet. Informants believed that they would remain with them after their return to the village.

No. 32 (ca. 1920). Wénak, a man from Hompokéi living at the Nelelum ward in Pasikni, had an adulterous affair with the wife of a man in the neighboring Womikma ward. One evening, after it had become dark, Foroxam, another Womikma man, shot and wounded someone near his ward whom he believed to be Wénak. The victim, however, was from the neighboring Longkopini ward and his kinsmen decided to avenge the injury. Since the wound was not fatal and Foroxam had mistaken the victim for a foreigner, the Longkopini men waylaid Savelep, another foreigner from the village of Tangkeam who lived at Womikma. Although Savelep survived, his condition was so serious that Womikma launched a revenge attack upon Longkopini. Other men's houses joined the fighting. Two Nelelum men who fought on the Longkopini side were killed. Fearing a catastrophic revenge, the Womikma people fled to the village of Toxong, where they stayed for several years. Foroxam and his agnates never returned to Pasikni.

The war continued nevertheless. One morning an army of men from Toxong and other villages in that district took up positions along a ridge bordering the village and challenged the Pasikni warriors to a battle. Roused by encouraging shouts from the old men to chase the enemy away, the combined forces of several men's houses in the village made a successful sally against the attackers and drove them into a hasty flight. Several teams went after small groups of enemies fleeing in different directions.

Three men, Timpa of Womikma and two allies from the Heriekpini ward in Pasikni, tried to reach the village of Waléi. Timpa had been wounded and, losing strength, could not keep pace with his companions. Finally, he lay down near the path and asked them to cover him with grass and branches. A pursuit party arrived in Waléi after the Heriekpini men had entered a men's house, whose residents closed the entrance as soon as the pursuers came in sight and resisted their demands to turn the refugees over to them. The frightened Heriekpini men finally told their pursuers where they could find a wounded man of the ward responsible for the war. The party left and succeeded in finding the spot where a heap of grass and branches betrayed Timpa. After they had pierced him with numerous arrows, they tied his body to a pole and carried it toward Pasikni. When the procession approached the village, the frenzied men gathered greens because they intended to cook the victim. However, several Pasikni elders furiously objected to their plan because the eating of a local man would have started an intra-village *soli* war. Since Timpa was an extraordinarily strong and healthy man, the Nelelum men's house group considered his killing adequate revenge for the death of their two members.

No. 33 (ca. 1930). Background: An intra-village war in the village of Nisikni had forced a lineage to emigrate to Pasikni. One man, Wamné, settled at the Jekjekpini ward. Two of his kinsmen, Sépsép and Kéléangéi, first lived at Kénanghólómó, but moved to the village of Savilivi after some years.

Wamné commited adultery with Ikinen, a woman from the district of Wanjok who was married to Pakóak of Kénanghólómó. In retaliation, Pakóak together with his friend, Avésa of the neighboring Halepini ward, the son of an immigrant from Wanjok, ambushed and killed Wamné. The subsequent fight between Jekjekpini and Kénanghólómó ended after a brief skirmish, because the Jekjekpini group had no interest in battles without the prospect of any compensation. Later Sépsép and Kéléangéi demanded and obtained a 'wergild' pig from Pakóak. Ikinen returned home after Jekjekpini men had threatened to kill and eat her.

A few years later Jekjekpini men executed Avésa for his participation in Wamné's killing. At that time several Halepini families lived at a garden hamlet. One day two men from this hamlet seized and stealthily cooked a pig that belonged to Ovoluk, a Halepini man who had remained in Pasikni. In retaliation Ovoluk clandestinely seized a pig in the hamlet which he shared with his co-residents in Pasikni. Although Avésa participated in the meal, he nevertheless betrayed Ovoluk, who then encouraged the Jekjekpini men to kill this foreigner.

No. 34 (ca. 1935). Wamenek of the Seraxanpini ward in Pasikni killed a pig of Pasinajek because the animal had bitten his own pig.

Pasinajek was a man from the village of Kaliepini who lived uxori-patrilocally at Nelelum. In retaliation the Nelelum men killed a pig belonging to a Seraxanpini man. The raiders wounded the latter's wife and Wamenek's father's brother with arrows when they tried to interfere with their plan. Both sides met in battle for several days, each aided by other wards. Nelelum warriors from the branch village of Tengkeléi (built during a great influenza epidemic of the early 1920's) attacked a Seraxanpini garden hamlet, seized several pigs, set fire to one hut, and drove the people back to Pasikni. Pasinajek's kinsmen from Kaliepini killed a pig belonging to one of Wamenek's agnates, who lived at another hamlet.

The first victim to die was a man from the Heriekpini ward who fought on the Seraxanpini side. Soon after his death the fighting stopped under fortuitous circumstances: when Nelelum men had unintentionally killed one of his pigs in their raid, Jéngkélek, a man from their allied Savéapini ward in Tengkeléi, switched to the Seraxanpini side. On his way to the battlefield he was killed from ambush by Musamet of Heriekpini, who supported Nelelum because men from that ward had once protected his mother, a woman from Waléi in the Ovaxak Valley, when other Pasikni men wanted to kill her in a war against her natal village. When Musamet informed the Nelelum men of his feat, they feared that the inevitable restructuring of inter-ward alliances would mean their certain defeat and decided to end the war by a trick. They announced that Seraxanpini men had killed Jéngkélek on his way to aid their enemies. With one man dead on either side, both parties agreed to lay down their weapons. When the truth became known several years later, Jéngkélek's death was reckoned as a revenge killing for the Heriekpini man. [My informants regarded the Nelelum men's deceit as a singularly successful example of information control.]

No. 35 (1963). Walusa, a man from the Womikma ward in Pasikni who lived uxori-patrilocally at the neighboring ward of Seraxanpini, abducted Wampexasa, the wife of a man from the village of Angkuruk. Her husband, Avenek, went to the village of Klengleng to solicit help from two brothers whose father's killing in an inter-regional war he had revenged. Reminding them of his status as "head man," Avenek asked that they claim a pig from Walusa on his behalf. The Klengleng men refused the request and sent Avenek away. They did not want to take sides with Avenek openly and decided to seize a pig by stealth because of the many kinship links between Klengleng and Seraxanpini.

Therefore, they went to Pue-Ikma, a Seraxanpini garden hamlet where Walusa was at that time staying. By mistake the two men killed, carried away, and presented to Avenek a pig that belonged to Selelemangke of the Nelelum ward in Pasikni, who was living at a nearby hamlet. In the evening Selelemangke and his family searched for the pig. The discovery of blood traces convinced him that someone had seized the animal. When the circumstances of the case became known a few days later, Selelemangke and his wife, who had painted her body with yellow ochre to show her grief over the lost animal, went to Pue-Ikma and claimed a pig from Walusa. Walusa complied with their demand although he had already provided a 'marriage' pig for Wampexasa. (See also Case *8.)

No. 36 (1964). A dog belonging to Savulaxe of the Halepini ward in Pasikni killed a dog owned by Pakóak of the neighboring Kénanghólómó ward that was famous in the village for its hunting skill. Pakóak's sons killed one of Savulaxe's pigs in retaliation and cooked it in front of their men's house. The men who took care of the dog's funeral were so aggrieved that Pakóak cooked one of his own pigs for the mourners. When Savulaxe heard that the Kénanghólómó men had seized his pig, he simply said, "They have cooked my pig because of their great grief; it's all right what they have done."

*No. *37 (1965).* Background: In 1963 Nengkesa of the Masaxavil ward in Pasikni became liable for the death of his sister's husband, Fovole of the neighboring Savéapini ward, but he refused to deliver a "guilt" pig (Case 26).

On January 18, Fovole's fourteen-year-old son and another Savéapini boy shot a small pig which they believed to be Nengkesa's and presented it to Wamné, Fovole's younger brother. The pig, however, belonged to Selexenéi of the neighboring Jekjekpini ward, who missed it in the evening. The following morning, the Jekjekpini people heard that Wamné was preparing to cook a pig in front of his men's house for no apparent reason. Together with his elder brother's sons, Selexenéi went over to Savéapini and recognized the dead animal as his own. Wamné quickly promised restitution. Selexenéi accepted the proposal, saying, "Today I have given a pig to you; you will give a pig to me." [Later that day the Jekjekpini people told me that they had not insisted on immediate compensation in order to avoid a conflict with their neighbors at a time when their village was fighting a war against Savilivi (Case *50).] On May 10, 1965, the Jekjekpini men helped with the rebuilding of the Savéapini men's house, although Wamné had not yet fulfilled his promise.

*No. *38 (1965).* In the morning of May 2, while playing in the fields near Pasikni, some children noticed that a pig belonging to Hosiek, a sixteen-year-old boy of the Nelelum ward, was bleeding from a wound obviously inflicted with a steel axe. The children shouted their discovery toward the village, and, within a few minutes, several men, women, and children came to look at the pig. Hosiek, who was working in the gardens when the news reached him, arrived an hour later and took the pig to its pen in his mother's hut.

For the rest of the day, most of the Nelelum men remained inside or around their men's house and engaged in long discussions attempting to find out who might have wounded the animal. The case concerned the whole group because the animal was a "sacred" pig—one they had subjected to a special growth ritual inside the men's house. [Though owned individually, a "sacred" pig in a way belongs to all residents, and females and uninitiated boys may not eat any part of it.]

In the afternoon they heard a rumor that Pakóak of the Kénanghólómó ward had beaten the pig. Several men and some older boys questioned Pakóak, whom they found in his garden just outside the village. Pakóak admitted the offense, but complained that Hosiek's pig had attacked his own as he took it to the foraging area in the morning. An altercation ensued between the Nelelum men and Pakóak and his sons, who had arrived on the scene. When the younger Nelelum men threatened to inflict a similar wound on one of Pakóak's pigs, Hosiek's old father shouted at his own followers to keep silent. He objected to their threats and reminded them that any reprisal in this form would lead to more trouble that might invite their common enemy to attack the village (see Case *50). In the end, Pakóak offered to eat the wounded pig if it died and return a live one to Hosiek. The Nelelum men accepted his proposal. Hosiek's mother treated the injured pig twice a day and after two weeks the wound had healed.

No. *39 (1965). During the early night hours of May 23, someone tried to enter the hut of Wamovok in the Seraxanpini ward. Her husband, Leveng, an immigrant from the village of Waléi, was staying at a garden hamlet at that time. The following morning Wamovok informed her mother of the incident. When the latter discovered footprints leading from her daughter's hut toward the Nelelum ward, she began to rail against Nelelum, accusing Jóukmó, a young man, of having attempted to seduce her daughter. Wamovok vociferously supported her mother and asked, "Why did you throw a lump of soil at me the other day [a customary technique of inviting sexual intercourse]?" The Nelelum men repudiated the charge with a few sporadic shouts. Jóukmó himself did not respond, but he told his co-residents that the women were lying.

In a somewhat longer statement, Savéavangke of Nelelum, who had persistently agitated against my presence in the village, suggested that I had visited Wamovok on one of my nocturnal aerial travels as a "ghost." Seraxanpini men who examined the footprints discredited this allegation. Some doubt remained, however, because Wamovok's mother had told people that she had heard her daughter ask me for salt during a previous night.

In the evening of May 24, Leveng returned to Pasikni. After a discussion of the affair in the Seraxanpini men's house, he launched a verbal attack against Nelelum. Soon several men on both sides participated in the altercation, which included the following exchanges:

Leveng to Nelelum: "Have you been thinking, 'he doesn't do anything about it, because he came to Pasikni only recently?' I have become a true Pasikni man. I am going to fight you!"

Avajek of Seraxanpini to Leveng: "You, who have come to stay with us, kill him when you have learned his face [know the intruder]!"

Wali of Nelelum to Wamovok: "Now that you have spoken bad language about [slandered] us, tell us: 'I saw the face of Jénguruk, I saw the face of Avele, I saw the face of Pavéon, I saw the face of . . . [listing all young adult males of the Nelelum men's house].' Tell us his name!"

Wali to Leveng: "I have been telling the boys here, 'Don't bother their women lest they refuse to share their pigs, their pandanus, their food with us.' "

Avele of Nelelum to Leveng: "We all have been sleeping together in our house until that woman woke us up with her shouting."

Pavéon of Nelelum to Leveng: "I, who have been eating your food—you have been eating my food—I, your 'younger brother' [son of Leveng's mother's sib sister, a woman from Waléi], don't copulate with your wife."

Leveng to Nelelum: "I have come from Waléi mourning the death of my elder brother after men from Sangkalpunu killed him; he [the intruder] must not come to my hut and remove the door boards again. As for this time, it may pass."

Usaxón of Nelelum to Leveng: "We did not run away from your hut."

Leveng to Usaxón: "Are you speaking as if you didn't know? One day he came here, another day he came here, still another day he came here, last night it was the seventh time he came. Don't come again to copulate with my wife!"

Hosiek of Nelelum to Leveng: "Seven times you say? And she did not see the man who copulated with her? Did he do it from the rear?" [Laughter among the Nelelum men.]

Wali to Leveng: "When he comes again, ambush him! Your wife,
let her say who it was. Whose face did she see?"

Avele to Seraxanpini: "Your wives are just talking bad about us."

Leveng to Nelelum: "You keep bothering our wives. We don't do
that to yours."

Wali to Seraxanpini: "Because Silóxóp [a Womikma man] once
copulated with Saxavak [wife of the Seraxanpini man Sóxól], you are
now accusing us! Jóxóliangke [of Womikma] was badly wounded
in your war [Case *50]. I and Hónómó [another Nelelum man] as
well."

Leveng to Nelelum: "I have been talking to you because the
footprints run toward your place."

The shouting lasted for nearly an hour and ended when all
participants had drifted back to the fireplace of their men's houses.

No. *40 (1966). Background: In a recent war between Pasikni and
the village of Savilivi (Case *50) Pue of the Seraxanpini ward in
Pasikni took up residence at the neighboring Longkopini ward, where
his wife Angke, a woman from Savilivi, stayed with Aphéra, the
wife of Seleven, who had lived in Savilivi before the war. Since
the principal parties in this war were Seraxanpini and Angke's
lineage, Longkopini afforded her greater safety. Pue's widowed father
lived in the Seraxanpini adjunct men's house of his sib brother
Avésangéi. His sister, Filikon, living with Avésangéi's wives, was
betrothed to Seleven's son Léalék, whose younger sister, Musanen,
was married to Jénguruk of the Nelelum ward.

On January 4, Jénguruk arranged a picnic at his shed in a garden
near Savilivi. Among the people who participated in the outing were
Jénguruk's mother and his wife's parents, Seleven and Aphéra, who
came with their daughter, the wife of Avésangéi's son Ómpalielek,
and Angke, who brought her little son along.

When Angke went to gather firewood, Jénguruk clandestinely
followed her into the bush. Pue, who came to join the party and by
chance observed their movements from afar, rushed through the
brushwood toward the place where he had seen his wife and
Jénguruk disappear. While Jénguruk escaped unharmed, Pue's
arrow hit Angke in her right shoulder, but she managed to get back
to the garden. Aphéra extracted the arrow and hid her behind a
bush. The party broke up immediately. [Pue later told his co-residents
that he had deliberately spared Jénguruk, lest an intra-village war
arise, for which he could not afford to become the "man of the arrow's
stem" after the killing of his elder brother had resulted in great
battles during the recent war.]

When Pue arrived at the shed, he found only his son. He carried the little boy to Pasikni, where he left him with Avésangéi's wives, and raced back to the garden bent on punishing his wife. In the meantime Aphéra had guided Angke to a nearby rock shelter, but footprints betraying her refuge soon brought Pue to her hiding place. He first attacked her with his stone adze, then he pulled her into the open, jumped back and drew an arrow. At this moment a small party of Pasikni men appeared on a nearby ridge. Their shouts distracted Pue; his arrow hit Angke in her right lumbar region. A better aimed second shot penetrated her left breast but lacked thrust, because the approaching men compelled Pue to retreat from the scene.

Informants differed in their opinion as to whether or not Pue intended to kill his wife. Some maintained that Pue only wanted to "tie a rope to her," bind her to the house for a while, and take advantage of her condition by having frequent intercourse to impregnate her again. Although the gravity of Angke's injuries seems to contradict this view, the particular circumstances of the couple's conjugal relations make it plausible. While the boy had reached the age at which his parents could resume sexual intercourse, their residential arrangement precluded any opportunity for cohabitation at night. Another, perhaps more credible, interpretation of why Pue did not kill the woman was that Angke's death would have meant an undesirable addition to the list of victims on the Savilivi side in the war (Case *50).

The men and boys who came to Angke's rescue were from the Nelelum ward and from Longkopini. The Nelelum men had heard about the incident from Jénguruk, who told them upon his return to the village, "Pue has killed his wife because he thinks I have copulated with her." When they reached the injured woman [minutes before me], she had already extracted the two arrows. She was sitting on the ground bleeding, her legs and apron besmeared with feces and urine. While we discussed how to carry her back to Pasikni, other Longkopini men arrived. One of them demanded to know from Angke whether she had copulated with Jénguruk before. With great effort she whispered, "Only today."

The men finally managed to place the woman on a crude stretcher. Walking in heavy rain, we reached Pasikni after one hour. Men and women from Longkopini and the neighboring wards of Kénanghólómó and Halepini stood waiting. Some older women cried. The Seraxanpini men had gathered in front of their house and watched from afar, but went inside as soon as we reached the village. The stretcher was put down at the hut of Aphéra, who helped Angke creep inside. Aphéra and other Longkopini women wailingly derogated the "bad, bad fellow, the evil ghost-like man," who had injured the woman. They voiced no complaint about Jénguruk.

Throughout the afternoon, everybody carried his bow and arrows, even on short walks in the village. Jénguruk had stayed at Nelelum only long enough to inform the men there. He spent the afternoon with relatives in the village of Klengleng, whose readiness to support him in case of trouble he reported to his men's house group when he returned in the late evening. He denied that he had actually copulated with Angke, but admitted that he had tried to seduce her.

After dark, Avésangéi's brother's son, Somónak (who had shared a hamlet men's house with Pue's dead brother) addressed the village with a formal statement: "He has wounded his wife in anger. For his brother I [meaning: we] killed people [referring to the revenge killings of Angke's agnates in the recent war]. This time he has wounded just his wife in a rage because her behind was eaten [cryptonymic expression for copulation]. Pasikni men, don't go after our wives! You, Jénguruk, kill a pig of yours for the woman's kinsmen if they come; because you ate her behind, she [Angke] has been injured!"

The next day, January 5, all Pasikni wards guarded their pigs, and no man walked about without his weapon. At Nelelum the men avoided talking about the affair. Pue stayed inside Avésangéi's men's house for several days and the Seraxanpini men tried to keep his presence secret. For a few days people in other Pasikni wards believed him to be in a different part of the valley. Somónak scolded Pue for his excessive punishment. He told him that Seraxanpini had fought enough battles for his elder brother and that this time he could fight alone. Since the Longkopini men wanted neither Musanen's marriage to Jénguruk to break up nor Léalék's betrothal to Filikon, they refrained from any action. Jénguruk visited the Longkopini men's house less than three weeks after the incident. As informants put it, "The men did not speak a bad word, thinking 'our brother-in-law has come to us again.' " Angke stayed in Aphéra's hut, where Seleven and I treated her regularly. She made a surprisingly quick recovery, and within a week she was able to sit outside for a few hours a day.

On January 6, a man from the village of Toxong arrived at Longkopini to inquire about Angke, who was his wife's father's sister's daughter. He briefly talked to her through the closed door of the hut and then went over to the men's house, where he discussed the case with Seleven. The Longkopini people later heard that Angke's elder brother, Pintelu, who since the recent war had been living with his wife's kin in the village of Mere, located near Toxong, had sent this man to find out if Angke and Pue would resume their marital relationship. Pue, in fact, tried to reconcile his marriage and talked to his wife on several clandestine visits to the Longkopini ward around noon, when everybody else was in the gardens. Angke rejected his proposal. On January 15, Pintelu came to Pasikni and took his sister to Mere, where he put her up with his wife and her mother. Two days later an elder brother of Pintelu's wife abducted Angke.

No. *41 (1966). In the afternoon of January 9, Lilen, the daughter of Taling of the Nelelum ward in Pasikni, was weeding in her father's garden. Wéak of Kénanghólómó came by and threw a tiny stone at her [a common way of proposing sexual intercourse]. Lilen did not respond, but told her husband, Óngkólili of Seraxanpini, about the incident in the evening. After nightfall the Seraxanpini men started a mass shouting against their neighboring wards. Because their initial complaints singled out Wéak and his kinsmen, the Kénanghólómó group assembled at the Longkopini men's house, which was located nearer to Seraxanpini and from where they could be heard better. As the altercations wore on, several men from the Halepini and Womikma wards joined them there. Some Nelelum men participated in the dispute without leaving their ward. Nobody from the Longkopini men's house came outside, for the elders of its founding lineage had reminded the younger men that Seraxanpini was their original home (see Case 5).

Although the Seraxanpini men first accused only Wéak, they subsequently complained about several other villagers who had, in the past, tried and often succeeded in seducing their wives. They further asserted that their neighbors had failed to reciprocate the "parsley" pigs they received after a recent war against Savilivi with "stump" pigs (Case *50). Speakers on the other side resorted to customary tactics. They vehemently rejected the charges, made repetitious counter-accusations, scorned, insulted, and shamed their opponents in statements like the following:

Wéak's elder brother, Hóló, accused Óngkólili: "You, Óngkólili, made Lólómen [wife of Apering, Hóló's father's father's brother's son's son] leave her husband. Because you did that, we thought, 'Let's copulate with your wife,' and have done likewise." [Some time ago Óngkólili had seduced Lólómen. Because Apering refused to take food from her afterward, she deserted him.]

One of Óngkólili's sib brothers, who is a weakling and afflicted with chronic asthma, heard: "You with a little leaf in your throat, shut up! You did not fight against the Savilivi men but stayed home and kept copulating with your wife! Senile fellow, evil one! For just one 'marriage' pig that you gave for your wife, you keep begetting a child?"

A collective imitation of his voice silenced an old Seraxanpini man who stuttered a little when he began to speak. He was told:

"You, whose speech goes [imitating gurgling sounds], shut up! Senile, decrepit fellow, your speech is bad!"

Several men shamed Leveng, a Seraxanpini resident who immigrated to Pasikni after his brother's death: "When your elder brother was slain by men from Sangkalpunu, did you also kill [take revenge]?"

Usaxón of Nelelum reprimanded Leveng, who had falsely accused his co-residents of adultery some months before (see Case *39): "Leveng, you man over there, it was Ólóvéng who copulated with your wife at night, but you spoke to us." [This statement incriminated Ólóvéng of the Masaxavil ward in connection with Case *39. After Leveng had moved his family hut closer to other huts in the Seraxanpini ward, Ólóvéng remarked to some Nelelum men that he thought the old place a better location. They considered this comment evidence that he had visited Leveng's wife.]

A while later, Usaxón raised his voice again to challenge Leveng: "If I, Usaxón, have incited your wives, just say so! If my elder brother, Sintuk, has incited your wives, just say so! If my 'son' Pavéon [his mother's father's sister's son's son] has incited your wives, just say so! just say so! . . . [listing all younger Nelelum men]."

Others derided Sóxól of Seraxanpini about his wife's adulterous conduct (see Case *12): "Sóxól, you man over there, at Singkenkenma Ólóvéng copulated with your wife for you! Sóxól, you man over there, at Sóvóróatok-Ikma, Selon copulated with your wife for you! Sóxól, you man over there, at Pangkoleméi they copulated with your wife for you today! Go away and cry! That defiled food which is cooked for you!"

Wéak's father, Pakóak, criticized the whole Seraxanpini group: "Whenever we suffer from illness, whenever we are at war, whenever we make a new garden, you just go up to Pue-Ikma [a Seraxanpini garden hamlet], you go up there to hide yourselves. Your Seraxanpini homes down here, we shall burn down; in a raid we shall drive you away. The kind of people you are, where will you go, where will you hide? We shall fight you, we shall fight you!"

An hour after it began, the shouting faded. Occasional outbursts of complaints interrupted pauses which grew longer and longer. At this point a "big man" of the Halepini ward made a brief final speech, in which he exhorted both sides not to molest each others' women and reminded the villagers, as had others before him, that their enemies were waiting to exploit the conflict between the wards in a sudden revenge raid.

No. *42 (1966). Background: In September 1965 Jóukmó of the
Nelelum ward began to court Ampentak of the neighboring Womikma
ward. His delivery of a 'marriage' pig, a few months later, confirmed
the marriage. Ampentak continued to live at her natal ward.

On March 9, Jóukmó and Ampentak prepared a picnic in
Ampentak's father's garden shed. While Jóukmó was heating the
stones, his wife went to a nearby spring to wash sweet potatoes.
There Tilip of Womikma, the younger brother of Ampentak's elder
sister's husband, sneaked up to her from behind and shoved his
hand under her apron. Ampentak swerved around and shouted, as
she later reported, "Did they teach you to do that, man Tilip, you?"
Tilip replied, "Jóukmó will not provide the [initiation] pig for your
younger brother's initiation. When I shall have killed the pig for
your younger brother, will I have you?" Ampentak disliked his talk.
She hastily gathered the tubers in her net and ran back to the shed,
where she told her husband of the encounter. Jóukmó took his bow
and arrows and went to search for the pig that Tilip had brought to
the garden area. He saw Tilip, who pretended to be on his way home
and carefully kept his distance, but he could not find the animal.

Jóukmó decided to leave the picnic for another day and went home
to discuss the incident with his father, Alóat, and other residents
of their adjunct men's house. Finally, Alóat announced that he just
wanted to tell Tilip he could have Ampentak, got up, took his stone
adze, and walked toward the Womikma ward, followed by Jóukmó,
who also carried a stone adze.

Although the other men suspected that Alóat would attack Tilip,
whose elder brothers happened to be away from the village, no
fighting took place. Leaving Jóukmó behind, Alóat entered the
Womikma men's house, where he found Tilip in the company of two
other residents. A short while later Pavéon, another Nelelum man,
came up to Jóukmó and both of them climbed into the house. Alóat
finished the cigarette he had rolled and lit after entering and then
addressed Tilip, "Have you done it thinking, 'I am going to copulate
with Ampentak, her vulva having become big' [metaphorical
reference to Ampentak's recent menarche], after you gave up that
large vulva, Faxemak [a woman from the village of Kéveangken
whom Tilip abducted while she was staying with her father's sister at
Nelelum, and who deserted him after two months because he failed
to provide a 'marriage' pig for her]?"

Tilip replied, "Is Nelelum your true home, man Alóat? If I had
copulated for you, I would have come to the big Nelelum men's
house. You would have had the little house. We would have had a
fight. Is it the [big] Nelelum house where you, man Alóat, keep taking
pork?" Alóat answered, "To hear him say this, we have come. Let's

go home, Jóukmó, come on!" When both had left, Pavéon deplored Jóukmó's single 'marriage' pig and assured Tilip that some of the members of the Nelelum men's house would have sided with him in a fight with Alóat's group.

No. 43 (ca. 1925). A man from the Helók Valley, south of the Central Range, 'eloped' with a girl from the village of Kaliepini, where he had visited trading partners. Later the girl was killed, cooked, and eaten. Since no hostilities existed between the two regions, her slaying was without cause, and not "for an eye"—an act of revenge.

Years later, during an especially good salt season, another man from the Helók Valley came to Pasikni together with his wife, his daughter, his wife's mother, and his brother's daughter. They stayed at the Savéapini ward, where the man's elder sister was married to Saxaléi. When Erekien, the slain girl's elder brother, heard that Helók Valley people were around, he came to Pasikni. At the Nelelum ward lived his father's sister's son Hampok, with whom he could talk about a plan to revenge his sister's death. The following morning Erekien returned to Pasikni with a party of Kaliepini warriors. Hampok met the men outside the village and led them to a place near the Savéapini ward, where the visiting women were spreading out the saliferous banana fibers for drying. Numerous arrows felled the two women; the two girls were left unharmed and later escorted home by people from the village of Savilivi. The man, who was in the Savéapini men's house when the attack began, escaped and returned to his village.

The same day a man of the Heriekpini ward in Pasikni who had joined the Savéapini group in their pursuit of the attackers seriously wounded a man from Kaliepini. [Informants attributed the readiness of Pasikni men to revenge the killings of the foreign women to their desire to continue their trips to the ratan groves in the lower Helók Valley. They considered the following events macabre but related them with great hilarity.] A while later, a revenge party from Kaliepini searched the valley for a victim. At a Heriekpini hamlet, located halfway between Kaliepini and Pasikni, they met Héxérek, a man from the village of Savilivi who lived there with the kinsmen of his wife. Héxérek asked the men what the shouting he heard was all about. The wounded man's mother's brother recounted the events in great detail, ending his explanation with a demonstration of how his "son" had been shot. Motioning Héxérek to assume the role of his "son" for the sake of re-enacting the circumstances of the shooting, he suddenly took aim and killed him with a single arrow.

Since Héxérek had not yet begotten a child, the Heriekpini people decided to leave his cremation to the Savéapini people. During the

night, his wife's mother's brother carried the corpse in a big net
to Pasikni and managed to hang the load unnoticed at one of the
four inner poles of the Savéapini adjunct men's house. The residents
were so horrified at their discovery of the corpse the next morning
that they fled to the neighboring Seraxanpini men's house, whose
group afterward helped them with the funeral.

Héxérek had been an immigrant in Savilivi, where he lived at
the Avirévam ward with the sons of a sib sister. When these men
later demanded compensation, Saxaléi gave them a "guilt" pig.
Erekien rewarded the Nelelum group for their part in the slaying
of the two Helók women with a "head" pig, which they shared with
all other Pasikni men's houses except Savéapini, a procedure that
defined the pig as "parsley" tribute. Since Erekien realized that
the Nelelum men shared the meat in an effort to disclaim their
participation in the killing, he later invited Hampok and his co-
residents to prepare a garden for him. On this occasion he presented
them with a second "head" pig, which they could eat alone because
it overtly represented their compensation for garden work.

No. 44 (ca. 1925). Avéné, a man from the district of Wanjok,
abducted the wife of Mólón of the Usapini ward in the village of
Móxéimó. When a group of Usapini men came to Wanjok to claim
a compensatory pig, Avéné and his kinsmen drove them away with
arrows, but the fleeing men waylaid one of their pursuers and killed
him. The following day Wanjok warriors attacked the Usapini settlement. The battle ended with the exodus of the Usapini people to the
village of Savilivi after three of their men had been killed and their
homes burnt to the ground. The subsequent ambush killing of another
Wanjok man by Usapini men started a war that lasted for several
months. Pasikni men's house groups joined forces with Savilivi; a
Seraxanpini man and a Nelelum man died from their battle wounds.
During the truce that followed the cessation of daily fighting,
Usapini men revenged their deaths with the ambush killings of two
enemies.

Following mutual promises to cease hostilities, both sides resumed
visits to relatives and friends across the Jaxólé River. Before long,
however, further killings ended the truce. One day a small group
of Wanjok men invited two Pasikni men, Jalé of Longkopini and
Karéon of Seraxanpini, who were working in gardens near the river,
to come over and accept some pandanus nuts. Then they attacked
the men as soon as they had crossed the water, hitting each with
several arrows when they tried to escape. Karéon collapsed on the
bridge and fell into the river, but Jalé managed to get across with the

help of his son, who had been working nearby and raced down the slope when he heard the shouts of the wounded men.

News of the incident spread rapidly through the whole garden area. Several small bands pursued the treacherous men but failed to reach them. However, a pursuit party discovered a woman from their village in a garden not far from the bridge, shot her and carried her body to Savilivi, where it was cooked and eaten. A large portion of meat was given to Jalé, who lived for several years, enduring great pain from the arrow points which could not be extracted. The same day the woman's kinsmen killed and ate a Pasikni woman, who happened to be on a visit in Wanjok. No battles followed these killings, but traffic between Wanjok and the villages in the Pasikni district ceased for many years.

No. 45 (ca. 1940). At a dance of men from the village of Waléi in her home village of Savilivi, a young woman, married to Selelemangke of the Nelelum ward in Pasikni, let herself be abducted by one of the visitors. When a party of Nelelum men came to Waléi to demand a pig, the abductor and his co-residents threatened to attack them. Some time later, Selelemangke abducted a woman in a garden near her home village of Waléi, where she was married to a local man. When her husband, accompanied by a party of supporters, arrived in Pasikni and claimed a pig, the Nelelum group retaliated the treatment they had received in Waléi. However, the woman's agnates gave the first of Selelemangke's 'marriage' pigs to her former husband. This transaction settled the dispute.

No. 46 (ca. 1945). A man from the village of Kaliepini abducted the wife of Talo of the Nelelum ward in Pasikni, who lived at the neighboring Seraxanpini ward. Although the abductor gave a pig to a party of Seraxanpini men when they demanded compensation, a coincidence led to a war. While the Seraxanpini men were negotiating for the pig in Kaliepini, Talo's kinsmen who lived in Tengkeléi, a branch village settled by Nelelum people, anticipated a battle and crossed the Jaxólé River, where they cut calami needed for bowstrings which had been planted by a man from the village of Élintam. They were surprised by a local woman, who misunderstood their motions to keep quiet and ran off to alarm her village. The same day small bands of armed men from Élintam and neighboring villages moved through the valley. A party from Kaliepini, among them Enexon of the Longkopini ward in Pasikni who lived there at that time, killed a man from the village of Nisikni living at Nelelum. Elsewhere, a small group of men from the Heriekpini ward in Pasikni who were enjoying a picnic in the gardens shot a woman whose husband, a Nelelum man, lived in Tengkeléi.

These killings precipitated a war that lasted for several months and took the lives of men, women, and children on both sides. Divided alliances tore apart the village of Pasikni: Heriekpini, Jekjekpini, and Halepini supported Élintam and Kaliepini; Nelelum, Kénanghólómó, and Savéapini joined forces with Seraxanpini. Womikma men fought on both sides. During this war the Heriekpini and Jekjekpini people, most of whose family huts were plundered and destroyed by fire, dispersed throughout the valley except for a few men and their families who were given asylum by relatives in other Pasikni wards. The battles ceased only after Pasikni warriors had set fire to huts in the villages of Kaliepini, Toxong, Sengfeng, and Angkuruk and forced an exodus of many inhabitants to Hélariki, half a day's walk to the north. The refugees returned after several months and rebuilt their homes.

From Jekjekpini only two brothers and their agnatic cousin came back to Pasikni; the others founded a new Jekjekpini men's house in Kaliepini. The Heriekpini people abandoned their ward forever; the adjunct men's house Masaxavil remained the domicile of a lineage with close putative links to one sib fragment at Nelelum. For several years the others lived in Angkuruk and Kaliepini until they founded the Oloruk and Pantele settlements. Around 1953 they established a new Heriekpini ward on the south side of the Tuluk stream, which by 1964 had grown into the village of Tuluk-Ikma. The great war with the Sévé Valley (Case *53) prompted a peace ceremony for which a Womikma man, whose sib brother had been eaten by the enemy, provided the "kidney" pig.

No. 47 (ca. 1955). When Avésa of the Kénanghólómó ward in Pasikni was a thirteen-year-old boy he lived in the village of Klengleng, where several members of his men's house had settled after a great influenza epidemic in the 1920's. One evening a "net" pig, which he had received from his sister after the death of her daughter, did not return from the foraging grounds. An extensive search of the area was unsuccessful. The following day the wife of his father's father's brother's son, Ulaxón of Kénanghólómó, told Avésa that she had seen Seraxanpini men on their way to their garden hamlet carrying a slaughtered pig. A large party of Klengleng men went to the hamlet, where they accused the Seraxanpini men of having stolen Avésa's pig and claimed restitution. Hélémó, who had killed the animal, provided the demanded live "ear" pig.

However, angry over its poor quality, the Klengleng men stopped at Seraxanpini on their way home and claimed another pig from

Méléirek, a Heriekpini man who had moved to that ward in the course
of an intra-village war (Case 46). When Méléirek, whose son had
participated in the theft, refused to comply, the men killed one of his
pigs and cooked it after their return to Klengleng. Méléirek never
demanded restitution. Informants explained that he could neither
get a pig from his Seraxanpini neighbors, because his son had eaten
part of Avésa's animal, nor obtain their support against Klengleng,
because he was a "lone man."

No. 48 (1961--1965). Wiemaxe, the wife of Palésék from the village
of Angkuruk, refused to let her new co-wife live in her hut. She
could afford to remain obstinate because Palésék lived at her own natal
ward in the village of Élintam. Yet, after several days of quarreling,
she left herself and moved into an unoccupied hut nearby. Since
Wiemaxe had been badly bruised by her co-wife, Palésék feared for
his relationship with her agnates and provided a huge pig for the
initiation of her younger brother—the same pig he had planned to
present as a 'marriage' pig to his junior wife's kinsmen.

About a month later, Amólé, a man from the village of Tuluk-
Ikma, abducted Wiemaxe. When Palésék and his kinsmen came to
claim compensation, Amólé and his co-residents attacked him. The
skirmish, in which men on both sides suffered injuries, led to a war
lasting for three days. Contingents of warriors from Pasikni and
several other villages participated in the fighting. On the fourth day,
Palésék came to Angkuruk very early in the morning. He asked
his brother for a pig, which he needed to compensate his supporters.
When he announced that he did not want the war to continue, a
"big man" from Angkuruk shouted the peace offer toward Tuluk-
Ikma. Amólé's father answered him and urged both sides to stop
fighting and resume garden work. Both speakers referred to the
ongoing *soli* war with the Sévé Valley which threatened their common
safety (Case *53).

Amólé expelled Wiemaxe half a year later because she did not
conceive. [Informants claimed that Wiemaxe's father had cursed
his daughter after her abduction.] She stayed with the wife of her
mother's sister's son at a garden hamlet for two months, until a
man from Pasikni abducted her. When Wiemaxe's father received
a 'marriage' pig from the abductor, he had it delivered to Amólé, who
had given him a pig after the war. Four years later, Palésék moved
to Tuluk-Ikma, where his married younger sister lived. After Palésék
had built his family hut, Amólé gave him a 'welcome' pig. This gift
ended their enmity.

*No. *49 (1962–1966)*. On his way back home from the Angkuruk
mission station, where he had accompanied mission personnel as a

carrier, Asengseng, a seventeen-year-old boy from the Usapini exile settlement in the district of Wanjok, seized a pig belonging to Aliek from Angkuruk. [Several years earlier the Usapini people had fled to Wanjok from Savilivi in a war against their neighboring ward Seleriek (Case 9).] When Asengseng returned to Angkuruk about a week later with another party of carriers, Aliek waylaid him on his walk home and shot an arrow into his lumbar region. Asengseng managed to extract the arrow and fled to Pasikni, where he stayed at the Seraxanpini ward with his maternal kinsmen.

The whole Seraxanpini group welcomed Asengseng because his quest for protection provided them with an opportunity for demonstrating their intention to make peace with the Usapini people, whom they had helped to defeat in their war against Seleriek. Next morning Asengseng's maternal kinsmen and many of their co-residents descended toward Angkuruk. The altercation over claims for compensation and counter-claims for restitution soon developed into a battle. Both sides were supported by warriors from surrounding villages. One arrow hit Kalpun from Kaliepini, fighting on the Angkuruk side, through the eye. The Angkuruk force believed that Kalpun was dead and made an all-out attack against the Pasikni lines which quickly disintegrated in a general flight. [Later that day Kalpun was brought to the mission station, where he stayed under medication for three days until a plane took him to the coast for further treatment lasting about two weeks. His brain damage caused a permanent loss of muscular coordination in the lower extremities and partial aphasia.]

Kalpun's father's sister's son, bent on avenging the injury, seriously wounded Asólóm from the Nélampoma ward in the village of Savilivi although both had fought on the same side. [Informants explained this revenge with the fact that ancestors of the Usapini and Nélampoma ward had once occupied the same settlement (see Case *51).] In spite of his wounds, Asólóm crossed the Jaxólé River twice and via Wanjok reached a Nélampoma hamlet, where Asengseng's sister's husband provided the "guilt" pig that a medicine man used for a curing ceremony.

The battle made travel between Pasikni and Angkuruk a precarious enterprise. All Seraxanpini men stopped working at the mission station and people from other wards did not venture into the vicinity of Angkuruk and Kaliepini whenever Kalpun's condition deteriorated into a coma—which happened twice between January 1965 and July 1966. In February 1966, Kalpun's injury was revenged with the killing of an Usapini man who had fled to Angkuruk after he had become the "man of the arrow's stem" in another inter-village war (Case *51).

*No. *50 (1964–1966).* Background: The Longkopini ward in the village of Pasikni was founded by jóal and kénangalem lineages from the neighboring Seraxanpini ward. In a great influenza epidemic of the early 1920's, the jóal people settled at Seleriek in Savilivi and the kénangalem people moved to garden hamlets from where they later returned to Seraxanpini. Around 1946 a kénangalem lineage rebuilt the Longkopini ward.

One day in January 1964, Selon and his half-brother, Pintelu, members of the Seleriek jóal lineage, assaulted Axavéak of Seraxanpini after another Seraxanpini man, Sinamók, an immigrant from the Helók Valley, had told them that Axavéak had seduced Selon's junior wife. [Informants agreed that Axavéak had sought opportunities to approach the woman, but had never succeeded in his endeavors.] Sinamók absconded to the village of Toloping after he realized the consequences of his gossip.

In two separate revenge actions, Seraxanpini men injured the wife of one of Selon's agnatic cousins, and another member of his lineage. [Informants considered these attacks excessive but understandable because the Seleriek group had failed to provide a "head" pig after Seraxanpini men had killed an enemy for them in a recent war (Case 9).] These attacks led to a battle near the village of Savilivi, which ended with mutual assurances not to continue the fighting the following day. However, because his sib brother had been injured in the fighting, Ómalo of Seraxanpini ambushed Selon the same evening and hit him with an arrow. During the night and in the early morning many people from Seraxanpini and Seleriek staying at distant garden hamlets returned to their villages after they had been warned that a war was imminent.

Warriors from both wards supported by allied men's houses met near Savilivi the following day. Although men on each side suffered injuries, the Seraxanpini group decided not to continue the fighting. However, an attack force from Savilivi rejected their peace offer the next day, and another battle took place. The Seraxanpini man Savi was hit in the throat by Féré of the Longkopini ward in Pasikni, who aided the jóal group. [Féré lived in Tuluk-Ikma at that time. His kinsmen regarded his fatal shot as an unfortunate incident and for many months his part in the war remained unknown to most villagers.]

Now the last families who had continued to stay at hamlets or homesteads returned to their villages. When Savi died three days later, the war entered a new phase: a death had to be revenged. The Seraxanpini warriors performed an elaborate revenge ceremony. For several weeks battles in which contingents of warriors from most Jaxólé Valley villages participated were fought almost every day.

Over a dozen Pasikni men still persisted in their support of affinal relatives on the jóal side. Several huts in garden hamlets between Pasikni and Savilivi were burned down or dismantled as a convenient source of firewood, a pig was seized in Savilivi, and many men were wounded, some of them seriously. An informal agreement ended the fighting when the long neglect of garden work threatened famine. During the truce, which lasted for nearly a year, the only Pasikni men who traveled to Savilivi were those who had aided affinal kinsmen on the jóal side and a few others—though they had supported Seraxanpini—who had close relatives at Seleriek.

In January 1965, when the new gardens were ready for harvesting, the younger men at Seraxanpini agitated for a resumption of open warfare, since all attempts to ambush a jóal man had failed. Several elders, including Savi's father, disapproved of their talk but they, too, had occasionally deplored the unrevenged death. On January 17, three Seraxanpini men seized two pigs near Savilivi. As soon as the animals were missed, several men followed the raiders' tracks. Near Pasikni the pursuers came upon other Seraxanpini men, who managed to escape to their village. The Seraxanpini group cooked the pigs the same evening and distributed most of the meat to other Pasikni wards as "parsley" compensation.

The following day a great battle took place halfway between Pasikni and Savilivi. The jóal men lost the support of many men because they resented their meager reward. When the fighting ended in the late afternoon, the Savilivi force had drawn back across the ravine bordering the north side of the village. On the next day, the Savilivi warriors did not leave their village, but small groups of defenders gathered in protected places between the huts and behind fences. The Pasikni attackers were angry about these tactics, and without success urged the jóal men and their allies to fight on open ground. When more and more Pasikni men entered the village and combat deteriorated to sniping, women and children who were still staying in their huts left their wards and assembled in gardens located on the far side of the village.

The defenders took refuge in the men's houses, from where they shot occasional arrows through gaps made by pulling ajar boards in the wall. When the fighting stopped, the invaders had burnt down three Seleriek huts, plundered many others in the ward, captured four pigs, and killed two jóal boys, both agnatic cousins of Selon. They had discovered the older one on the sleeping floor of a family hut, and found his younger brother as he left the village with the wife of his eldest brother, who wanted to return to her home village of Hélariki. In the evening the Seraxanpini group conducted a ceremony that informed Savi's ghost of their revenge.

The following day, the Pasikni force encountered hardly any defense. When the first attackers entered the village, the Seleriek men fled into a neighboring men's house, which they were forced to leave again after a fire-brand hit the roof. The nefarious act of setting fire to a "sacred" house enraged the besieged men. While a few put the flames out, many others made a sudden sally and succeeded in driving the enemy back across the ravine. The fighting continued until the early afternoon, when the Seraxanpini men and their allies walked home.

When the first Pasikni warriors approached Savilivi the following morning, the village was empty. During the night most Seleriek people had fled to relatives in various villages in the Angkuruk district. The other wards had moved to their garden hamlets in the Móxéimó area. One more man, Wempa, an immigrant from a village south of the Central Range, whose sister was married to a jóal man, lost his life. He was on his way to his brother in the village of Sangkalpunu when men from the abandoned ward Usapini in Savilivi killed him to revenge an action stemming from another war (Case 9).

The Seraxanpini group was content with the outcome of the war. Therefore, when the next day men from the village of Angkenteng ambushed a man from another village, who had lived at Seleriek in the past, they refused to acknowledge his death as a revenge killing on their behalf. They knew that the man had been slain by the brother of a woman whom he had killed in an earlier war (Case 46). A Seraxanpini "big man" addressed the village in the evening and announced that Savi's death had been revenged by the Seleriek victims and that the new killing was a separate affair. [Informants explained that the Angkenteng men wanted to conceal their motive because their action constituted a breach of a formal peace agreement.]

The war ended all travel by Seraxanpini men and their Pasikni allies to the Angkuruk district, where the jóal men had settled. By the end of June 1966, only very few Seraxanpini men, who had affinal relatives in this area, and nobody from their neighboring wards who had participated in the actual killing of the boys, had ever been in Angkuruk again. First contacts, however, had long since been made. When on August 19, 1965, a jóal woman, who was married at Seraxanpini, died, her parents and brothers came to the funeral. On this occasion some elders urged both sides to make peace. In February 1966, the people of two wards who had fled from Savilivi returned from their hamlets and reoccupied their houses. Two months earlier the Pasikni men's houses and their main allies from

the village of Tengkeléi had celebrated their victory in dance
festivals.

*No. *51 (1965–1966)*. Background: In a war with Pasikni several
generations ago, the ancestors of the people who later lived at the
wards of Usapini and Nélampoma in the village of Savilivi were
driven from their original settlements at Wisalek, near the present
village of Tuluk-Ikma. They settled in the Wanjok district. Years
later, after another war, most lineages moved to Savilivi, but some
people stayed behind in Punumó and Wampérek. After their exodus
from Savilivi during an intra-village war (Case 9), the Usapini people
resettled in the Wanjok district at Iktélfél, not far from Wampérek
and adjacent to a garden hamlet of the village of Kisilpini.

In early December 1965, a young Usapini man named Kóxal took
refuge at the Wanjok outpost of the Angkuruk mission station.
Kóxal was a man of ill repute. A year before he had seriously
wounded his pregnant wife in a fight that he started by attempting
to force her to sexual intercourse. Public indignation, fear of revenge
by his wife's kinsmen, and a rumor that inculpated him with incest
brought him to Pasikni. There he stayed at the Halepini ward with
his father's sister's husband for several months before returning
to Wanjok. When Kóxal again got into trouble after seducing the wife
of his elder brother, Ngékngok, he went back to the mission outpost.
Pleased about the new pupil, the catechist, a coastal man, gave
Kóxal shorts and a shirt. A few weeks later, mission boy Kóxal
ventured back to Iktélfél.

In early February 1966, Kóxal began a series of nightly intrusions
into the family hut of a Kisilpini man named Lévélek. Informants
thought that particular circumstances protected Kóxal for a while.
Because he had a private domicile in the hut of his wife, who had
deserted him, the residents of the men's house remained ignorant of
his doings. Furthermore, the woman believed the clothed intruder
to be the catechist and, therefore, was afraid to inform her husband.
However, on February 14, after Kóxal had again sneaked up to
her sleeping floor, the woman recognized him and raised a clamorous
tirade. Lévélek, on hearing her screams, grabbed his bow, rushed
out of the men's house, and shot an arrow into Kóxal's thigh before
he could escape. Kóxal himself did nothing to avenge the wound, but
his younger brother retaliated the injury by shooting an arrow into
Lévélek's thigh when he found him in his garden shed the following
day.

Out to revenge the injury, Lévélek's co-residents attacked Iktélfél.
They had already encircled the settlement when a relief party of
Usapini men from Wampérek arrived. In the skirmish one of them

suffered a fatal injury. His body was cremated on a pyre erected with planks ripped off Kóxal's hut. The killing ended the fighting. Knowing that the Usapini men would seek to revenge the death, the Kisilpini people evacuated the hamlet and returned to their village.

The same day Ngékngok came back from an expedition into the ratan groves of the Helók Valley, south of the Central Range. When he was told that Kóxal had caused the death of a man, he thought up what later turned out to be an ingenious scheme of revenge. After Ngékngok had publicly reprimanded his brother for his mischievous conduct and expressed regret that Kóxal had not been killed, he went to Kisilpini, where his wife had sought refuge with her kinsmen. He explained that he had come to stay and would fight with them against his own people, because Kóxal had seduced his wife. And indeed Ngékngok actively supported the Kisilpini warriors in the battles that took place during the following days.

On February 20, the Usapini families evacuated Iktélfél and fled to Móxéimó on the other side of the Jaxólé River, where they found refuge with the Nélampoma people from Savilivi living in their garden hamlet. Kóxal, the "man of the arrow's stem," went back to Pasikni because he feared the kinsmen of the slain Usapini man after the fighting had not yielded a revenge killing. However, when his host scolded him for having neglected to bring part of the 'marriage' pig that he and his brothers received for their sister after her recent marriage, he traveled on to the Angkuruk mission station. His protector, the catechist from the Wanjok outpost, was staying there at that time and could give him shelter. Kóxal was killed at the station the same day by men from the village of Kaliepini.

His death revenged the tragic injury of Kalpun (see Case *49), whose brother announced their view of the situation in the following words: "I [meaning: we] did not kill a man of Walipini, I did not kill a man of Avirévam, I did not kill a man of Nélampoma, I did not kill a man of Hiktóxéi, I did not kill a man of Longkopini, I did not kill a man of Seleriek [naming the wards in Savilivi]. He [Kóxal] was caught by the *pangke* tree at Poarikma, whose bark had been removed, when it fell down." [This statement means that the Kaliepini men took revenge only on Usapini and not the other Savilivi wards. The *pangke* tree stands for Kalpun, who was maimed at a place called Poarikma. The Jalé people prefer this wood for its good combustibility and often remove the bark to cause its dehydration with the result that strong winds sometimes break off a dried bough. Kalpun's condition resembled that of a dehydrated tree, whose fall symbolizes the revenge.]

The war continued nevertheless. The Usapini men now received extensive battle support from Savilivi men's house groups living in the various hamlets in the Móxéimó area. On March 18, Ngékngok finally had a chance to implement his plan. He induced a Kisilpini man to accompany him to a place where they would be able to ambush an enemy. Not far from Iktélfél, Ngékngok shot a bamboo-tipped arrow into his companion's back. Believing the victim to be mortally wounded, Ngékngok danced around and chanted victory stanzas. He then fled to Móxéimó, where the Usapini people welcomed him.

But the injured man survived, and the war dragged on. Battle days alternated with short periods of garden work. By the end of March, the Usapini and Nélampoma groups had built two new bridges across the Jaxólé River which considerably eased their movements to and from the battlefield. Since Ngékngok feared that he and his brother might become liable for another killing, he conceived a scheme that would lead to the desired revenge killing not on the battlefield but by another piece of trickery. In the afternoon of March 28, a small party crossed the Jaxólé to execute the plan. While Ngékngok and the others stayed behind and hid themselves in a thicket near the path, one man sneaked into the village of Kisilpini and shot an arrow through the entrance of the main men's house. Several men pursued him as he made his escape. When he approached the spot where Ngékngok and his party were waiting in ambush, only one man by the name of Kirisiong still trailed him. A series of arrows brought him down as soon as he had passed the trap.

The revenge party ran back to the Jaxólé. They had hardly crossed the bridge into Móxéimó territory when their pursuers arrived on the opposite side of the river. Ngékngok shouted at them, "The *punum* fruit was split in two; the *sak* is not to be divided!" [*Punum* and *sak* are different pandanus species. Before roasting, the globular *punum* fruit is usually divided into two more or less equal sections, while the elongated cone-shaped *sak* fruit is split up into three sections. Ngékngok's metaphorical warning meant that since each side had revenged a death, no other killing should occur.] Informants believed that the Kisilpini men launched no further attacks because Kirisiong was a "lone man" and belonged to the sib of Lévélek, "the man of the arrow's stem" on his side.

*No. *52 (1966).* On January 14, Wal of the Kénanghólómó ward in Pasikni heard that Hingkéen, a girl from the village of Angkuruk whom he had courted for over a year, had let herself be abducted by a man from her own ward. The following day his kinsmen together with friends and affines in other Pasikni wards accompanied him to Angkuruk. As Wal had given one 'marriage' pig for Hingkéen (who had no living male agnates) to her elder sister's husband, they now demanded a pig from this man. Since Wal's recently deceased mother was from Angkuruk, the presence of maternal relatives favored their successful negotiations.

*No. *53 (1940–1966).* Around 1940, at a time when inter-regional trade still linked the Jaxólé, Sévé, and Balim Valleys, men from the village of Piliam in the Sévé Valley killed a Dani man. About four years later, men from the village of Kénanghólómó in the Wanjok district of the Jaxólé Valley, who were on a trading trip into Dani country, killed a Piliam man, and delivered his body to their Dani trading friends. Richly rewarded with "head" pigs and gifts, the party returned to Wanjok. The subsequent revenge killing of the Wanjok man Mejumingkik in Porongkoléi, a village located near Piliam, resulted in intermittent *soli* warfare which by 1966 had lasted for more than twenty years. [The following case history presents a mere outline of this war. A complete description would require an account of nearly monographic size.]

At first only men's house groups from the Wanjok district made revenge expeditions across the Fungfung forest, which separates the Jaxólé Valley region from the Sévé Valley. After their enemy had killed two more men, contingents from the Jaxólé Valley villages of Savilivi, Tengkeléi, and Pasikni participated in the forays. When these villages, too, had lost some warriors, they began to organize their own vengeance parties. By ca. 1949, more than a dozen people from the Jaxólé Valley region had been killed and eaten, including three men from Pasikni. Only a few people died on the other side. One man was killed in battle; the widow of Mejumingkik, being a Porongkoléi woman, was put to death and cooked by the kinsmen of a victim from Savilivi; and a man from another Sévé Valley village was slain by men from Tangkeam, a village located between the Sévé and Jaxólé Valleys. These Tangkeam men brought the body to Pasikni because Pasikni contingents had supported their ward in a past war with Hélariki, another Jaxólé Valley village.

One village in the Jaxólé Valley, Hompokéi, attempted to stay out of the war because several local lineages had earlier migrated to Piliam. The Hompokéi men maintained a neutral position even after Tengkeléi men had killed the wife of Loloxon, a Piliam man living in Hompokéi, upon their return from another revenge expedition into the Sévé Valley that had ended in a disastrous defeat. However, one day it became known that some men in Hompokéi, who had never been able to revenge the death of a woman once killed by a Savilivi man, had eaten the leg of this man's father's brother's son, who died in a battle with Sévé Valley warriors. After a revenge attack on

Hompokéi by a combined force of Savilivi, Tengkeléi, and Pasikni
warriors, in which only Loloxon was killed because his hosts refused
to fight, the villagers evacuated their homes and fled to Piliam.

Their departure incensed the Pasikni people and heir allies because
several men had brought pigs to their affines in Hompokéi the day
after Loloxon's killing in an effort to dissuade them from leaving
the valley. Therefore, as soon as news of the exodus reached them,
bands of warriors from several Jaxólé Valley villages pursued the
refugees, now considered *soli* enemies, and killed several men
and women, whose bodies were cooked by the relatives of men
who had died on past revenge expeditions. All domiciles in Hompokéi
except the sacred men's houses were burned to the ground.

Revenge parties continued to cross the Fungfung ridge in search
of victims, and sporadic killings of careless visitors and hunters
added a few casualties on both sides. When about three years after the
destruction of Hompokéi five people from the Sévé Valley were
ambushed on their return from a trading trip to Dani country,
the Sévé Valley villages also organized revenge expeditions. In 1959
a raiding party killed two Pasikni women whom they surprised
on Hompokéi territory. Tengkeléi men working in nearby fields
quickly banded together, pursued the enemy, and succeeded in
shooting four men. One body was cooked in the Tengkeléi branch
village Klengleng, one was given to the Womikma ward in Pasikni,
and a third was delivered to Wanjok. The fourth body went to
Angkuruk, not as a revenge victim, but in compensation for the loss
of hunting grounds on the west side of the Jaxólé River, where the
war prevented any further exploitation. A fifth man wounded in the
fighting made it to Tangkeam, where Angkuruk men, informed of his
presence there, killed him and later ate his body.

Although occasional revenge expeditions took place during the
following months, the Savilivi, Tengkeléi, and Pasikni people were
satisfied with the death balance. While Wanjok still counted a number
of unrevenged killings, the Tengkeléi people began to urge peace
negotiations. One day in 1960, three women with relatives among
the Hompokéi refugees traveled to Piliam with a peace message. Since
they returned unharmed and reported that the enemy also wanted
to end the war, a group of Tengkeléi men crossed the Fungfung forest
a few days later and sang peace stanzas within shouting distance
of Piliam. Two men came up to them, and with mutual embraces
the parties assured each other that they wanted to end the war.
One member of the group, a man from the Nelelum ward in
Pasikni, objected to his companions' sudden disregard of their slain
neighbors. He threatened the Piliam men, and oblivious to his companions' warnings, he pursued them when they fled. At an opportune

place they ambushed him and carried his body home to be eaten. His kinsmen in Pasikni claimed and received two "guilt" pigs from their Tengkeléi allies and seized a third from a man who had eagerly supported the peace move.

No further killings occurred until the arrival of the mission in Jalémó in the spring of 1961. The anxiety created by low-flying reconnaissance planes and the people's subsequent discovery of strange men and things effected an immediate and general desire to end all hostilities. Partly facilitated by travels of mission personnel between Piliam and Angkuruk, people from the Jaxólé and Sévé Valleys resumed mutual visits of relatives. Although they occasionally exchanged pigs, no formal peace ceremony took place.

The truce ended abruptly in July 1963. One day two women, Sineng, a young widow from Angkuruk, and her friend Laxasa from Tuluk-Ikma, who had frequent fights with her husband, traveled to Piliam, where both had relatives among the settlers from Hompokéi. Since the women had not told anyone of their plan, people assumed that they did not intend to come back. A few days later two coastal men in the employ of the mission went to Porongkoléi, where a landing strip was under construction, accompanied by two carriers from Angkuruk. One of them was Ómalo, an agnatic cousin of Sineng's husband, who wanted to bring the widow back so that he might marry her himself. A small group of Tengkeléi and Angkuruk people followed them at a distance.

It happened that the day on which the visitors arrived in Piliam Sineng and her new husband underwent the connubial purification ceremony that the remarriage of a widowed person requires. When Ómalo interfered with the proceedings, Sineng's new husband killed him. Hompokéi men, who had urged the villagers not to harm anybody, then shot Sineng, avenging Ómalo's death on her new husband. This killing precipitated a hunt for all other people from the Jaxólé Valley who were around. Altogether four men, five women, and a small child lost their lives.

The following day, the parents of one of the victims traveled to Piliam. They were worried about the safety of their son and believed that the presence of his mother, a Hompokéi woman, would protect him from any attack. While her husband, Saling, stayed behind in the forest, the woman walked to the village. Some men, suspecting that her husband was in the vicinity, went on a search and killed him after they had tracked him down. When his wife, who was mourning the fate of her son in the company of her kinsmen, heard of his death, she approached the place where the feast was taking place and asked to be eaten along with the others. Her lamentations annoyed the men. They teased her with pieces of meat cut from her

son's body, and then drove her away with sticks and stones. Her
agnates created another disturbance at the feast when they seized
two pigs from the slayers of her son. The woman remained in Piliam
until she heard that her husband's death had been avenged a year
later.

The kinsmen of the dead blamed the mission people for the
massacre because their assurances that nothing would happen to
them in Piliam had lured the victims into making the trip. After
the pastor had paid death indemnification in the form of a cymbium
shell and a steel axe for each of the two carriers, a party of Tengkeléi
men arrived at the mission station one morning and demanded
compensation for all other victims. When their request was refused,
the enraged men threatened to break into a storage room to get the
shells and steel axes themselves. The station radioed for government
protection from Wamena in the Balim Valley. For the second time
policemen were flown into the valley; they gave a rifle-shooting
demonstration and became known as "bum-bow carrying men." [The
police had visited Angkuruk shortly after the massacre. They stayed
half an hour to draw up a report of the event.]

During the following year Jaxólé Valley warriors made many
unsuccessful forays into enemy territory. Then, in June 1964,
Tengkeléi men killed an older Dani boy from the Mukwi Valley,
east of the Balim, and presented his body to Saling's sister's son in
Klengleng, who rewarded them with a "head" pig. (The boy, whose
father once lived uxori-patrilocally in Hompokéi, had previously
visited a maternal kinsman who had settled in Tengkeléi after the
raid on his home village.) Two months later a party of men from
Angkuruk and Tuluk-Ikma killed a woman from Piliam who had
married in the village of Tangkeam. Her body was cooked on the
Angkuruk air-strip by relatives of Sineng and Ómalo, who shared
the meat with the kinsmen of a victim from the Nelelum ward in
Pasikni. In September 1964, men from Tangkeam informed friends
in Tuluk-Ikma that several women from the Sévé Valley were on a
visit in their village. A few men from Tuluk-Ikma followed them to
Tangkeam and ambushed two of the women on their way home. A
year later men from their home village killed a Tangkeam man. This
revenge led to *wim* warfare between Tangkeam and Sévé Valley
villages. The next victim was a Piliam man whom a small revenge
party from Wanjok surprised in the Fungfung forest in November
1964. Fearing a pursuit, the raiders left the body behind after cutting
off one arm, which they presented to a relative of Laxasa's brother,
who had been killed in the massacre. A year later Piliam men killed
a boy from Wanjok after he had strayed from a group that was
gathering pandanus nuts in the Fungfung forest.

In March 1966, a party of Piliam men crossed the Fungfung ridge and, staying at a safe distance from a Tengkeléi garden hamlet on the west side of the Jaxólé, sang peace stanzas, but no direct contact was made since each side feared the other's treachery. One of the shouted messages explained the sudden desire to make peace: "bum-bow carrying men" were on their way to the Jalémó, killing people and pigs and burning down houses wherever they appeared. [This rumor referred to recent pacification activities of the army and police of the Balim Valley.]

Fear of punitive police actions did indeed promote a new peace effort. When in April 1966 people in the Tengkeléi branch village of Klengleng gave an unfriendly reception to a visiting European from the Angkuruk mission station, the schoolboys who accompanied him assumed that their lives were threatened by men seeking to revenge the death of a man recently killed on the station (see Case *51). Therefore, the mission again radioed for police protection. Three policemen arrived early in May. During the following weeks the Jalé people experienced for the first time the power of foreign political control in four separate events.

The first event was the overnight detention of a "big man" from Angkuruk in the house that served as a temporary police station, following an ill-fated intervention by policemen in a dispute over a pig; the second involved the fatal shooting of a man in another abortive attempt to settle a dispute. The third occasion was a peculiar "peace meeting" between Pasikni and Angkuruk ordered by the police to end the hostilities stemming from unresolved inter-village conflicts (Cases *49 and *51). The meeting was arranged through two coastal catechists and involved readings from the Bible as well as the display of the national flag. The fourth event was the payment of compensation by the mission to relatives of all victims in the Piliam massacre. [The police did not directly participate in this settlement; the European agricultural engineer on the station arranged an equitable distribution of cymbium shells and steel axes after consultations with me about the matter.]

The activities of the police created widespread fear that the "bum-bow carrying men" would settle in Angkuruk. The Jalé of the Jaxólé Valley realized that a new kind of stranger who neither spoke nor understood their language would punish any form of violent behavior. Therefore, when toward the end of June two old women from Wanjok who were married in Piliam visited their kinsmen to deliver another peace message, a group of Wanjok men crossed the Fungfung ridge and sang peace stanzas. The Pasikni people appeared to welcome any settlement that could be reached between Wanjok and Piliam. However, the kinsmen of those whose death had not been revenged prepared a joint journey to Wanjok to present their demand for "guilt" pigs. [According to information received after my departure, a peace ceremony was held at a place in the Fungfung forest on Piliam territory around the middle of July. However, in April 1967, Pasikni men killed and ate a Piliam man who had traveled to the Jaxólé Valley.]

Appendix B Demography of the Village of Pasikni

On December 31, 1965, 463 people lived in the village of Pasikni; approximately 40 percent (180) were initiated males.* The size of men's house groups varied from two for the remnant ward of Masaxavil to 66 for the populous Seraxanpini ward. A majority of seven wards had less than twenty men's house residents. The 283 women and children who lived in 109 family huts included 55 uninitiated boys and 9 infants whose sex I did not ascertain. Except for Seraxanpini, which had 41 huts, all wards had less than 20, the clusters ranging from 3 to 19.

I have computed sib and lineage affiliation and residential association for all adult men. Fifty-two distinct lineages belonging to thirteen different sibs and of whom a whole quarter is non-autochthonous, lived in the nine wards of the village. Given a population of 107 married or widowed men's house residents, the limited political significance of traceable agnatic descent lines becomes obvious. Genealogical links, however, facilitate the incorporation of immigrant lineages into the ward community. The affinal relationships between immigrant lineages and autochthonous villagers reflect this particular connection between kinship and residence. Of the thirteen original immigrants of non-autochthonous lineages in my sample two settled with maternal kinsmen, two uxori-patrilocally, and two with more distant affines. One man who belongs to a lineage in another village became a resident when his widowed mother remarried a Pasikni man from her natal ward. This distribution leaves only six immigrants who came to live at the wards of their trading friends. Furthermore, genealogical data for the thirteen immigrant lineages suggest a marked tendency in their first marriages concluded after settling in Pasikni toward local endogamy—if compared with the overall marriage pattern (see Koch 1968a). But immigration is not the only process that produces a residential accretion of different lineages. Intra-village warfare, unresolved conflict between agnates, and, rarely, a man's decision to build his family hut at his wife's natal ward may induce a single man or a whole lineage to leave their ancestral men's house and take up residence at a neighboring ward. Thirteen such cases have occurred in Pasikni

* All statistical data derive from genealogical records in Koch 1967.

over the span of a generation, and my informants believed that all but two or three shifts were "final"—a judgment with little predictive value under the circumstances.

The following tables (1 to 4) summarize the details of my demographic survey.

Table 1. Settlement and Residence in Pasikni

Ward	Adjunct Men's Houses	Family Huts	Men's House Residents	Family Hut Residents[a]	Married Men	Monogamous Unions	Polygynous Unions
Womikma	0	8	16	30	9	6	3
Halepini	2	8	17	20	7	7	0
Kénanghólómó	1	11	14	22	8	8	0
Longkopini	0	12	18	26	11	8	3
Nelelum	2	19	30	49	14	12	2
Savéapini	0	5	9	15	4	3	1
Masaxavil	0	3	2	7	2	1	1
Jekjekpini	0	4	8	14	7	6	1
Seraxanpini	2	41	66	100	42	38	4
Total	7	111[b]	180	283	104	89	15

[a] Table 2 contains detailed data on these residents.
[b] This figure includes the vacant family huts of a Kénanghólómó widow and a Seraxanpini wife who died in 1965 and the family hut of a Nelelum man who uses it as an adjunct men's house. The huts of four women (two widows and two wives) were built by their still unmarried sons for future accommodation of their own wives.

Table 2. Residents in Family Huts

Ward	Residence of Wives					Residence of Widows				Children				Total
	Separate	With co-wife	With husband's brother's wife	With husband's mother	Other	Separate	With son's wife	With married daughter	Other	Unmarried daughters	Uninitiated sons	Infants (sex?)	Others	
Nomikma	7[a]	4	1	0	0	0	1	0	1[b]	8	6	3	0	31
Halepini	7	0	0	0	0	1	0	0	0	8	4	0	0	20
Kénanghólómó	8	0	0	0	0	0	0	1	1[c]	7	3	1	0	21
Longkopini	12	0	0	1	1[d]	0	0	0	0	5	6	0	1[e]	26
Nelelum	15	0	0	0	1[f]	3	1	1	1[g]	14	12	0	1[h]	49
Javéapini	3	2	0	0	0	1	0	0	0	7	0	2	0	15
Masaxavil	2	0	0	0	1[i]	0	0	0	0	2	2	0	0	7
Tekjekpini	4[j]	2	0	2	0	0	0	0	0	4	2	1	0	15
Seraxanpini	37[k]	4	1	2[l]	2[m]	1	1	0	2[n]	28	20	2	2[o]	102
Total	95	12	2	5	5	6	3	2	5	83	55	9	4	286[p]
			119					16			147		4	

[a] Including one woman whose husband built his family hut at her natal ward of Kénanghólómó, where her widowed mother stayed with her before moving to the hut of her son's wife, who died in 1965.

[b] Residing with the wife of her father's brother's son who adopted her children.

[c] Living in the family hut of her son to care for his children after his wife's death in 1965; cf. note a.

[d] Residing with her adoptive mother after her husband, a Seraxanpini man, abandoned his homestead during a war in 1964 and moved to Longkopini.

[e] An unmarried, decrepit woman living with her sister.

[f] The wife of a polygynous man living with her daughter-in-law.

[g] Residing with her widowed mother after her husband immigrated from the village of Kévéangken.

[h] A married woman living with her mother's sister's daughter after she deserted her husband in another village.

[i] The wife of a polygynous man residing with her daughter-in-law in the village of Tuluk-Ikma, where her son has settled.

[j] Including one woman residing at her homestead near the village.

[k] Including the wife of a polygynous man living in the Masaxavil family hut of her brother, who settled in the village of Tuluk-Ikma.

[l] One of these women living alone after her husband's mother's death in 1965.

[m] One wife of a polygynous man residing with her daughter-in-law, and one old woman living with her sister-in-law in another village after her husband abandoned his homestead during a war in 1964.

[n] One widow residing with her brother's wife, the other with a neighbor who is a widow herself.

[o] One decrepit woman residing with her mother's sister after the death of her mother, and one girl engaged to a Longkopini man living with the wife of her father's sib brother after her mother refused to move to Pasikni when their homestead was abandoned during a war in 1964; cf. note m.

[p] The difference of 3 between this total and the number of family hut residents given in Table 1, column 4, results from including three nonresident wives in this table. Discrepancies between wards are explained in notes a, j, k, and m.

Table 3. Distribution of Sibs, Lineages, and Their Adult Male Membership in Pasikni Wards

Ward	Number of Resident Sib-Fragments	Number of Resident Lineages	Number of Adult Men
Womikma	3	6	9
Halepini	4	6	7
Kénanghólómó	2	3	9
Longkopini	5	5	11
Nelelum	4	8	15
Savéapini	4	4	4
Masaxavil	1	1	2
Jekjekpini	3	3	7
Seraxanpini	9	22	43
Total	35	58	107

Table 4. Distribution and Adult Male Membership of Lineages Resident in Pasikni[a]

Moiety	Name of Sib	Number of Lineages in Pasikni	Number of Married or Widowed Males	Number of Wards Where Resident
	amoxoso	3	3	3
	élintam	7 + (1)	13 + (1)	5
	hampasingkik	1	4	1
wanta	helempo	1 + (1)	1 + (2)	1
	(nélampo)	(1)	(1)	1
	paxavol	1 + (2)	1 + (4)	3
	sama	9	20	4
	(sélép)	(1)	(2)	1
	6 + (2) = 8	22 + (6) = 28	42 + (10) = 52	
	kavak	11 + (2)	26 + (2)	5
	kénangalem	6	20	5
waja	(móxéi)	(3)	(4)	2
	(ólóngéi)	(1)	(1)	1
	(séréngon)	(1)	(2)	1
	2 + (3) = 5	17 + (7) = 24	46 + (9) = 55	
Total	8 + (5) = 13	39 + (13) = 52[b]	88 + (19) = 107	

[a] A parenthesis indicates non-autochthonous residence in Pasikni.
[b] There is a discrepancy between this figure and the number of resident lineages listed in Table 3 because six men live separately from their descent group in other Pasikni wards.

Appendix C Kinship Terminology

The following tables and figures summarize taxonomic and semantic features of the Jalé classification of consanguineal relatives (Table 5 and Figures 14 to 16) and affinal relatives (Table 6 and Figures 17 and 18).

Table 5. Terms for Consanguineal Relatives

Terms Singular	Plural	Kin Types
1. *oe*	*oesi*	ebr, esi, efabrso[a], efabrda[a]
2. *ot*	*otsi*	ybr, ysi, yfabrso[a], yfabrda[a]
3. *ikni*	*iknisi*	fa, fabr, fafabrso, famosiso
4. *ésénga*	*éséngasi*	mo
5. *óan*	*óansi*	fasi, fafabrda, famosida
6. *amé*	*amusi*	mobr, mofabrso, momosiso, mobrso, mobrsoso
7. *ómóm*	*ómómsi*	mosi, mofabrda, momosida, mobrda, mobrsoda
8. *axavilie*	*axaviliesi*	mosiso, mosida, mofasiso, mofasida, mobrdaso, mobrdada
9. *amloxo*	*amloxoki(si)*	so, brso, siso, fabrsoso, fabrdaso, fasiso, fafasiso, mosisoso, mosidaso; soso, daso, brsoso, brdaso, sisoso, sidaso, fasisoso, fasidaso (female Ego)
10. *axaloxo*	*axolané*	da, brda, sida, fabrsoda, fabrdada, fasida, fafasida, mosisoda, mosidada
11. *ómpósak*	*ómpósaksi*	fafa, fafabr, famobr, mofa, mofabr, momobr, famobrso, momobrso; soso, soda, daso, dada, brsoso, brsoda, brdaso, brdada, sisoso, sisoda, sidaso, sidada, fasisoso, fasisoda, fasidaso, fasidada (male Ego)
12. *émpéanga*	*émpéangasi*	famo, fafasi, famosi, momo, momosi, mofasi, famobrda, momobrda; soda, dada, brsoda, brdada, sisoda, sidada, fasisoda, fasidada (female Ego)

[a] If two patrilateral parallel cousins are considered to be of the same age, the Jalé substitute the terms *are*, *exe*, or *erek*.

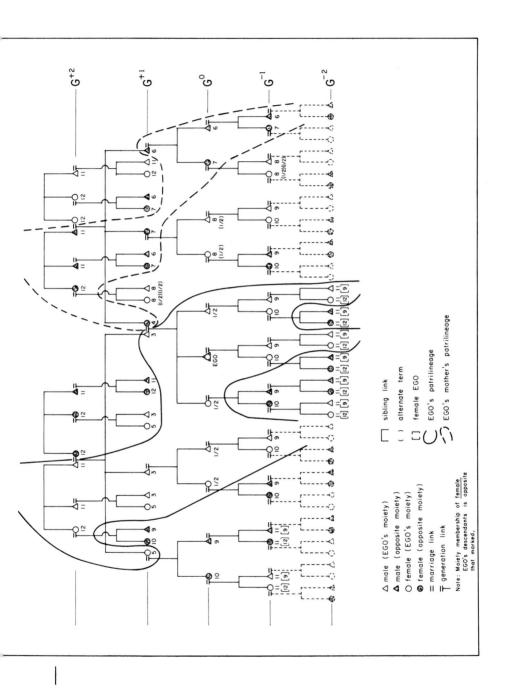

Note: Moiety membership of female
EGO's descendants is opposite
that marked.

△ male (EGO's moiety)
▲ male (opposite moiety)
○ female (EGO's moiety)
◉ female (opposite moiety)
= marriage link
⊤ generation link

⊓ sibling link
( ) alternate term
[ ] female EGO
∪ EGO's patrilineage
⌒⌒ EGO's mother's patrilineage

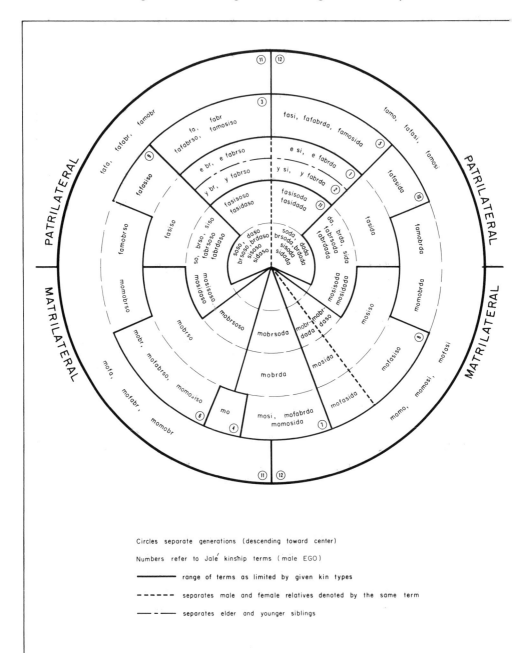

Circles separate generations (descending toward center)

Numbers refer to Jalé kinship terms (male EGO)

————————— range of terms as limited by given kin types

- - - - - - separates male and female relatives denoted by the same term

——— – ——— separates elder and younger siblings

16 Consanguineal relatives: semantic features of classification

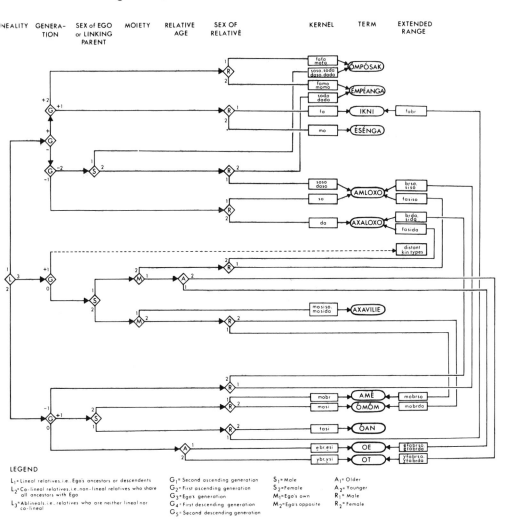

LEGEND

L_1 = Lineal relatives, i.e., Ego's ancestors or descendents

L_2 = Co-lineal relatives, i.e., non-lineal relatives who share all ancestors with Ego

L_3 = Ablineals, i.e., relatives who are neither lineal nor co-lineal

G_1 = Second ascending generation

G_2 = First ascending generation

G_3 = Ego's generation

G_4 = First descending generation

G_5 = Second descending generation

S_1 = Male

S_2 = Female

M_1 = Ego's own

M_2 = Ego's opposite

A_1 = Older

A_2 = Younger

R_1 = Male

R_2 = Female

Table 6. Terms for Affinal Relatives

| Terms | | Kin Types | | | |
Singular	Plural	Spouse Linked Male Ego	Female Ego	Consanguineally Linked Male Ego	Female Ego
axón	axónsi		hu		
óxe	óxesi	wi			
antélaxa	antélaxaki(si)		co-wife		
éamal	éamalsi	wifa, wifabr, wimobr, wimobrso	hufa, hufabr, humobr, humobrso	brwifa, sihufa, sowibr, dahu, dahubr, brdahu, sidahu, fasidahu	dahu, sidahu, fasidahu
éamalhe	éamalhómé	wimo, wimosi, wimobrda	humo, humosi, humobrda	sowi, brsowi, sisowi, fasisowi	sowi, sisowi, fasisowi
ómparik	ómpariki(si)	wibr, wisi, wifabrso, wifabrda, wimosiso, wimosida		brwibr, brwisi, sihu, sihubr, sihusi, fabrdahu, mosidahu, sowifa, dahufa	brwibr, sihu, sihubr, fabrdahu, mosidahu
axaruk	axaruki(si)		husi, hufabrda, humosida		brwi, brwisi, sihusi, fabrsowi, mosisowi, sowimo, dahumo
ómaeng	ómaengsi	wifasiso, wifasida, wibrso, wibrda, wisiso, wisida		fasihu, mosihu, mobrdahu	fasihu, mosihu, mobrdahu

Table 6. (continued)

| | | Kin Types | | | |
| | | Spouse Linked | | Consanguineally Linked | |
Singular	Plural	Male Ego	Female Ego	Male Ego	Female Ego
erek	erekisi	wibrwi	husihu	brwimo, sihumo, sowimo, dahumo	sowifa, dahufa, sowibr, dahubr
exe	exevisi		hubrwi		brwimo, sihumo, sowisi, dahusi
ikni	iknisi		huebr, ehufabrso, ehumosiso		
ésénga	éséngasi	wifasi	hufasi	fabrwi, ebrwi efabrsowi, emosisowi	fabrwi
óan	óansi			mobrwi, mobrsowi	mobrwi, mobrsowi
axavilie	axaviliesi	wisihu			
amloxo	amloxoki(si)		huybr, yhufabrso, yhumosiso, hufasiso, hubrso, husiso		brdahu
axaloxo	axolané		hufasida, hubrda, husida	ybrwi, yfabrsowi ymosisowi	brsowi
ómpósak	ómpósaksi			sowisi, dahusi	brwifa, sihufa

17 Affinal relatives linked by spouse

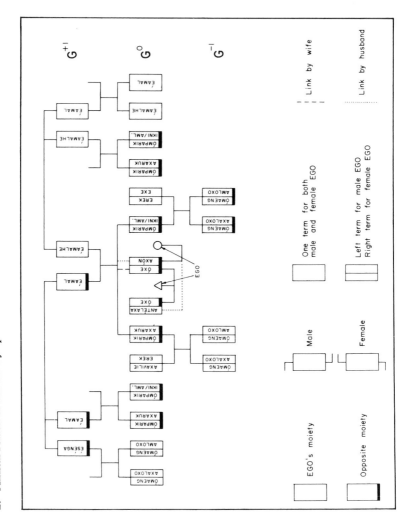

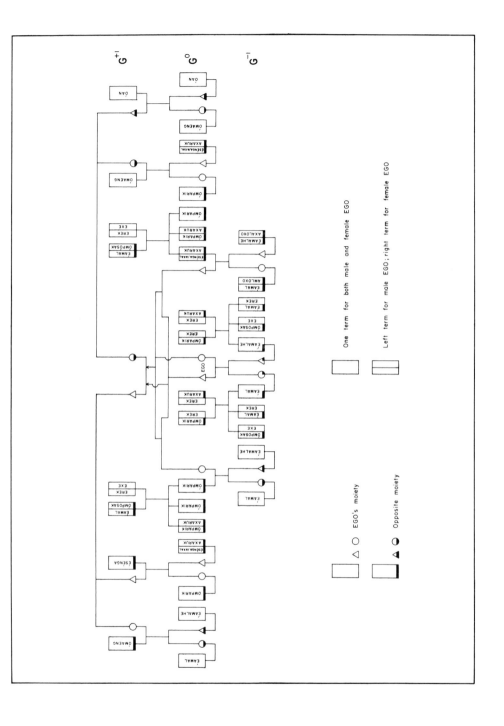

Bibliography

Allott, A. N., A. L. Epstein, and M. Gluckman. 1969. "Introduction."
  Ideas and Procedures in African Customary Law, ed. Max
  Gluckman, pp. 1–96. London: Oxford University Press.
Arendt, Hannah. 1969. *On Violence*. New York: Harcourt, Brace
  and World.
Ayoub, Victor F. 1965. "Conflict Resolution and Social Reorganization
  in a Lebanese Village." *Human Organization* 24, 1: 11–17.
Barnes, J. A. 1962. "African Models in the New Guinea Highlands."
  Man 62, 2: 5–9.
————— 1969. "The Politics of Law." *Man in Africa*, ed. Mary Douglas
  and Phyllis M. Kaberry, pp. 99–118. London: Tavistock.
Barton, R. F. 1969. *Ifugao Law*. Berkeley and Los Angeles: University
  of California Press. (First published in 1919 in University of
  California Publications in American Archaeology and Ethnology
  15, 1.)
Beals, Alan R. 1969. "Social Structure and the Prediction of Conflict:
  A Test of Two Hypotheses." *Contributions to Indian Sociology,*
  n.s., no. 3: 32–44.
Beattie, J. H. M. 1957. "Informal Judicial Activity in Bunyoro."
  Journal of African Administration 9, 4: 188–195.
Benedict, Ruth. 1934. *Patterns of Culture*. Boston and New York:
  Houghton Mifflin.
Berndt, Ronald M. 1962. *Excess and Restraint: Social Control among
  a New Guinea Mountain People*. Chicago: University of Chicago
  Press.
————— 1964. "Warfare in the New Guinea Highlands." *American
  Anthropologist* 66, 4 (part 2): 183–203.
Biller, Henry B. 1970. "Father Absence and the Personality Develop-
  ment of the Male Child." *Developmental Psychology* 2, 2: 181–
  201.
Black, Cyril E., and Richard A. Falk, eds. 1971. *The Future of the
  International Legal Order*, vol. III, *Conflict Management*.
  Princeton: Princeton University Press.
Blumberg, Abraham S. 1967. "The Practice of Law as a Confidence
  Game: Organizational Cooptation of a Profession." *Law and
  Society Review* 1, 2: 15–39.

Bohannan, Paul. 1960. "Theories of Homicide and Suicide." *African Homicide and Suicide*, ed. Paul Bohannan, pp. 3–29. Princeton: Princeton University Press.

———— 1969. "Ethnography and Comparison in Legal Anthropology." *Law in Culture and Society*, ed. Laura Nader, pp. 401–418. Chicago: Aldine.

Boorman, Scott A. 1969. *The Protracted Game: A "wei-ch'i" Interpretation of Maoist Revolutionary Strategy*. London: Oxford University Press.

Boulding, Kenneth E. 1962. *Conflict and Defense: A General Theory*. New York: Harper & Brothers.

Bozeman, Adda, B. 1971. *The Future of Law in a Multicultural World*. Princeton: Princeton University Press.

Bramson, Leon, and George W. Goethals, eds. 1968. *War: Studies from Psychology, Sociology, Anthropology*, rev. ed. New York and London: Basic Books.

Brandewie, Ernest. 1971. "The Place of the Big Man in Traditional Hagen Society in the Central Highlands of New Guinea." *Ethnology* 10, 2: 194–210.

Broekhuijse, J. Th. 1967. *De Wiligiman-Dani: Een cultureel-anthropologische studie over religie en oorlogvoering in de Baliem-Vallei*. Tilburg: H. Gianotten.

Brögger, Jan. 1968. "Conflict Resolution and the Role of the Bandit in Peasant Society." *Anthropological Quarterly* 41, 4: 228–240.

Bromley, H. Myron. 1960. "A Preliminary Report on Law among the Grand Valley Dani of Netherlands New Guinea." *Nieuw-Guinea Studiën* 4, 3: 235–259.

———— 1961. *The Phonology of Lower Grand Valley Dani: A Comparative Structural Study of Skewed Phonemic Patterns*. Verhandelingen van het Koninklijk Instituut voor Taal-, Land- en Volkenkunde 34. The Hague: Martinus Nijhoff.

———— 1967. "The Linguistic Relationships of Grand Valley Dani: A Lexico-Statistical Classification." *Oceania* 37, 4: 286–308.

Brongersma, L. D., and G. F. Venema. [1960]. *Het Witte Hart van Nieuw-Guinea: Met de Nederlandse Expeditie naar het Sterrengebergte*. Amsterdam: Scheltens & Giltay.

Brookfield, H. C., and Paula Brown. 1963. *Struggle for Land: Agriculture and Group Territories among the Chimbu of the New Guinea Highlands*. Melbourne: Oxford University Press.

Brown, Paula. 1962. "Non-Agnates among the Patrilineal Chimbu." *The Journal of the Polynesian Society* 71, 1: 57–69.

———— 1964. "Enemies and Affines." *Ethnology* 3, 4: 335–356.

Brown, Paula, and H. C. Brookfield. 1959. "Chimbu Land and Society." *Oceania* 30, 1: 1–75.

Chao, Yuen Ren. 1968. *Language and Symbolic Systems:* London: Cambridge University Press.

Clarke, William C. 1971. *Place and People: An Ecology of a New Guinean Community.* Berkeley, Los Angeles, and London: University of California Press.

Cohen, Jerome Alan. 1966. "Chinese Mediation on the Eve of Modernization." *California Law Review* 54, 3: 1201–1226.

Colson, E. 1953. "Social Control and Vengeance in Plateau Tonga Society." *Africa* 23, 3: 199–212.

Corbett, Percy E. 1971. *The Growth of World Law.* Princeton: Princeton University Press.

Coser, Lewis A. 1956. *The Functions of Social Conflict.* Glencoe: Free Press.

Coult, Allan D. 1967. "Lineage Solidarity, Transformational Analysis and the Meaning of Kinship Terminologies." *Man* 2, 1: 26–47.

de Lepervanche, Marie. 1967–1968. "Descent, Residence and Leadership in the New Guinea Highlands." *Oceania* 38, 2: 134–158; 38, 3: 163–189.

Douglas, Jack D. 1967. *The Social Meanings of Suicide.* Princeton: Princeton University Press.

Dundas, Charles. 1921. "Native Laws of Some Bantu Tribes of East Africa." *Journal of the Royal Anthropological Institute* 51: 216–278.

Durand, Paul. 1958. "Conciliation and Mediation in Collective Industrial Disputes." *International Social Science Bulletin* 10, 4: 544–603.

Dynes, Russell R., and E. L. Quarantelli. 1971. "The Absence of Community Conflict in the Early Phases of Natural Disasters." *Conflict Resolution: Contributions of the Behavioral Sciences,* ed. Clagett G. Smith, pp. 200–204. Notre Dame and London: University of Notre Dame Press.

Eckhoff, Torstein. 1966. "The Mediator, the Judge and the Administrator in Conflict-Resolution." *Acta Sociologica* 10, 1–2: 148–172.

Ekvall, Robert B. 1964. "Peace and War among the Tibetan Nomads." *American Anthropologist* 66, 5: 1119–1148.

Ember, Melvin, and Carol R. Ember. 1971. "The Conditions Favoring Matrilocal versus Patrilocal Residence." *American Anthropologist* 73, 3: 571–594.

Epstein, A. L. 1967a. "Injury and Liability: Legal Ideas and Implicit Assumptions." *Mankind* 6, 9: 376–383.

—— 1967b. "The Case Method in the Field of Law." *The Craft of Social Anthropolgy,* ed. A. L. Epstein, pp. 205–230. London: Tavistock.

—— 1969. "Injury and Liability in African Customary Law in

Zambia." *Ideas and Procedures in African Customary Law*, ed.
Max Gluckman, pp. 292–304. London: Oxford University Press.

————— 1971. "Dispute Settlement among the Tolai." *Oceania* 41,
3: 157–170.

Firth, Raymond. 1961. "Suicide and Risk-Taking in Tikopia Society."
Psychiatry 24, 1: 1–17.

Fortes, M., and E. E. Evans-Pritchard, eds. 1940. *African Political
Systems*. London: Oxford University Press.

Fried, Morton H., Marvin Harris, and Robert Murphy, eds. 1968.
War: The Anthropology of Armed Conflict and Aggression.
Garden City: Natural History Press.

Fuller, Lon L. 1963. "Collective Bargaining and the Arbitrator."
Wisconsin Law Review 1963, 1: 3–46.

————— 1971. "Mediation—Its Forms and Functions." *Southern
California Law Review* 44, 2: 305–339.

Gallin, Bernard. 1967. "Mediation in Changing Chinese Society in
Rural Taiwan." *Journal of Asian and African Studies* 2, 1–2:
77–90.

Galtung, Johan. 1965. "Institutionalized Conflict Resolution." *Journal
of Peace Research* 4:348–397.

Gardner, Robert, and Karl G. Heider. 1968. *Gardens of War: Life
and Death in the New Guinea Stone Age*. New York:
Random House.

Gibbs, James L., Jr. 1963. "The Kpelle Moot: A Therapeutic Model
for the Informal Settlement of Disputes." *Africa* 33, 1: 1–11.

Glasse, Robert M. 1968. *Huli of Papua: A Cognatic Descent System*.
Cahiers de l'Homme, n.s. VIII. Paris and the Hague: Mouton
& Co.

Gluckman, Max. 1959. *Custom and Conflict in Africa*. Glencoe:
Free Press.

————— 1965. *Politics, Law and Ritual in Tribal Society*. Chicago:
Aldine.

————— 1973. "Limitations of the Case-Method in the Study of Tribal
Law." *Law and Society Review* 7, 4: 611–641.

Gulliver, Philip H. 1963. *Social Control in an African Society: A Study
of the Arusha, Agricultural Masai of Northern Tanganyika*.
Boston: Boston University Press. London: Routledge and
Kegan Paul.

————— 1969. "Case Studies of Law in Non-Western Societies." *Law
in Culture and Society*, ed. Laura Nader, pp. 11–23. Chicago:
Aldine.

————— 1971. *Neighbors and Networks: The Idiom of Kinship in
Social Action among the Ndendeuli of Tanzania*. Berkeley, Los
Angeles, and London: University of California Press.

——— 1973. "Negotiations as a Mode of Dispute Settlement:
Toward a General Model." *Law and Society Review 7*, 4: 667–691.

Hart, H. L. A. 1968. *Punishment and Responsibility: Essays in the
Philosophy of Law.* Oxford: Clarendon Press.

Healey, Alan. 1964. "The Ok Language Family in New Guinea,"
unpub. diss., Australian National University.

Heider, Karl G. 1968. See Gardner, Robert, and Karl G. Heider.

——— 1970. *The Dugum Dani: A Papuan Culture in the Highlands
of West New Guinea.* Viking Fund Publications in Anthropology
49. New York: Wenner-Gren Foundation for Anthropological
Research.

Hippler, Arthur E. 1969. "Fusion and Frustration: Dimensions in the
Cross-Cultural Ethnopsychology of Suicide." *American
Anthropologist 71*, 6: 1074–1087.

Hoebel, E. Adamson. 1954. *The Law of Primitive Man: A Study in
Comparative Legal Dynamics.* Cambridge, Mass.: Harvard
University Press.

Hogbin, H. Ian. 1938. "Social Reaction to Crime: Law and Morals in
the Schouten Islands, New Guinea." *Journal of the Royal
Anthropological Institute 68*: 223–262.

Holmes, O. W. 1881. *The Common Law.* Boston: Little, Brown
& Co.

Holsti, K. J. 1966. "Resolving International Conflicts: A Taxonomy
of Behavior and Some Figures on Procedures." *The Journal of
Conflict Resolution 10*, 3: 272–296.

Holý, Ladislav. 1967. "Social Consequences of *dia* among the Berti."
Africa 37, 4: 466–479.

Howell, P. P. 1954. *A Manual of Nuer Law: Being an Account of
Customary Law, Its Evolution and Development in the Courts
Established by the Sudan Government.* London: Oxford
University Press.

Jaspan, M. A. 1965. "West Irian: The First Two Years." *The
Australian Quarterly 37*, 2: 9–21.

Jeffreys, M. D. W. 1952. "Samsonic Suicide or Suicide of Revenge
among Africans." *African Studies 11*, 3: 118–122.

Kaberry, Phyllis M. 1967. "The Plasticity of New Guinea Kinship."
Social Organization: Essays Presented to Raymond Firth, ed.
Maurice Freedman, pp. 105–123. Chicago: Aldine.

Kelly, Raymond C. 1968. "Demographic Pressure and Descent Group
Structure in the New Guinea Highlands." *Oceania 39*, 1: 36–63.

Koch, Klaus-Friedrich. 1963. "Legal Implications of Suicide." Ms.

——— 1967. "Conflict and Its Management among the Jalé People
of West New Guinea," unpub. diss., University of California,

Berkeley. (Facsimile produced and distributed by University Microfilms, Ann Arbor, Michigan.)

—— 1968a. "Marriage in Jalémó." *Oceania* 39, 2: 85–109.

—— 1968b. "On 'Possession' Behaviour in New Guinea." *The Journal of the Polynesian Society* 77, 2: 135–146.

—— 1970a. "Cannibalistic Revenge in Jalé Society." *Natural History* 79, 2: 40–51.

—— 1970b. "Structure and Variability in the Jalé Kinship Terminology: A Formal Analysis." *Ethnology* 9, 3: 263–301.

—— 1972. "Semantics of Kinship Terms: The Jalé Case." *Bijdragen tot de Taal-, Land- en Volkenkunde* 128, 1: 81–98.

—— in press a. "Incest and Its Punishment in Jalé Society." *The Journal of the Polynesian Society.*

—— in press b. "Sociogenic and Psychogenic Models in Anthropology: The Functions of Jalé Initiation." *Man.*

Kooijman, S. 1962. "Material Aspects of the Star Mountains Culture." *Nova Guinea*, Anthropology no. 2: 15–44.

Kroeber, A. L. 1928. "Law of the Yurok Indians." *Proceedings of the Twenty-Second International Congress of Americanists* (Rome 1926), vol. II: 511–516. Rome: Instituto Christoforo Colombo.

Landheer, Bart. 1966. *On the Sociology of International Law and International Society.* The Hague: Martinus Nijhoff.

Langness, L. L. 1964. "Some Problems in the Conceptualization of Highland Social Structures." *American Anthropologist* 66, 4 (part 2): 162–182.

—— 1972. "Political Organization." *Encyclopaedia of Papua and New Guinea.* Carlton, Victoria: Melbourne University Press.

LeVine, Robert A. 1965. "Socialization, Social Structure, and Intersocietal Images." *International Behavior: A Social-Psychological Analysis*, ed. Herbert C. Kelman, pp. 45–69. New York: Holt, Rinehart and Winston.

Lijphart, Arend. 1966. *The Trauma of Decolonization: The Dutch and West New Guinea.* New Haven and London: Yale University Press.

Lorentz, H. A. 1913. *Zwarte Menschen—witte bergen: verhaal van den tocht naar het Sneeuwgebergte van Nieuw-Guinea.* Leiden: E. J. Brill.

Lowman-Vayda, Cherry. 1968. "Maring Big Men." *Anthropological Forum* 2, 2: 199–243.

Luard, Evan. 1968. *Conflict and Peace in the Modern International System.* Boston: Little, Brown & Co.

Lubman, Stanley. 1967. "Mao and Mediation: Politics and Dispute Resolution in Communist China." *California Law Review* 55, 5: 1241–1359.

Malcolm, L. A. 1966. "The Age of Puberty in the Bundi People."
   Papua and New Guinea Medical Journal 9: 16–20.
Malinowski, Bronislaw. 1926. *Crime and Custom in Savage Society.*
   New York: Harcourt, Brace & Co. London: Kegan Paul, Trench,
   Trubner & Co.
Manning, Helen. 1969. *To Perish for Their Saving.* Eastbourne,
   Sussex: Victory Press.
McKinley, Robert. 1971. "Why Do Crow and Omaha Kinship
   Terminologies Exist? A Sociology of Knowledge Interpretation."
   Man 6, 3: 408–426.
Mead, Margaret. 1968. "Alternatives to a War." *War: The
   Anthropology of Armed Conflict and Aggression,* ed. Morton
   Fried, Marvin Harris, and Robert Murphy, pp. 215–237. Garden
   City: Natural History Press.
Megargee, Edwin I., and Jack E. Hokanson, eds. 1970. *The Dynamics
   of Aggression: Individual, Group and International Analyses.*
   New York: Harper and Row.
Meggitt, M. J. 1965. *The Lineage System of the Mae-Enga of New
   Guinea.* New York: Barnes and Noble.
———— 1967. "The Pattern of Leadership among the Mae-Enga of
   New Guinea." *Anthropological Forum* 2, 1: 20–35.
Montagu, M. F. Ashley, ed. 1968. *Man and Aggression.* London,
   Oxford, and New York: Oxford University Press.
Moore, Sally Falk. 1970. "Politics, Procedures, and Norms in
   Changing Chagga Law." *Africa* 40, 4: 321–344.
Murphy, Robert F. 1957. "Intergroup Hostility and Social Cohesion."
   American Anthropologist 59, 6: 1018–1035.
Nader, Laura. 1965. "Choices of Legal Procedure: Shia Moslem and
   Mexican Zapotec." *American Anthropologist* 67, 2: 394–399.
———— 1969. "Styles of Court Procedure: To Make the Balance."
   Law in Culture and Society, ed. Laura Nader, pp. 69–91. Chicago:
   Aldine.
Nader, Laura, Herma Kay, et al. 1966. "Comparative Village Law
   Project: Field Manual on Law." Department of Anthropology,
   University of California, Berkeley. Mimeographed.
Nader, Laura, and Duane Metzger. 1963. "Conflict Resolution in Two
   Mexican Communities." *American Anthropologist* 65, 3:
   584–592.
Newman, Donald J. 1956. "Pleading Guilty for Considerations: A
   Study of Bargain Justice." *Journal of Criminal Law, Criminology,
   and Police Science* 46, 6: 780–790.
Newman, Philip L. 1965. *Knowing the Gururumba.* New York: Holt,
   Rinehart and Winston.

Otterbein, Keith F. 1968a. "Cross-Cultural Studies of Armed Combat." *Buffalo Studies* 4, 1: 91–109.

———— 1968b. "Internal War: A Cross-Cultural Study." *American Anthropologist* 70, 2: 277–289.

———— 1970. *The Evolution of War: A Cross-Cultural Study.* New Haven: HRAF Press.

Otterbein, Keith F., and Charlotte Swanson Otterbein. 1965. "An Eye for an Eye, a Tooth for a Tooth: A Cross-Cultural Study of Feuding." *American Anthropologist* 67, 6 (part 1): 1470–1482.

Peristiany, J. G. 1954. "Pokot Sanctions and Structure." *Africa* 24, 1: 17–25.

Peters, E. L. 1967. "Some Structural Aspects of the Feud among the Camel-Herding Bedouin of Cyrenaica." *Africa* 37, 3: 261–282.

Peters, H. L. 1965. *Enkele Hoofdstukken uit het sociaal-religieuze leven van een Dani-groep.* Venlo: Dagblad voor Noord-Limburg.

Ploeg, A. 1969. *Government in Wanggulam.* Verhandelingen van het Koninklijk Instituut voor Taal-, Land- en Volkenkunde 57. The Hague: Martinus Nijhoff.

Plucknett, Theodore F. T. 1956. *A Concise History of the Common Law,* 5th ed. Boston: Little, Brown & Co.

Pospisil, Leopold. 1958. *Kapauku Papuans and Their Law.* Yale University Publications in Anthropology, no. 54. New Haven: Yale University for the Department of Anthropology.

Power, Jan. 1964. "A Social System in the Star Mountains: Toward a Reorientation of the Study of Social Systems." *American Anthropologist* 66, 4 (part 2): 133–161.

———— 1966. "Toward a Configurational Approach to Society and Culture in New Guinea." *The Journal of the Polynesian Society* 75, 3: 267–286.

Radcliffe-Brown, A. R. 1941. "The Study of Kinship Systems." *Journal of the Royal Anthropological Institute* 71: 1–18.

Rappaport, Roy A. 1967. *Pigs for the Ancestors: Ritual in the Ecology of a New Guinea People.* New Haven and London: Yale University Press.

Read, K. E. 1954. "Cultures of the Central Highlands, New Guinea." *Southwestern Journal of Anthropology* 10, 1: 1–43.

———— 1955. "Morality and the Concept of the Person among the Gahuku-Gama." *Oceania* 25, 4: 233–282.

———— 1959. "Leadership and Consensus in a New Guinea Society." *American Anthropologist* 61, 3: 425–436.

Reay, Marie. 1959. *The Kuma: Freedom and Conformity in the New Guinea Highlands.* Carlton: Melbourne University Press.

Reisman, W. Michael. 1971. *Nullity and Revision: The Review and*

Enforcement of International Judgments and Awards. New Haven and London: Yale University Press.

Reynders, J. J. 1962. "Shifting Cultivation in the Star Mountains Area." *Nova Guinea,* Anthropology no. 3: 45–73.

Ryan, John. 1969. *The Hot Land: Focus on New Guinea.* New York: St. Martin's Press.

Schapera, I. 1956. *Government and Politics in Tribal Societies.* London: C. A. Watts & Co.

Shepperdson, M. J. 1969. "Political Conflict in Ten Villages in India, Pakistan and Ceylon." *Contributions to Indian Sociology,* n.s., no. 3: 45–75.

Sherif, Muzafer. 1966. *In Common Predicament: Social Psychology of Intergroup Conflict and Cooperation.* Boston: Houghton Mifflin.

Simmel, Georg. 1908. *Soziologie: Untersuchungen über die Formen der Vergesellschaftung.* Leipzig: Duncker and Humblot. (Parts published in 1950 in *The Sociology of Georg Simmel,* translated and edited by Kurt H. Wolff, Glencoe: Free Press; and in 1955 in *Conflict* [and] *The Web of Group-Affiliations,* translated by Kurt H. Wolff and Reinhard Bendix, Glencoe: Free Press.)

Skolnick, Jerome. 1967. "Social Control in the Adversary System." *The Journal of Conflict Resolution* 11, 1: 52–70.

Stauder, Jack. 1972. "Anarchy and Ecology: Political Society among the Majangir." *Southwestern Journal of Anthropology* 28, 2: 153–168.

Strathern, Andrew. 1966. "Despots and Directors in the New Guinea Highlands." *Man* 1, 3: 356–367.

————— 1969. "Descent and Alliance in the New Guinea Highlands: Some Problems of Comparison." *Proceedings of the Royal Anthropological Institute of Great Britain and Ireland for 1968:* 37–52.

————— 1971. *The Rope of Moka: Big-Men and Ceremonial Exchange in Mount Hagen New Guinea.* London: Cambridge University Press.

Thoden van Velzen, H. U. E., and W. van Wetering. 1960. "Residence, Power Groups and Intra-Societal Aggression: An Enquiry into the Conditions Leading to Peacefulness within Non-Stratified Societies." *International Archives of Ethnography* 49 (part 2): 169–200.

United Nations. 1969. "Report of the Secretary-General Regarding the Act of Self-Determination in West Irian." United Nations General Assembly, twenty-fourth session, agenda item 98, agreement between the Republic of Indonesia and the Kingdom of the Netherlands concerning West New Guinea (West Irian).

———— n.d. *The United Nations in West New Guinea: An Unprecedented Story.* New York: United Nations, Office of Public Information.

van der Kroef, J. M. 1970. "West Irian Redeemed?" *New Guinea* 4, 4: 62–72.

van der Sprenkel, Sybille. 1962. *Legal Institutions in Manchu China: A Sociological Analysis.* London School of Economics Monographs on Social Anthropology, no. 24. London: Athlone Press.

van der Stap, P. A. M. 1966. *Outline of Dani Morphology.* Verhandelingen van het Koninklijk Instituut vor Taal-, Land- en Volkenkunde 48. The Hague: Martinus Nijhoff.

van der Veur, Paul W. 1964. "The United Nations in West Irian: A Critique." *International Organization* 18, 1: 53–73.

van Nouhuys, J. W. 1913. "Der Bergstamm Pěsěgěm im Innern von Niederländisch-Neu-Guinea." *Nova Guinea*, VII, 1-[36]. Leiden: E. J. Brill.

van Velsen, J. 1969. "Procedural Informality, Reconciliation, and False Comparisons." *Ideas and Procedures in Africian Customary Law*, ed. Max Gluckman, pp. 137–152. London: Oxford University Press.

Vayda, Andrew P. 1971. "Phases of the Process of War and Peace among the Marings of New Guinea." *Oceania* 42, 1: 1–24.

Vicedom, Georg F., and Herbert Tischner. 1943. *Die Mbowamb: Die Kultur der Hagenberg-Stämme im östlichen Zentral-Neuguinea*, vol. II (by Georg F. Vicedom). Hamburg: Friederichsen, de Gruyter & Co.

Wagner, Roy. 1967. *The Curse of Souw: Principles of Daribi Clan Definition and Alliance in New Guinea.* Chicago and London: University of Chicago Press.

Watson, James B. 1970. "Society as Organized Flow: The Tairora Case." *Southwestern Journal of Anthropology* 26, 2: 107–124.

Weber, Max. 1956. *Wirtschaft und Gesellschaft: Grundriss der verstehenden Soziologie*, ed. Johannes Winckelmann. Cologne and Berlin: Kiepenheuer & Witsch.

Wedgwood, Camilla H. 1930. "Some Aspects of Warfare in Melanesia." *Oceania* 1, 1: 5–33.

Westermarck, Edward. 1908. "Suicide: A Chapter in Comparative Ethics." *The Sociological Review* 1, 1: 12–33.

Whiting, Beatrice B., ed. 1963. *Six Cultures: Studies of Child Rearing.* New York and London: John Wiley and Sons.

———— 1965. "Sex Identity Conflict and Physical Violence: A Comparative Study." *American Anthropologist* 67, 6 (part 2): 123–140.

Whiting, John W. M. 1941. *Becoming a Kwoma: Teaching and Learning in a New Guinea Tribe*. New Haven: Yale University Press.

Zöllner, Ilse. 1972. "Taufe in Angguruk." *In die Welt für die Welt: Berichte der Vereinigten Evangelischen Mission* (Essen) 8, 6: 4–7.

Notes

Introduction: Fieldwork in Jalémó

1. The former colony of Nederlands-Nieuw-Guinea became the provisional province of Irian Barat (now called Irian Jaya) after the transfer of administration to the government of Indonesia on May 1, 1963, which succeeded the United Nations Temporary Executive Authority (UNTEA) that had been in office since October 1, 1962. Several revolts against Indonesian rule occurred after 1964. In the summer of 1969, Indonesia, with the assistance and participation of a United Nations representative, organized the "act of free choice," which entitled the people of West New Guinea to decide whether or not they wished to remain with Indonesia under the 1962 "Agreement between the Republic of Indonesia and the Kingdom of the Netherlands concerning West New Guinea (West Irian)." The "consultative assemblies" established for that purpose in each of the eight regencies reached unanimous affirmative decisions by the Indonesian practice of *musjawarah*, or mutual consultations. These were "implemented in accordance with the social situation and conditions in West Irian" (United Nations 1969: 38), where "approximately 80 per cent . . . [of] the population is illiterate and little concerned with political matters" (ibid.: 45). The following publications deal with this recent history: Jaspan 1965; Lijphart 1966; Ryan 1969: Part 3; United Nations 1969, n.d.; van der Kroef 1970; and van der Veur 1964.

2. The following recent studies relate to these areas: Broekhuijse 1967; Bromley 1960, 1961, 1967; Brongersma and Venema 1960; Heider 1968, 1970; Kooijman 1962; Peters 1965; Ploeg 1969; Power 1964; Reynders 1962; van der Stap 1966.

3. Many data concerning the initial history of contact came from the Reverend S. Zöllner, Angkuruk.

4. In 1972 the first Jalé people were baptized in Angkuruk (Zöllner 1972).

5. I shall treat this initial phase in the pacification of the Jalémó in a separate study. However, a few additional observations concerning police activities and the mission's relationships with the local people appear in Case *53.

6. The Jalé expression combines the Indonesian word for "school" and the Jalé verb for "speak."

7. These records appeared in Koch 1967.

I. An Anthropological View of Conflict

1. See the perceptive analysis by Boorman 1969.

2. Litigation in small claims courts in the U.S., for example, often involves judicial mediation. Lubman (1967) has described the political context of judicial mediation in Communist China.

3. A special kind of mediation is the practice of arguing over a grievance in a public assembly, as in the neighborhood councils among the Banyoro (Beattie 1957), in the village assembly among the Tolai (Epstein 1971), and in moots among the Kpelle (Gibbs 1963), where several participants in the proceedings may effect a conciliation. Eckvall (1964) has provided an illustrative ethnographic example of peace mediation among Tibetan nomads.

4. Fuller has described an essential difference between arbitration and mediation in the following words: "The procedures appropriate for mediation are those most likely to uncover that pattern of adjustment which will most nearly meet the interests of both parties. The procedures appropriate for arbitration are those which most securely guarantee each of the parties a meaningful chance to present arguments and proofs for a decision in his favor" (1963: 24).

5. For a comparative study of different procedures for settling industrial disputes in North America and Europe see Durand 1958. In international conflicts a plebiscite represents a special case of arbitration (Holsti 1966).

6. I have described this method in Koch in press a.

7. For studies of bargain justice in U.S. courts see Blumberg 1967, Newman 1956, Skolnick 1967.

8. Gulliver's discussion of this problem reaches a similar conclusion, and his studies of the Arusha (1963) and Ndendeuli (1971) of Tanzania describe the fusion of political and judicial methods of dispute settlement in societies without formal forensic institutions. Moore (1970) has analyzed the political nature of judicial activities in a historical study on the Chagga legal system (see also Barnes 1969).

9. Other formal models of conflict resolution have been devised by Eckhoff (1966), Galtung (1965), Gulliver (1973), and Pospisil (1958).

10. For ethnological examples of this approach see Nader 1969, Nader and Metzger 1963, van Velsen 1969.

11. See Cohen 1966; Gallin 1967; Gibbs 1963; Gulliver 1963, 1971: Chapter 5; van der Sprenkel 1962.

12. Fuller (1971) has observed that mediation may also facilitate the termination of a contractual relationship to the benefit of both principals. One recurrent function of mediated conflict resolution is the beneficial effect of this method on the preservation and support of cooperative relationships among members of a local community.

Consequently, as Gallin's work on a village in Taiwan (1967) and Ayoub's study of a Lebanese community (1965) demonstrate, when political and economic changes reduce the scope of mutual dependence and weaken the need for communal solidarity, the effectiveness of mediation in the resolution of disputes declines, while the people's reliance on adjudication by agencies of the national government increases.

13. The fact that other New Guinea Highlands societies which have judicial authorities—notably the Kapauku (Pospisil 1958) and the Kuma (Reay 1959)—also have a body of legal rules supports my view that adjudication and a formal code are interdependent aspects of a legal system.

14. Pertinent reviews of the "case method" approach are Epstein 1967b and Gulliver 1969. See also Gluckman's (1973) critique of this method.

II. The Jalé Way of Life

1. The settlement of Pamóxók, located approximately one mile north of Pasikni, founded by people from the Pasikni ward of Halepini, is an example of this type of branch village.

2. Appendix B records a demographic survey that shows the distribution of the population in Pasikni over its nine wards and the residence patterns of individual families.

3. A man's dress consists of over a hundred feet of split ratan lengths coiled around the body from hips to chest. A woman's apron consists of several layers of rushes that are separately tied around her hips in such a way that one bunch covers her pubes and the other the lower part of her buttocks.

4. These bundles consist of banana-stalk fibers that have been soaked in the brine and then dried in the sun.

5. I have described Jalé initiation ceremonies in Koch in press b.

6. I have published a detailed analysis of Jalé marriage patterns in Koch 1968a.

7. The Jalé word for the 'marriage' pig signifies the "handing over" of a woman, and the attribute for the 'dowry' pig expresses the notion of "securing" the arrangement.

8. While all "men of knowledge" are capable of performing the more common ceremonies, any rite involving a direct confrontation with a ghost and the restoration of a sick person's soul to full strength requires the intervention of a curer or medicine man; see Koch 1968b.

9. For example, in the early 1920's a great influenza epidemic led to a temporary abandonment of the village of Pasikni. Most people

who sought refuge in other villages later returned, but a few lineages from the wards of Nelelum and Savéapini settled permanently at Tengkeléi, a place located approximately one mile south of Pasikni. Around 1954 the people abandoned Tengkeléi in the course of another epidemic and rebuilt their homes at the nearby places of Klengleng and Angkenteng. Although these new settlements have since become separate villages, their inhabitants are still collectively referred to as "the Tengkeléi people."

10. Appendix B contains tables that record the distribution of sibs, lineages, and their adult male membership in the village of Pasikni.

11. "Descent" denotes genealogical continuity expressed in a culturally relevant idiom of identifying ancestral linkages. The Jalé assign descent by tracing the biological link between a father and his children; for them the idiom of paternity defines descent. Their conceptualization of agnatic descent lines is quite similar to our metaphor of a genealogical tree. They refer to the line as "stem" and to offspring as "branch." A person's natal affiliation to a descent line, transmitted at birth, is permanent and changes neither by adoption nor by expatriate residence.

Detailed taxonomic and semantic analyses of the Jalé kinship terminology have appeared in Koch 1970b and 1972. Appendic C summarizes these data.

12. The nature of Omaha terminologies as an ideological correlate of the solidarity of agnatic lineages has long been recognized (Coult 1967, McKinley 1971, and Radcliffe-Brown 1941).

13. The widespread practice of incorporating non-agnates in patrilineal descent groups and erratic fission processes unlike the pattern of chronic segmentation known from Africa and certified as textbook examples of social structure have left the picture of New Guinea kinship systems muddled. The apparent discrepancy between ideational representation of descent lines as localized groups and the observed flexibility in an individual's residential association and political alignments have confused many ethnographers whose genealogical models of tribal organization made little sense in the Highlands. Some of these problems and their implications for comparative research are discussed in Barnes 1962, Brown 1962, de Lepervanche 1967, Kaberry 1967, Langness 1964 and 1972, Power 1966, Strathern 1969, Watson 1970.

14. Although everywhere in the New Guinea Highlands the "big men," who possess conspicuous physical strength and rhetorical skill, achieve positions of leadership, the scope of their exercise of power varies from one place to another; however, their tenuous control over a small local group always derives in large measure from their

clever management of pigs and other goods needed in obligatory exchange transactions.

15. In contrast to the political control exercised by leaders among the Kapauku (Pospisil 1958) and the Kuma (Reay 1959), whose "big men" adjudicate disputes among the constituents of their realm, political control in most Highlands societies lacks consistency, as among the Daribi (Wagner 1967), the Gahuku (Read 1959), the Gururumba (Newman 1965), the Wanggulam Dani (Ploeg 1969), the Mbowamb (Brandewie 1971; Strathern 1966, 1971: Chapter 10), and the Maring (Lowman-Vayda 1968, Rappaport 1967).

III. Methods and Ideology of Conflict Management

1. A superficial analysis of several dozen recorded standard insults in relation to the sex of the parties involved in the exchange showed, for example, that opponents of the same sex insult each other with remarks depreciating their health and looks or with scatophagous suggestions, while antagonists of the opposite sex focus on each other's genitals in their verbal attacks. Cases *39 and *41 contain translations of typical altercations between neighboring wards.

2. The metaphorical signification of the Jalé expression *héléroxo* derives from *hélé*, the ditch which separates two adjacent garden plots; the suffix *-roxo* corresponds to the English "-wise."

3. A woman may resort to a special way of expressing her intent to terminate a trading partnership. If her request for a pig fails, she may defecate on the sleeping floor or in the fireplace of her host's hut before returning to her home village.

4. The other eight known cases involved women from other villages who threw themselves into the Jaxólé, five in anger and three from fear.

5. My limited case data do not suffice for reliable sociological and psychological analyses concerning the etiology and jural consequences of suicide among the Jalé. The specific problems mentioned here have been studied in different cultures; see, for example, Berndt 1962, Douglas 1967, Firth 1961, Jeffreys 1952, Malinowski 1926, and Westermarck 1908. Bohannan (1960) and Hippler (1969) have reviewed additional studies. My own cross-cultural research on suicide yielded the general hypothesis that "where suicide is legally recognized . . . as constituting the result of an injury inflicted by another person, this person and his kin group respectively are held responsible to satisfy claims made by the deceased's relatives" (Koch 1963: 75). The Jalé cases support this view. For example, if a marital dispute drove the woman into the river, her agnates demanded compensation in pigs from her husband; and in one case a man obtained a pig from

the father of his wife after she killed herself following a fight with her mother.

6. I have mentioned such a case in Koch 1968b.

7. Case *53 records the history of this great war.

8. A description of Jalé anthropophagy has appeared in Koch 1970a.

9. I distinguish between "liability" as a jural obligation and "responsibility" as moral fault or mental disposition. For a useful semantic analysis of the legal implications of the term "responsibility," see Hart 1968: Chapter 9.

10. Critiques of these methodological defects have appeared in Allott, Epstein, and Gluckman 1969; Bohannan 1969; and Epstein 1967a, 1969. Especially relevant is Gluckman's statement, "Each offense is relative to its context of social relationships, and the chances of securing redress for a wrong in the absence of a governmental organization depend on the social relations between offender and injured" (1965: 206).

11. Few ethnographers have dealt explicitly with this problem. Dundas (1921) describes the consequences of accidental killing in East African tribes, Hogbin (1938) relates modes of retaliation for adultery and theft to different social and political contexts on Wogeo Island in Melanesia, Barton (1969) lists rules of liability among the Ifugao of Luzon in the Philippines, and Kroeber (1928) examines this concept among the Yurok Indians of California. Other studies analyze the relationship between social organization and patterns of vengeance or indemnification among the Huli of New Guinea (Glasse 1968), the Berti (Holý 1967) and the Nuer (Howell 1954) of the Sudan, the Pokot of Kenya (Peristiany 1954), and the Bedouins of Cyrenaica (Peters 1967). Gluckman (1965) discusses concepts of injury and liability in the law of the Zambian Barotse in a comparative ethnological and historical framework.

12. Ideas similar to the Jalé doctrine of effective action have appeared in the development of the Common Law. Whether or not Anglo-Saxon law included an identical principle is still a matter of scholarly debate over presumably inadequate sources (Plucknett 1956: Chapter 4), but the modern idea of "liability without fault" bears a certain resemblance to the Jalé theory. Holmes's conclusion that "the various forms of liability known to modern law spring from the common ground of revenge" (1881: 37) suggests an intriguing comparison of the sociological conditions that produce such similar jural principles.

13. My friends' unrealistic fear of having to compensate me for any injuries I might sustain led them to object vehemently, if unsuccessfully, to my walking across battlefields or joining them on raiding expeditions.

VII. Conclusion: Theoretical Implications

1. For a comparative review of warfare patterns see Berndt 1964.

2. In another study Meggitt reports that "a clan seriously threatened by invasion by a clan of another phratry [a group of localized patriclans related through a putative agnatic ancestor and usually occupying a contiguous area] may rally all its brother clans to its defense" (1967: 25–26).

3. More careful studies on the possible relationship between population size and the incidence of conflict by Beals (1969) and Shepperdson (1969) show the complexity of this problem as related to political organization.

4. In his Mbowamb monograph Vicedom explains that wars could arise out of any kind of dispute, but he, too, adds the dubious inference from a population movement of the past that "in earlier times land shortage and want of space seem to have often represented a cause of war" (1943: 146).

5. See the description of this system among the Chimbu by Brown (1964). If, indeed, the Enga and Maring once fought for land, an interesting question inviting comparative research concerns the relationship of conquest warfare to the political organization of local groups. In this connection it may be significant that in the densely settled Maring areas "clan clusters are the largest named group with recognized territorial boundaries and with members that act together in war and in ceremonies" (Vayda 1971: 3). Without a broader base Vayda's ecological theory of warfare remains, at best, an interesting if one-sided speculation. In view of the quality of available data regarding the effects of war on the distribution of land, I readily accept Vayda's own appraisal of his theory that "oversimplification is unavoidable, since the post-refuging distribution processes [among the Maring] have hardly been operating recently, and details about them are, accordingly, hard to come by" (ibid.: 18).

Stauder's (1972) study on feuding and ecology among the Majangir of Ethiopia actually reverses Vayda's theory. He explains the prevalence of feuds by the lack of political integration resulting from the great residential mobility that follows from an abundance of arable land.

6. See, for example, Barnes 1962; Berndt 1962; Read 1954, 1955.

7. In the writings of zoologists, anthropologists, and psychologists the word "aggressive" has so many different meanings that its use inevitably invites criticism (see the recent anthologies by Bramson and Goethals 1968, Fried, Harris, and Murphy 1968, Megargee and Hokanson 1970, and Montagu 1968). Within the limitations of my

explorations the term denotes a hostile attitude expressed in violent attacks against an opponent.

8. Colson uses the term "clan" for the type of descent group that I call a "sib."

9. Wedgwood (1930) and J. Whiting (1941) suggested a similar explanation of warfare and headhunting in Melanesian societies.

10. In his study of the relationship between forms of social organization and inter-group conflict management, LeVine suggests an extension of the divided loyalties hypothesis to stratified societies including tribal monarchies, where "the control maintained by the central authority rested on a social underpinning of cross-cutting kin and territorial ties" so that "the pacifying effect of multiple loyalties, although seen in clearest form where a central authority is absent, may be operative in a politically amalgamated group as well" (1965: 54).

11. Subsequent cross-cultural studies by Otterbein (1965, 1968a, 1968b, 1970) confirmed this hypothesis. I should add, however, that Otterbein's conclusions concerning the more complex relationships between the existence of "fraternal interest groups," the level of "political organization," and "armed combat" are suspect. His codifications of these variables suffer from the difficulties inherent in many comparative library studies—ranging from the vastly diverging use of terms like "tribe" by ethnographers to questionable inferences and scaling of frequencies and ad hoc fabricated distinctions, such as between "feuding" and "internal war," that have no comparative analytical meaning. When computer programs rather than ethnographic context prescribe the rules of anthropological reasoning, a study may find that "the greater the percentage of professionals in the military organization, the more likely that cavalry is used" (1970: 57), whereas I would naively think that the Marshall Islanders or the Mundurucú—to mention only two societies in Otterbein's sample—failed to deploy cavalry because they had no horses.

Cross-cultural computations of residence patterns, division of labor, and warfare by Ember and Ember also confirmed Thoden van Velzen and van Wetering's discovery that patrilocality is correlated with violent intra-societal conflict. Their interpretation of this correlation, however, reverses the latters' and my own explanation by concluding that "patrilocal residence is favored by the presence of at least some internal warfare (that is, warfare within the society), whether or not such warfare interferes with a patridominant division of labor; and matrilocal residence is favored by purely external warfare if such warfare compels the divsion of labor to become matridominant" (1971: 593). Since their deductions completely ignore the conditions under which conflicts escalate into warfare, they apparently assume that some peoples suffer from an innate pugnacity and that societies cope with this predicament through rules of residence and division of labor.

12. See Simmel's observations in 1908: 103–111; 1950: 145–153.

13. Similarly, matrilocality itself does not lead to intra-societal peacefulness. Rather, this form of conjugal residence widens the circle of men who share those common interests that demand the repression of open hostilities between local communities.

14. In this form the hypothesis concurs with the established theory that political integration promotes the development of specialized agencies of conflict management (see Fortes and Evans-Pritchard 1940, Hoebel 1954, Schapera 1956).

15. B. Whiting's hypotheses include the assumption that violent conflict management correlates with more formalized legal codes and procedures—an infelicitous formulation because it contradicts the implications of her other propositions. For detailed ethnographies of the six communities see B. Whiting 1963. On the whole, the correlation between the development of "protest masculinity" and aggressiveness rests on fairly solid empirical data (see Biller 1970).

16. See, for example, Black and Falk 1971, Bozeman 1971, Corbett 1971, Landheer 1966, and Reisman 1971.

17. See especially Sherif 1966. Relevant to this problem also are studies describing how natural disasters reduce conflict within a community (Dynes and Quarantelli 1971).

Index